HOME ON THE STAG

As a serious drama set in an ordinary middle-class home, Ibsen's *A Doll's House* established a new politics of the interior that was to have a lasting impact upon twentieth-century drama. In this innovative study, Nicholas Grene traces the changing forms of the home on the stage through nine of the greatest of modern plays and playwrights. From Chekhov's *The Cherry Orchard* through to Williams's *A Streetcar Named Desire*, domestic spaces and personal crises have been employed to express wider social conditions and themes of class, gender and family. In the later twentieth century and beyond, the most radically experimental dramatists created their own challenging theatrical interiors, including Beckett in *Endgame*, Pinter in *The Homecoming* and Parks in *Topdog/Underdog*. Grene analyses the full significance of these versions of domestic spaces to offer fresh insights into the portrayal of the naturalistic environment in modern drama.

NICHOLAS GRENE is Professor of English literature at Trinity College Dublin, a Senior Fellow of the College, a Member of the Royal Irish Academy and a Life Member of Clare Hall, Cambridge. He has published widely on Shakespeare, drama and Irish literature, and his books include *Bernard Shaw: a Critical View* (1984), *Shakespeare's Tragic Imagination* (1992), *The Politics of Irish Drama* (Cambridge, 1999) and *Shakespeare's Serial History Plays* (Cambridge, 2002). Among his most recent books are *Yeats's Poetic Codes* (2008), the New Mermaids edition of *Major Barbara* (2008), *Synge and Edwardian Ireland* (coedited with Brian Cliff, 2011) and a memoir, *Nothing Quite Like It: An American-Irish Childhood* (2011). He has been a visiting professor at the University of New South Wales, Dartmouth College and the University of Paris IV (Sorbonne).

HOME ON THE STAGE

Domestic Spaces in Modern Drama

NICHOLAS GRENE

CAMBRIDGE
UNIVERSITY PRESS

CAMBRIDGE
UNIVERSITY PRESS

University Printing House, Cambridge CB2 8BS, United Kingdom

Cambridge University Press is part of the University of Cambridge.

It furthers the University's mission by disseminating knowledge in the pursuit of
education, learning and research at the highest international levels of excellence.

www.cambridge.org
Information on this title: www.cambridge.org/9781107078093

© Nicholas Grene 2014

First published 2014

Printed in the United Kingdom by Clays, St Ives plc

A catalogue record for this publication is available from the British Library

Library of Congress Cataloging in Publication data
Grene, Nicholas.
Home on the stage : domestic spaces in modern drama / Nicholas Grene.
pages cm
ISBN 978-1-107-07809-3 (Hardback)
1. Domestic drama–History and criticism.   2. Drama–20th century–History and criticism.
3. Drama–21st century–History and criticism.   4. Home in literature.
5. Families in literature   I. Title.
PN1954.G74 2014
809'.829355–dc23   2014014324

ISBN 978-1-107-07809-3 Hardback

In memory of Andrew Grene (1965–2010)

Contents

Illustrations

The author and publishers acknowledge the following sources of copyright material and are grateful for the permissions granted. While every effort has been made, it has not always been possible to identify the sources of all material used, or to trace all copyright holders. If any omissions are brought to our notice, we will be happy to include the appropriate acknowledgements on reprinting.

Acknowledgements

I gratefully acknowledge a term's leave of absence from Trinity College Dublin in the autumn of 2012 and to Clare Hall, Cambridge once again for providing a congenial place to write during that time. I wish to acknowledge a grant from the Trinity Arts, Humanities and Social Sciences Benefaction Fund for support towards the funding of research visits to the United States and the United Kingdom. I would like to thank the following for their help in sourcing illustrations for the book: Erin Lee of the National Theatre in London, Michael Kantor of Ghostlight Films, Jeremy Megraw of the New York Public Library for the Performing Arts, Judith Seeff of Sydney Theatre Company, and Dale Stincomb of Harvard University Library. A part of Chapter 4 first appeared as an essay in the *Hungarian Journal of English and American Studies* and I am grateful for the opportunity to redeploy it here.

I have benefited from the help and advice of a number of friends and relations. Lucy McDiarmid, always stimulating, commissioned an essay from me which, though it is not part of this book, gave me the idea for writing it. Adrian Frazier was once again enormously helpful, with much-needed encouragement and marvellously shrewd, detailed editing suggestions on the early chapters he read in draft. Jean Chothia kindly gave me the benefit of her Eugene O'Neill expertise and saved me from several gaffes in her comments on Chapter 4. I had help in tracking down sources from both Lisa Coen and Sophia Grene: thanks to both of them. To the groups of students in the Trinity School of English with whom I debated the ideas in this book in classes over the period 2011–13, I am collectively grateful.

Vicki Cooper at Cambridge University Press has been a helpful and supportive editor and I have benefited from the anonymous readers' reports she commissioned. I am also very grateful to Fleur Jones for her prompt and efficient help in the final stages of preparing the manuscript.

The book is dedicated to the memory of my dear brother Andrew, much loved and much missed.

Introduction: Ibsen and after

> The future is with naturalism. The formula will be found; it will be proved that there is more poetry in the little apartment of a bourgeois than in all the empty, worm-eaten palaces of history; in the end we will see that everything meets in the real. – Émile Zola[1]

Naturalism in the Theatre, from which this famous quotation is taken, originally appeared in 1881 as the first of a two-volume collection of Zola's theatre reviews.[2] Like Shaw, writing for the *Saturday Review* in the 1890s, Zola, by his negative notices of the standard stage fare of his time, was clearing a space for his own avant-garde practice. Or rather, he cast himself as a voice crying in the wilderness, preparing the way for the messiah of naturalism to come. The book opens with a spectacle of expectation constantly disappointed:

> Each winter at the beginning of the theatre season, I fall prey to the same thoughts. A hope springs up in me, and I tell myself that before the first warmth of summer empties the playhouses, a dramatist of genius will have been discovered. [. . .] I picture this creator scorning the tricks of the clever hack, smashing the imposed patterns, remaking the stage until it is continuous with the auditorium, giving a shiver of life to the painted trees, letting in through the backcloth the great, free air of reality. Unfortunately, this dream I have every October has not yet been fulfilled, and it is not likely to be for some time. I wait in vain.[3]

Of course, unknown to Zola, the wait was over; the dramatist of genius had already arrived, but in Scandinavia, not in France – 1881 was the year of the publication of *Ghosts*. Two years before, *A Doll's House* had been produced.

The target of Zola's attack in *Naturalism in the Theatre* was the still canonised neoclassical drama and the romantic forms of Victor Hugo and Alfred de Musset that had partially replaced it in the French theatre: hence the scornful reference to 'the empty, worm-eaten palaces of history'. The new drama of naturalism was to be contemporary, but it was also to be

I

staged in the ordinary living space of the bourgeois. There was nothing revolutionary in itself about the idea of a domestic middle-class drama; it had been theorised long before by Diderot in the eighteenth century. The stage means necessary for naturalism were already available. The box set constructing a solid illusionist interior, as an alternative to the traditional painted backcloth and side wings, had been introduced in the London theatre in the 1830s, making possible the concept of the 'fourth wall', another notion anticipated by Diderot.[4] Even in the highly stylised French theatre, real items of furniture had begun to appear by the 1850s.[5] What is radical in Zola's programme for a naturalist drama of the interior is its claims to significance and aesthetic value. The familiar space of ordinary middle-class life, 'the little apartment of bourgeois', is to be valued with the dignity and meaning accorded in the past only to tragedy. 'Poetry is everywhere', Zola claims, 'in everything, even more in the present and the real than in the past and the abstract.'[6]

In this drama of middle-class life, the setting itself is of resonant significance, not merely a backdrop to the action as in the traditional well-made play. 'In high naturalism', as Raymond Williams puts it, 'the lives of the characters have soaked into their environment. [...] The relations between men and things are at a deep level interactive, because what is there physically, as a space of a means for living, is a whole shaped and shaping social history.'[7] A Doll's House carries in its very title the issue of how the marital home is to be viewed and evaluated. Ibsen's revenants in Ghosts walk not on the battlements of a castle, where you might expect them, but in Mrs Alving's well-appointed conservatory. The attic in The Wild Duck and the inner room in Hedda Gabler bespeak the psychological condition of those who occupy them. The naturalistic home on the stage, as conceived by Zola and realised by Ibsen, figures both the outer world that surrounds it and the interiority of the private lives it houses. Insofar as the stage is made 'continuous with the auditorium', it implies a mirroring identity between the experience of the characters represented and that of the contemporary audience that watches them, the audience that stands in for a wider society beyond. At the same time, the intimacy to which the removed fourth wall gives access takes us into the recesses of hearts and minds.

Of all this Miss Julie (1888) is paradigmatic, and Strindberg, then at the height of his zeal for naturalism, is its most articulate exponent in the preface to the play.[8] The single set, the below-stairs kitchen where the servants Jean and Kristin live and work and to which Miss Julie descends, provides a topography for the play's class dynamics. Strindberg reveals a

significant source for his scenic concept: 'As for the scenery, I have
borrowed the asymmetry and cropped framing of impressionist painting,
and believe that I have thereby succeeded in strengthening the illusion.'⁹
As the impressionists with their cut-off perspectives challenged conventional principles of composition, Strindberg gives a more authentic sense
of lived space by its fragmentation. A glimpse of Jean's arm as he changes
in his bedroom next door, the count's boots that wait so menacingly for his
valet's attention, vividly realise the offstage spaces and all that they signify.
Julie and Jean as mistress and man are created as 'characters' in the very
special sense Strindberg gives to that term in the preface. He scornfully
dismisses theatrical 'characters', the one-note stereotypes of traditional
dramaturgy. Instead, he says, 'My souls (characters) are conglomerates of
past and present stages of culture, bits out of books and newspapers, scraps
of humanity, torn shreds of once fine clothing now turned to rags, exactly
as the human soul is patched together.'¹⁰ This is a characteristic statement
in its naturalist's irony at the idea of the God-given disembodied soul, its
challenge to the Romantic cult of the unique individual. Such stage figures
are not only products but patchwork quilts of their environment.

The dramaturgical revolution that put the middle-class home and the
occupants' inner lives at the centre of drama reflected the social reality of
the time, as the historian Michelle Perrot makes clear:

> The nineteenth century was the golden age of private life, a time when the
> vocabulary and reality of private life took shape. Privacy as an idea was
> elaborated with great sophistication. Civil society, private life, intimate
> relations, and the life of the individual, though conceptualised as concentric
> circles, actually overlapped.¹¹

This development is variously explained and dated. Catherine Hall, for
example, looking at the case of England, sees the rise of the domestic ideal
of the family as a feature of the early nineteenth century resulting from the
growth of Evangelicalism, with its emphasis on the godly life based on
individual conviction, at the same time as the development of separate
spheres of public and private life for men and women, with middle-class
men working exclusively in marketplace and factory, while women were
confined to managing the household.¹² She points to the fact that the
British census of 1851 introduced the category of 'housewife' for the first
time and in the introduction to its report stated: 'The possession of an
entire house is strongly desired by every Englishman; for it throws a sharp
well-defined circle round his family and hearth – the shrine of his sorrows,
joys and meditations.'¹³ Writing just a few years later, the American

preacher Henry Ward Beecher elaborated on that viewpoint: 'A house is the shape which a man's thoughts take when he imagines how he should like to live. Its interior is the measure of his social and domestic nature; its exterior, of his esthetic and artistic nature. It interprets, in material form, his ideas of home, of friendship, and of comfort.'[14]

In 'Paris, the Capital of the Nineteenth Century', Walter Benjamin declared that 'under Louis Philippe, the private citizen makes his entrance on the stage of history'. Benjamin went on to evoke the concept of the 'interior' that resulted:

> For the private individual, the place of dwelling is for the first time opposed to the place of work. The former constitutes itself as the interior. Its complement is the office. The private individual, who in the office has to deal with reality, needs the domestic interior to sustain him in his illusions. [...] From this arise the phantasmagorias of the interior – which, for the private man, represents the universe.[15]

Benjamin argued that this illusory bourgeois privacy was a specific historic phenomenon of the nineteenth century, in which the soft furnishings of the interior with its plethora of collected objects represented an attempted resistance to the alienation of the modern city: 'Against the armature of glass and iron, upholstery offers resistance with its textiles.' Charles Rice, who quotes this aphorism of Benjamin, follows him also in seeing the 'short historical life of the bourgeois domestic interior' as coming to an end with the modernism of the early twentieth century.[16]

Late nineteenth-century naturalism offered a critical representation of that bourgeois domestic interior, and for most theatre historians, it had an equally short life. As impressionism in the visual arts was rapidly succeeded by postimpressionism, then by Cubism and surrealism, so in drama naturalism was overtaken by expressionism, epic theatre and the theatre of the absurd. This view was fostered by theatre practitioners themselves, who inveighed against the naturalistic style as yesterday's fashion. 'We have endured too much from the banality of surfaces', declared Eugene O'Neill in 1924, in celebration of *The Ghost Sonata*, one of what he called Strindberg's 'behind-life' plays.[17] Brecht relentlessly attacked the bourgeois theatre of illusionism as the antithesis of his forms of alienated political engagement. In *Our Town*, Thornton Wilder lightly mocks the audience who expect a conventional set when he has his Stage Manager remark as two trellises are pushed out from the proscenium pillars: 'There's some scenery for those who think they have to have scenery.'[18] Antonin Artaud in his theory and practice represented the most vehement opponent of representational drama and as such was to become the standard-bearer for much postwar European avant-garde theatre. It is easy to see why it should have been so. The realistically rendered family interior in the twentieth century was to become the standard model not only for conventional theatre but also for most film and television drama. Its *reductio ad absurdum* is reality television, where the camera does not just take the audience through one 'fourth wall' but follows its victims into all the rooms in the house.

A great deal of work has been devoted to theatrical space in the last thirty years in the context of the new discipline of performance studies. Most of this has taken the form of semiotic theory that looks at the whole phenomenon of theatre rather than any one particular period. Anne Ubersfeld offered nothing less than a comprehensive methodology for 'reading theatre'.[19] Gay McAuley provided a taxonomy of different stage spaces, including the auditoria where performances take place, as well as discriminating between the 'presentational space' involving the arrangement of the set, actors' positioning, entrances and exits and the 'fictional space' of places represented on- and offstage.[20] Within such overarching treatments of the subject of theatre space, there could be little room for something as restricted as the realistic representation of domestic spaces in modern drama. Indeed, in David Wiles's history of Western performance space, the emphasis is not primarily on conventional mimetic theatre at all, but on alternative staging venues.[21]

The dominance of poststructuralism and postmodernism in academic scholarship has also influenced the way the story of modern drama is told. So, for instance, Una Chaudhuri in *Staging Place* links her study of modern drama to a 'postmodern critical geography' that draws upon the work of Edward Soja, Michel Foucault and Henri Lefèbvre.[22] It is not surprising, therefore, that her book, after an initial analysis of the realistic drama of Ibsen, Strindberg and Chekhov, should be largely concerned with anti-illusionist avant-garde theatre. She speaks of a 'hidden discourse of home and belonging that runs through modern drama from the nineteenth century onward'.[23] I would argue, in fact, that the representation of home in modern drama is by no means hidden; it is everywhere apparent, just overlooked and unexamined by theatre historians whose interests are elsewhere. It is the aim of this book to consider the persistent afterlife of the naturalistic home on the stage through the twentieth century. It is not only that the plays of Ibsen, Chekhov and Strindberg themselves have gone on being revived as part of the modern repertoire; the image of the family interior has continued to be adapted, reconceived or parodied right through into the contemporary period. What I want to investigate is why and how the form has proved so flexible, adaptable and tenacious.

Class, community, nation

Bert O. States identifies the characteristic mode of naturalist drama as metonymy: 'Metonymy and synecdoche, as we find them in the realistic style, are devices for reducing states, or qualities or attributes, or whole entities, like societies, to visible things in which they somehow inhere.'[24] The representative standing of the visible things the audience watches depends on them being individually specific and yet completely familiar. The Helmers' apartment expresses their own unique situation but is immediately recognisable as the type of any other middle-class professional home. It is designed to be so recognisable by virtue of its contemporaneity and its implied kinship with the comparable homes of its original audiences. That model of middle-class naturalism alters when the status of the home represented is changed and when the audience is distanced in class or social background from the characters.

It is different already in Chekhov's country houses, with their extended families including a wider class span from servants to landowners. The actions of the plays take place in the present, but one that is situated within a historical continuum. States observes that in Chekhov, furniture is 'visible history'.[25] *The Cherry Orchard* (1904) as a study in shifting patterns of ownership of the house and estate, looking before and after its own moment of modernisation, becomes a state of the nation play unlike the state of society plays of Ibsen or Strindberg. The bourgeois naturalist home, though individually realised, was representative in its ordinariness. In *Heartbreak House* (written in 1916–17, published in 1919), Shaw's very un-Chekhovian experiment in the style of Chekhov, we are confronted with an extraordinary living space, a house shaped like a ship. This necessarily moves the mode towards allegory and, in the context of the war crisis in which it was written, we are invited to see the houseful of cultured middle-class characters as embarked on a ship of state perilously out of control.

In the naturalistic drama, audiences are drawn into the observation of people more or less like themselves. This is not the case with Gorky's down-and-outs in the basement doss house of *The Lower Depths* (1902), nor yet with the peasants of Lorca's rural trilogy. At first glance, Lorca's work is stylistically remote from naturalism. *Blood Wedding* (1933) uses an elaborate colour coding for each of its scenes and personified figures of the

Moon and Death in its climactic third act. Its dramatic high points are expressed in verse arias and duets. However, this poetic dramaturgy is naturalised by its rural setting. Drama is built up from the traditional folk forms of lullabies and wedding songs, marriage rituals and wakes. The nature imagery of a heightened lyrical style is rendered plausible by the proximity of the natural world. In Lorca's most austere last play, *The House of Bernarda Alba* (1936), written almost all in prose, we are forced to endure the stifling claustration of the daughters within the house but are therefore all the more aware of the irrepressible powers of animal vitality that Bernarda seeks vainly to exclude. The play's subtitle, 'A Drama about Women in the Villages of Spain', suggests the quasi-ethnographic status of this study of the rural domestic interior.

Synge was evidently one of Lorca's models; the grieving Mother in *Blood Wedding* mourns in all but the same words as Maurya in *Riders to the Sea* (1904). For Synge, as for Lorca, the life of a peasant community remote from urban culture justified a highly wrought poetic speech and a dramatic action shaped by the traditions of folklore. In Synge's case, however, the context of a decolonising national culture complicated the plays' reception. The rural Irish country cottage, in which most of his plays were set, was an icon in the nationalist imaginary, the unspoiled antithesis of the Anglicised and modernised life of the city. As such, it stood as an ideal image of the nation, and Synge's plays were suspiciously scrutinised for un-Irish activities. Ibsen's Nora in *A Doll's House* shocked its original audiences by walking out on her sacred duties to husband and children. Synge's Nora, unhappily married to a pathologically jealous older man in *The Shadow of the Glen* (1903), scandalised its critics by leaving the marital cottage in the company of a tramp. Such an action was not only immoral; it disgraced the name of Irish women.[26]

Staged domestic spaces as images of the national life have had a remarkably prolonged life in Irish theatre for a century after Synge. The tenement dwellings of Sean O'Casey's Dublin plays (1923–26), in their very proximity to the urban violence of rebellion and civil war, challenged the rhetoric that animated those conflicts. Brendan Behan's *The Hostage* (1958) had a Republican safe house cum brothel as an ironic metaphor for postrevolutionary Ireland. Brian Friel's trademark setting of Ballybeg, literally 'small town', has been a prism for seeing the condition of the country, whether in the then-contemporary present of *Philadelphia Here I Come!* (1964) or in the retrospective memory play *Dancing at Lughnasa* (1990). Martin McDonagh's Leenane in the *Leenane Trilogy* (1996–97) is a savagely satiric version of the Connemara village imagined as Irish idyll.

The ultimate metadramatic parody of this form comes in Enda Walsh's *The Walworth Farce* (2006), in which a crazed father, locked up in a London flat, forces his two sons daily to enact a play of Irish exile. By this point in time, the Irish domestic space as an image of the nation has taken on its own intertextual life, reflecting more its theatrical predecessors than any social actuality. But what made this tradition possible is the social and/ or geographical gap between the middle-class urban audiences who watch these plays, whether in Dublin or London, and the stage spaces of their peasant or proletarian characters.

Radical realism

Benjamin maintains that the cherished bourgeois home of the nineteenth century is an attempt to cordon off private space from the anonymising modern city beyond. As such, according to Henri Lefèbvre, it was bound to failure because such divisions of private and public spheres are ultimately illusory:

> Visible boundaries, such as walls or enclosures in general, give rise [...] to an appearance of separation between spaces where in fact what exists is an ambiguous continuity. The space of a room, bedroom, house or garden may be cut off in a sense from social space by barriers and walls, by all the signs of private property, yet still remain fundamentally part of that space.[27]

A number of plays in the mid-twentieth century found ways of rendering that 'ambiguous continuity'. With the stage design of *A Streetcar Named Desire* (1947), it proved possible to represent simultaneously the constricted living quarters of the Kowalskis' one-bedroom flat and the New Orleans streetscape outside. What is more, Williams borrowed techniques from expressionism to convey inner psychological states within the framework of domestic realism. The 'station drama' had been the characteristic form of expressionism, tracing the emotional trajectory of the individual travelling through often nightmarish, distorted scenes of urban life, as in Georg Kaiser's *From Morning to Midnight* (1917). In *Streetcar*, such projections of Blanche's disturbed state are dramatised within the realistically rendered living space. This is, of course, the outstanding characteristic of *Death of a Salesman* (1949) also, which Miller first thought of calling *The Inside of His Head*.[28] This is a double drama of the interior, of the house and of the mind – the fluid space of the home, which dissolves into Willy's flashback scenarios, backed by the high-rise apartment blocks of the city looming beyond.

The realist dramatists of this mid-century period were fighting the battles of naturalism all over again. In the famous debate with Kenneth Tynan, Miller felt obliged to rebut the charge that you could not have a tragedy centred on a mere salesman like Willy Loman. He later responded sarcastically to the play's critics:

> [T]he academy's charge that Willy lacked the 'stature' for the tragic hero seemed incredible to me. I had not understood that these matters are measured by Greco-Elizabethan paragraphs which hold no mention of insurance payments, front porches, refrigerator fan belts, steering knuckles, Chevrolets, and visions seen not through the portals of Delphi but in the blue flame of the hot-water heater.[29]

We are back with Zola's declaration that 'there is more poetry in the little apartment of a bourgeois than in all the empty, worm-eaten palaces of history'. Once again, the democratising spirit of the realist drama protests against the hegemony of canonised forms of the past, claiming truth, depth and dignity for the ordinariness of modern private life.

The 1950s saw a series of plays that used naturalistic domestic drama as one form of the 'theatre of revolt'.[30] John Osborne's *Look Back in Anger* (1956) is always cited as a landmark in British postwar theatre. Its setting in an attic bedsit at the top of a Victorian house in a Midland town inaugurated the style of 'kitchen sink' realism. Osborne was reacting against the formulaic theatre of playwrights such as Somerset Maugham, then hugely popular. *Look Back in Anger*, Michael Billington says, 'was a riposte to the mechanical glibness of the Maugham school but also to the technical artifice of the post-war verse drama of Christopher Fry and Ronald Duncan'.[31] Even more striking was the case of Shelagh Delaney's *A Taste of Honey* (1958). The nineteen-year-old author supposedly wrote the play after seeing Terence Rattigan's *Variations on a Theme* in Manchester.

> To her, the polite drawing-room comedy, which was still at this time the staple diet available to the theatre-goer, was unrealistic – it 'depicts safe, sheltered, cultured lives in charming surroundings, not life as the majority of ordinary people knew it'.[32]

The result was the drama of the adolescent daughter of a 'semi-whore' mother, pregnant after a fleeting encounter with a black sailor, being cared for in a 'comfortless flat in Manchester' by a gay art student.[33]

Still more striking was another first play by a young woman playwright, Lorraine Hansbury's *A Raisin in the Sun* (1959). Most naturalistic domestic dramas from *A Doll's House* on feature more or less dysfunctional families. By contrast, Hansbury's Younger family, for all the stresses and friction between them, with mother, son, daughter, daughter-in-law and grandson all sharing the one two-bedroom apartment, are in the end a model of love and solidarity. Their only problems come from the fact that they are poor working-class African Americans living on the south side of Chicago. The plot turns on how the $10,000 insurance money received on the death of the father will be spent, whether on the college fees of Beneatha, the daughter who wants to be a doctor, or on the partnership in a liquor store that is the long-cherished dream of the son Walter. In the event, the mother Lena puts the down payment on a house in a white Chicago suburb, a move the family eventually decide to make in spite of the active discouragement of other residents and the possibility of fire-bombing. The play is completely conventional in its realistic representation of the home and the family, radical only in its claim by an African American underclass to the nineteenth-century bourgeois dignity of private space.

Reluctant returns to the home

In postwar Britain and America, it was possible to write challenging new plays in the realist mode. In France, the absurdists aggressively attacked the principle of representation in general and the bourgeois home in particular. In *Eleutheria* (written in 1947), Beckett's first standard-issue avant-garde play, the comme il faut home of the Krap family literally slides off the side of the stage as, from act to act, the space comes to be wholly occupied by the sordid apartment of their refusenik son Victor. In *The Bald Prima Donna* (1950), Ionesco reduces middle-class family life to the learned by rote exchanges of a language primer. But the iconic home on the stage remained a powerful part of the theatrical vocabulary of this sort of theatre. *Endgame* (1957), with its enclosed room in which Hamm sits with his aged parents in bins while the pseudo-son/servant Clov waits in his kitchen to be called, is a parody of the traditional residence of the nuclear family. Pinter in *The Homecoming* (1965) puts upon the stage the completely realistic ground floor of a North London house; it is only the dialogue and actions of its occupants that are bizarre. Pinter's destabilising version of realist representation was caught in John Bury's design for the premiere of *Old Times* (1971). The set beautifully reproduced the modernised farmhouse in which Deeley and Kate live, down to the discreet central heating pipes running along the walls. Its only oddity was that the room was tilted at a slight angle to the proscenium arch.

A surprising number of adventurously experimental modern playwrights have returned more or less reluctantly to the family home on the stage. The most famous is Eugene O'Neill. The man who disdained the 'banality of surfaces', who in the 1920s and 1930s went through expressionism, Freudian stage symbolism and masks, nine-act plays with stream of consciousness asides and modern remakes of Greek tragedy, belatedly created in *Long Day's Journey into Night* (1956) a classic naturalist drama: father, mother and two grown-up sons fighting it out in the living room. Tom Murphy, considering writing a play for the first time with a friend in 1959, was confident of one thing: '[I]t's not going to be set in a kitchen.'[34] Kitchen-sink drama might have been nouvelle vague in Britain at that time, but in Ireland it had become equated with the country cottage kitchen of the tired, formulaic 'Abbey play'. Instead, Murphy went on to write plays such as the Brechtian history play *Famine* (1968), the expressionist *A Crucial Week in the Life of a Grocer's Assistant* (1969), the dystopian fairy tale *The Morning after Optimism* (1971) and a theatrical version of film noir, *The Blue Machushla* (1980). Nevertheless, one of his most extraordinary plays, *Bailegangaire* (1985), is set in 'a country kitchen in the old style'.[35]

Caryl Churchill habitually uses non-naturalistic modes for her politically engaged work. *Top Girls* (1982) opens with the extravagantly surreal gathering in a London restaurant of outstanding women from all ages of history, literature and folklore invited to celebrate the appointment of the career woman Marlene to the managing directorship of the recruitment agency Top Girls. In later scenes, we are shown her at work in the agency. But the last act narrows down to the bleak Essex kitchen of her sister Joyce and the squalid and deprived family background with all its pathologies out of which Marlene has emerged. Maria Irene Fornes once reproached an interviewer for describing her plays as part of 'Off- Broadway'; no, she said, 'I'm part of *Off-Off* Broadway.'[36] Fornes's work has certainly been remote from mainstream styles of theatre. *Fefu and Her Sisters* (1978), however, not only puts the home of Fefu on the stage but takes the convention of the fourth wall to its ultimate limit when the audience is divided into four groups, each of which is led in turn to a different space in the house, where they watch a separate piece of the action. Sam Shepard seemed positively apologetic about the conventionality of *Buried Child* (1978): 'It's sort of a typical Pulitzer Prize–winning play. It wasn't written for that purpose; it was kind of a test. I wanted to write a play about a family.'[37] (It duly did win the Pulitzer Prize in 1979.) One of the theatrical pleasures of *True West* (1980) is seeing a nicely appointed California home thoroughly trashed by the viciously conflicting siblings. Many modern playwrights have been driven so to trash the naturalistic home on the stage, but they have had to return to it repeatedly as it refuses to stay trashed.

Gender dynamics

Women are, or might be expected to be, at the centre of domestic spaces as conceived in the nineteenth century, when this was first established as their distinctively separate sphere. *A Doll's House*, of course, polemically challenged this idea of woman's proper place in the home. Against what he saw as Ibsen's man-hating feminism, Strindberg reacted fiercely in *The Father* (1887) and *Miss Julie*. In the first half of the twentieth century, there were women playwrights who wrote back to these male-conceived versions of the marital situation. Susan Glaspell in her one-act play *Trifles* (1916) has a group of neighbours looking over the country farmhouse where a woman has just murdered her husband. The women see all the tokens of the wife's efforts to make it into a home, which the investigating sheriff and his men, looking only for evidence, dismiss as 'trifles'.[38] The women's key discovery is of the dead canary, evidently killed by the brutal husband. In *Miss Julie*, Jean's bloody onstage disposal of Julie's pet bird represents at once his deflowering of his mistress and the ascendancy he has over her that will allow him to order her death. In Glaspell's scenario, it is the woman who takes revenge for the symbolic death of the bird by the murder of the man.

If Glaspell rewrites Strindberg, Teresa Deevy in *Katie Roche* (1936) reimagines the Ibsenian position of the housebound housewife. Her central figure has none of the middle-class assurance of a Nora Helmer in her initial situation; as a servant and the illegitimate daughter of an unknown father, Katie Roche is expected to be very grateful to be offered marriage by a much older man. She is caught between an expected conformity on the one hand and her attachment to her neighbourhood and a potential young lover on the other; she is violently disciplined by the mysterious tramp figure who turns out to be her father. Katie, unlike Ibsen's Nora, has no reason to think it a happy ending when she leaves her home in the last scene because she is under the firm control of the husband who is to take her away from all she has ever known.

In spite of such female reconceptions of the male-imagined home on the stage, the form has perhaps surprisingly continued to be dominated by men. There are few major women dramatists in the first half of the twentieth century, and in the latter part of the period, feminist playwrights for political as well as dramaturgical reasons have favoured non-naturalistic modes and nondomestic settings.[39] That in itself provides an occasion for the study in gender dynamics that will be one of the concerns of this book. How do male playwrights imagine the dramatised domestic spaces in which women do – or do not – occupy a central position? How far is their perspective conditioned by personal prejudices or preoccupations? Gender roles are no more fixed than the domestic spaces in which they are played out; they vary according to social and cultural context and to the imaginative bent of the individual dramatist. In the analysis of the plays that serve as case studies for the varying representation of domestic spaces through this book, I will be concerned to show how gender figures in each.

This book began with a preoccupation with the afterlife of the Ibsenian home on the stage in the twentieth century and on into the twenty-first. The introduction has given some sense of the sheer range of plays that might have been used to illustrate the phenomenon. The nine texts I have picked for close scrutiny were chosen for a number of reasons. First, I wanted a spread of plays across the period to represent changing styles and contexts – social and political as well as theatrical contexts. It was necessary to begin, as the naturalist movement in theatre itself began, with two of the great landmark European plays. On the whole, thereafter, I have preferred Anglophone texts because of the dangers in attempting a close reading of plays known to me only in translation. Regretfully, I have left out some Irish plays by Synge and O'Casey that would have been very suitable because I have written about them elsewhere and felt I would be repeating myself.

I have chosen for the detailed case studies major plays by major playwrights – four of them Nobel Prize winners – and have tried to place the individual works in relation to their authors' evolving dramaturgy. As such, they can seen as landmark works within the overall history of modern theatre. The texts, however, were not selected simply because they were canonical but because they have had an afterlife of frequent revivals in different sorts of staging. The nineteenth-century domestic space has been variously adapted and reimagined in the modern period, and those adaptations reflect the changed cultural, political and social contexts of their time of composition. At the same time, plays originally created for the naturalistic illusionist theatre have had to be reconceived in later dramaturgical modes. Ingmar Bergman's *Doll's House* and Peter Brook's *Cherry Orchard* are very different works from the productions of the turn of the nineteenth into the twentieth century. This book, therefore, is designed to tell a double story: of the mutations of the naturalist interior as imagined by successive playwrights through the modern period and of the shifting theatrical realisation of that iconic form, home on the stage and its staging.

CHAPTER I

A Doll's House: *the drama of the interior*

'It is simply [...] as a mild picture of domestic life in Christiana [Oslo] that the piece has any interest at all. It is a little bit of genre painting, with here and there an effective touch.'[1] Even by the standards of the abusive criticism heaped on *A Doll's House* when it was first produced in London in 1889, this comment from the *Daily News* reviewer seems exceptionally obtuse. This, after all, was the play that had caused a sensation when published and performed in Scandinavia and Germany a decade before. The appearance of *A Doll's House* in 1879 is now regarded as a landmark in modern theatre, but even at the time it was hugely, controversially successful. Nora's slam of the door, the wife's desertion of her husband, became an instant, scandalous talking point. How could the *Daily News* reviewer have got it so wrong? A part of the answer lies in the condescending lines before those quoted. The 'starting point [...] has dramatic possibilities. A Sardou might conceivably turn it to excellent account on the stage.'[2] Victorien Sardou, along with his contemporary French dramatist Eugène Scribe, developed the model of the 'well-made play', collectively mocked by Shaw as Sardoodledom. Sardou and Scribe had made twists and turns of plot seem an obligatory feature of theatre, and it was these that the 1880s English critics found so signally missing in *A Doll's House*. But the terms of the dispraise in the *Daily News* also bring out how little expected was a play confined to the home. To later tastes, the action, with its sinister blackmailer, frenetic tarantella and 'strong' curtains to each act, may seem quite melodramatic enough. In 1889, it appeared no more than 'a mild picture of domestic life'. It had in fact taken Ibsen half a lifetime of more conventional playwriting to produce this new drama of the interior.

The breakpoint in Ibsen's career, according to many accounts, came with a negative review of his great poetic drama *Peer Gynt* (published in 1867). He reacted with fury in a letter to his sometime friend and rival Bjornson in much quoted terms: 'If I am not a poet, I have nothing to lose.

I shall try my hand as a photographer.' As J.W. McFarlane and Graham Orton point out, when quoting this letter, the force of the comment is appreciated only if you realise 'the weight of contempt with which Ibsen earlier in his career had loaded the term "photographic"'.[3] Ibsen through the first phase of his career had written poetic, romantic, or mythological plays, despising all public demands for photographic realism. If he decided in 1867 to work in the medium of contemporary, realistic prose, it was largely to take revenge upon those he thought of as his enemies.

And he did so effectively in *The League of Youth* (1870), with its satiric portrait of the opportunist politician Stensgard, widely regarded as a caricature of Bjornson – Bjornson, who had in fact written a glowingly enthusiastic review of *Peer Gynt*. (As with his later disciple Joyce, it was a dangerous business being a friend of Ibsen's.) *The League of Youth*, with its focus on the politics of a modern Norwegian small town and its lively conversational style, was closer to verisimilar realism than anything Ibsen had done before. But it has a (by modern standards) extravagantly large cast, with fifteen speaking principals, quite apart from a small army of servants, attendants and crowds. These are necessary because of the enormously complicated network of plots and subplots, all involving the traditional creaky mechanisms of nineteenth-century theatre – misunderstood speeches, misdirected letters, improbable coincidences. The fifth act culminates in the announcement of no less than three engagements, leaving Stensgard (who for self-interested reasons has courted all three of the prospective brides at one time or other in the course of the action) comically mateless. It is equally conventional in its use of five different settings for its five acts, each of them presumably a painted backdrop behind traditional side wings, each of them there merely to provide a strategic situation facilitating the necessary comings and goings of the play's intrigue.

In the early 1870s, Ibsen laboured on his huge 'world-historical drama' of ideas, *Emperor and Galilean* (published in 1873), and it was not until 1877 that he produced his next contemporary prose drama, *The Pillars of Society*. This is often considered the first in the sequence of modern problem plays of Ibsen's middle period that were to make him internationally famous. However, it also sticks with many of the theatrical norms of the time: large cast (nineteen in this case), melodramatic plot involving intertwined emotional relationships, murky property deals and unseaworthy ships, snatching from all of this an improbably 'happy' ending. *The Pillars of Society* does have a single setting, 'a spacious conservatory in the house of Consul Bernick' (Ibsen, v, 23), offering a view of the garden and the street beyond. Again, though, it works largely to facilitate the several plotted scenes, a meeting ground for the middle-class ladies who sew for the good of the poor in Act I, for the various members of Bernick's family, the business people in cahoots with the Consul on the property scam, Johan Tönnesen and Lona Hessel returned from America, Aune the shipyard foreman and the rest.

Its glass wall at the back, though, does make possible one very significant scene in Act IV. Rummel, the ringleader of the business cabal, has organised a torchlit procession of townspeople to come to Bernick's house to honour their most prominent citizen. 'When the garden is filled with a surging throng', he explains, 'then the curtains go up, revealing within a surprised and happy family. . . A man's home ought to be like a show-case' (Ibsen, v, 104). This icon of the perfect middle-class home is intended to provide such reassurance to the community that Bernick will be able to get away with announcing his profiteering land deal. In fact, of course, Bernick uses the opportunity to make his public confession of the corruption of his own life, the hypocritical sham of the model family home: 'Away with all this show', he exclaims (Ibsen, v, 123). It is the free-spirited Lona Hessel who is left to declare the moral of the story. It is not the supposedly upright Bernicks who are the pillars of society: 'No, my friend, the spirit of truth and the spirit of freedom – *these* are the pillars of society' (Ibsen, v, 126).

The revolutionary innovation of Ibsen in *A Doll's House* was to turn that scene of the glass-walled conservatory the other way around, to put the audience of the play in the position of the townspeople gazing in at the middle-class marital home, with no indication that this is a theatrical setup. The stage feature of the back glass wall of *Pillars of Society* becomes the imagined 'fourth wall' of naturalist convention, theorised originally by Diderot, as we have seen, which from André Antoine on was to become the norm for so much modern drama that followed. What is more, the title of the play, as it would have been originally received, can have given little away as to how the audience were to view the home into which they gazed. As Einar Haugen points out, the title *Et Dukkehjem* 'does not mean a house for dolls, which in Norwegian is *dukkehus*, or *dukkestue*. Before Ibsen, *et dukkehjem* was a small, cosy, neat home; his play gave it the pejorative meaning.'[4] As in *Pillars of Society*, Ibsen was still in the business of unmasking, of revealing the truth behind the appearance of happy propriety in the family home, but his title was not intended to make that as blatantly apparent as it does to us, conditioned by the play itself and its misleading English translation. Where in *League of Youth* and *Pillars of Society* Ibsen's target had been whole communities, with their hypocritical pretence of public probity and private morals, in *A Doll's House* he moved inward into a purely domestic space and created a drama of the interior that was to provide a new theatrical paradigm for a century to come.

Bringing it all back home

One measure of the shift of focus from town to home is the reduction in cast size. Instead of the fifteen named characters of *League of Youth*, the nineteen of *Pillars of Society*, there are just five principals in *A Doll's House*, all five of them with connections to the living room we watch through the play. It is the home of Nora and Torvald Helmer and their children; they are visited there daily by their very old friend Dr Rank. Kristine Linde, who appears in Act 1, is a school friend of Nora's with whom she has lost touch, but who rapidly becomes a close confidante. Even Krogstad, the sinister moneylender who appears as the strange intruder on the family scene, turns out to have known Helmer since college days and has a better sense of Torvald's character than Nora does. There is the plotted intrigue of Krogstad's hold over Nora, Torvald's determination to fire Krogstad from his position at the bank, the added complications of Nora's relationship with the dying Rank and the rapprochement between the former lovers Kristine and Krogstad, but all of it is played out within the Helmers' home and all of it is designed to illuminate the marriage at the centre of that home.

The setting of the play, the living room of the Helmers' flat, is very precisely realised. Ibsen spent a full year brooding on the subject before he began to draft it, but in that time he came to develop an intimate visual sense of the characters and their situation. There is a famous story of how he told his wife one day, 'Now I've seen Nora. She came right up to me and put her hand on my shoulder.' When Suzannah asked him what Nora was wearing, she was told 'a blue woollen dress'.[5] He seems to have been just as sure about the layout of Nora's living quarters. In the earliest extant draft of Act 1, the detailed description of the flat corresponds almost exactly to that in the final version (Ibsen, v, 289). Egil Törnqvist supplies a useful ground-plan, showing how the mimetic space of the represented living room is supplemented by the diagetic spaces just offstage.[6] (See Figure 1.1.[7]) At the back of the stage, both the entrance hall of the flat (stage right) and Helmer's study (stage left) are intermittently visible workable spaces. Indeed, in the first production at the Royal Theatre Copenhagen in 1879, the study and hallway were both painstakingly furnished to add to the sense of authenticity.[8] Other rooms in the flat are clearly indicated

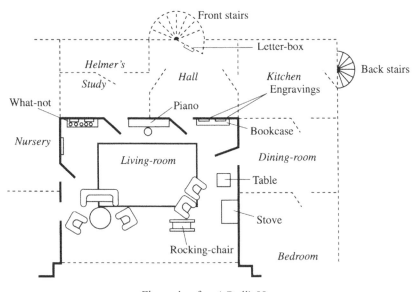

Floor plan for *A Doll's House*

Figure 1.1   Diagram of floor plan of *A Doll's House*.

though not seen. The door to the left leads to the nursery, which the three young children share with Anne Marie, their nursemaid. On the right of the entrance hall is the kitchen, with a back stairs that allows servants (and Krogstad at one point) a separate way into the apartment from the street. And the door from the living room on the right gives access both to the dining room and to a spare bedroom where Nora changes her clothes in Act III. There must be other rooms in the flat as well that are never evoked in the dialogue – the maids' room, for instance, and (strikingly omitted) the marital bedroom of the Helmers.

'The characteristic setting of the realistic drama is the living room', remarks Bert O. States, 'as the most versatile intersection of the private and the social spheres.'[9] The stage topography of *A Doll's House* well illustrates that proposition. Other lives and other inhabited spaces lie just outside the main frame of the living room of the Helmers. The maid Helene is hardly more than a name: bringing in the Christmas tree, answering the door, seen 'half dressed, in the hall' when she is roused up late at night to receive Krogstad's rescuing letter (Ibsen, V, 277). We are given a basic backstory for Anne Marie, the nursemaid to Nora's children, who also nursed Nora herself when, as a young unmarried mother, Anne Marie was forced to give up her own baby for adoption. The Helmers' is an apartment on the first floor of a building with other apartments above it, such as that of the Stenborgs, where they go to the fancy dress party on Boxing Day and where Nora dances her tarantella. The music can still be heard coming down from the party when the couple enter in Act III. And beyond the front door of the building, which so sensationally slams at the play's end, is the town – though we are never told what town. Krogstad can watch there to see that the coast is clear to return to talk to Nora in Act I: 'I was sitting in Olsen's café, and I saw your husband go down the road' (Ibsen, V, 224). This town (wherever it may be) is reachable for Kristine by steamer from an unnamed Norwegian elsewhere, at some distance also from the home district to which Nora plans to return.

It is not, however, merely in the interests of presenting a slice of life that Ibsen thus grounds the Helmers' doll's house in a larger social context. Richard Hornby is no doubt right to claim that 'what realism did for Ibsen was to provide him with new external forms – the everyday objects and events of contemporary bourgeois life – from which to fabricate his symbolism'.[10] What we are shown onstage, according to the opening stage direction, is 'a pleasant room, tastefully but not expensively furnished' (Ibsen, V, 201). The taste, represented in the first production by a bust of Venus and a reproduction of Raphael's *Madonna and Child*, would seem to be that of Helmer the aesthete, who cannot bear anything ugly or even functional in his environment: sewing must be hidden away from him, and ladies should indulge only in elegant embroidery, not in more homely knitting.[11] Helmer has his own separate male space in the study where he can shut himself away. It is significant, also, that the study can be accessed directly from the entrance hall: other men, such as Krogstad and Rank, are shown into the study that way. Nora never once enters the study, though she listens at its closed door to establish Helmer is there when she first enters in Act I. Helmer, on the other hand, is constantly bouncing out into the living room for all his declarations that he is not to be disturbed. Nora has in fact to bolt the door of the study when she needs to ensure an uninterrupted conversation with Krogstad. When it is unlocked, Helmer exclaims with mock indignation, 'Well, can a man get into his own living-room again now?' (Ibsen, V, 257). The male view of the shared space of the marital home is clearly 'what's yours is mine and what's mine's my own'.

Some areas of the stage are more specifically associated with Nora and feminine activity. So, for instance, the stove with the armchairs and rocking chair close to it, downstage right, are at a diagonal opposite corner from the male preserve of Helmer's study. It is here that Nora installs

Kristine when she welcomes her in Act I: 'Now let's sit down here in comfort beside the stove. No, here, you take the armchair, I'll sit here on the rocking-chair' (Ibsen, V, 207). After the disturbance of Krogstad's first entrance, she feels the need to fiddle with the stove, as though to warm herself against the chill of fear: 'There, it'll burn better now' (Ibsen, V, 217). A return to sitting in the rocking chair, associated as it is with a calm maternity, is a reassuring normalisation after the emotional upset of Rank's love declaration in Act II (Ibsen, V, 249). The game of hide and seek with her children in Act I spills over into the offstage nursery, making the living room into an extended play area. But by Act II, the nursery door is shut and the children excluded, as the terrified Nora contemplates the possibility of being separated from them forever.

'Theatre constructs space that is not only structured, but in which structures become signifying', says Anne Ubersfeld.[12] In the case of *A Doll's House*, the signifying structures are developed out of the latency of everyday living, in which stoves are sources of warmth and comfort on a northern winter's day, and studies are rooms where men work undisturbed. In the domestic space of the play, meaning is so vested in the ordinary that to speak of symbolic significance seems like an overstatement. Nora's initial entrance, with Christmas tree and presents, needs no decoding to bespeak the family holiday, though by now we probably need to be told that 'a Christmas tree around 1880 was a status symbol, an indication that you belonged to the better situated in society'.[13] Nora seeks to offset the threat to the security of the happy middle-class marital home posed by Krogstad's blackmailing with the decoration of the Christmas tree, which she instructs the maid to place in the middle of the living room:

> NORA [*busy decorating the tree*]. Candles here ... and flowers here. – Revolting man! It's all nonsense! There's nothing to worry about. We'll have a lovely Christmas tree. (Ibsen, V, 230)

By Act II, however, on Christmas Day itself, we are told that 'in the corner beside the piano stands the Christmas tree, stripped, bedraggled and with its candles burnt out' (Ibsen, V, 235).[14] In Act III, the Christmas tree has gone altogether and in its place in the centre of the living room is the round table which in Act I stood by the window downstage left. No doubt it had been temporarily moved from this, its normal position, to make way for the Christmas tree. But in the emotional development of the action, the central positioning of the table at which Nora and Torvald will have their final confrontation is highly significant in the disillusioned aftermath of Christmas.

The look of the Helmers' flat changes over the course of the play, as we move from the gaiety and warmth of Christmas Eve to the sober reckoning of Boxing Day. Throughout, we are also conscious of the contrast between inside and outside. Norwegian winter means that, apart from anything else, clothes mark that difference. Nora at her first entrance is 'in her outdoor things'; when Kristine arrives, Nora 'helps her' out of her 'things' and seats her by the stove to get warm (Ibsen, v, 201, 207). When Dr Rank is getting ready to leave, he 'fetches his fur coat from the hall and warms it at the stove' (Ibsen, v, 221). The credits sequence of the 1973 film, directed by Patrick Garland, showing a well wrapped-up Nora being driven on a sledge through the snow before coming into her warm and welcoming flat, makes actual what is implicit in the stage play. That sense of the home as a separated place of shelter is enforced by Nora's dismissive attitude towards anyone beyond the family. The creditors who would lose out in Helmer's hypothetical moral story, intended to teach Nora the dangers of borrowing, are of no importance: 'Them? Who cares about them! They are only strangers!' (Ibsen, v, 202). The world is divided into the happy home of the Helmers, their children and friends and an anonymous place of strangers beyond.

The appearance of Krogstad in Act I already brings that outside world with its claims upon Nora into the home. We see her at the beginning of Act II with 'her outdoor things [. . .] on the sofa' restlessly pacing up and down, picking up and putting down her coat, undecided whether to stay in or go out (Ibsen, v, 235).[15] Anne Marie tries to restrain her mistress from going out: 'Out again? In this terrible weather? You'll catch your death of cold, Ma'am' (Ibsen, v, 235). And the full horror of suicide is brought home to her by Krogstad with his scaremongering images of the winter realities: 'Under the ice, maybe? Down in the cold, black water?' (Ibsen, v, 254). Yet, as the stress builds on Nora, the place of cosy shelter becomes a place of confinement. In the hectic mood of the second act, she is steeling herself for an ultimate escape into death. And that helps to make plausible what is often thought of as implausible: her decision to leave at the end. When in the final scene we see her again in her 'outdoor things', it provides a rhymed closure for the opening entrance and marks just how far Nora has come since she skylarked onto the stage with the presents and Christmas tree.

The multiplicity of doors on the stage set of *A Doll's House* has been pointed out by Austin Quigley: we are shown a room with 'no fewer than four doors, one of which leads to a fifth and a sixth'.[16] The inner space of the living room is separated from the outside by three of these: the door out of the living room into the entrance hall of the flat, the door out of the flat onto the stairs and the door of the building. There are, therefore, a set of liminal spaces between the interior and the full exterior of which we are aware through the play. The hallway in particular is an important focus for attention, occupied in succession by the generously tipped porter bearing the Christmas tree in the opening moments: the maid who takes it from him; Rank and Kristine, who so awkwardly arrive together; and so on. The hall, with its own two doors, makes for a gender division, Rank being shown into the study, space of business and male intimates, Kristine into the living room. When Krogstad first appears in the hallway, Nora is afraid he is heading her way, but he reassures her that it is 'just routine business matters' that have brought him to the house, and she directs him accordingly into the study (Ibsen, v, 217). Beyond the outer hall door is the staircase. Rank, introduced to Kristine, realises who she is: 'I believe I came past you on the stairs as I came in' (Ibsen, v, 218). A strange woman who might have been calling on any of the families in the building is now placed in relation to the Helmers. That awareness of the staircase is crucial to the effect of the play's last speech. We see Nora leave through the hall door. There is then a moment of suspense long enough for Helmer to oscillate between despair at her leaving and renewed hope for 'the miracle of miracles' before 'the heavy sound of a door being slammed is heard from below' (Ibsen, v, 286). Nora has decisively abandoned the interior of home and marriage for an unknown space without.

Marriage reimagined

For all its innovative dramaturgy, *A Doll's House* retains several traditional features of nineteenth-century theatre including melodramatic plot props like the loan with the forged signature, the all-important letter that must be stopped and so on. It is startling, however, to realise that one of the most implausible and stagey-sounding pieces of the narrative – Nora's need to save her husband's life by secretly borrowing money to finance a trip to the south – was based on fact.[17] The story is well known but needs to be retold because of the implications for the way Ibsen used it in the play.[18] Laura Kieler, a young friend of Ibsen who had written a novel as a sequel to *Brand*, had done just what Nora does in the play and for similar reasons: she had borrowed to fund a health trip for her schoolteacher husband Victor but had not told him because he was neurotic about money. Desperate to repay the loan, she asked Ibsen to endorse a weak manuscript she had written in haste. Ibsen refused to do this, but sensing that there was something more behind the request, he urged her to tell her husband everything. Rather than do that, Laura burned the manuscript and forged a cheque. Victor, when he found out, refused to allow Laura to have anything to do with the children, and had her committed to a mental hospital when this precipitated a nervous collapse. Only after two years of separation was the family home reestablished.

In earlier plays, Ibsen had shown his sympathy for women oppressed by patriarchal codes. There is, for example, the figure of Selma, a relatively marginal figure in *League of Youth*, who welcomes the opportunity to share the troubles of her husband Erik, who has – guess what? – forged a bill: 'How I've longed for even a little share in your worries! But when I asked, all you did was laugh it off with a joke. You dressed me up like a doll. You played with me as you might play with a child. Oh, how joyfully I could have helped to bear the burdens!' (Ibsen, IV, 93). Betty Bernick, wife of Karsten in *Pillars of Society*, is also only too pleased to support her husband when he confesses his misdoings. The story of Laura Kieler must have foregrounded the plight of such disregarded and infantilised wives for Ibsen, the more so because of his personal involvement with her. In the playful relationship between them, he had nicknamed Laura 'skylark', as Torvald does Nora in the play.[19] He, like Kristine Linde, had insisted on the need for honest disclosure of wife to husband. Driving through the play is the urge to rewrite Laura's story, to turn it into an exemplary paradigm, the very opposite of the messy tale of misery and tyrannical domination it was in real life.

Initially it was the issue of law that preoccupied Ibsen in his contemplation of the play. His often quoted 'Notes for the tragedy of modern times', written months before he began actual composition, highlights this theme: 'There are two kinds of moral law, two kinds of conscience, one in man and a completely different one in women. [. . .] A woman cannot be herself in contemporary society, it is an exclusively male society with laws drafted by men, and with counsel and judges who judge feminine conduct from the male point of view' (Ibsen, V, 436). In his early draft, the behaviour of Nora was much closer to that of Laura Kieler; in Act II she appears to be on the verge of nervous collapse. The act was then set on New Year's Eve and the prolonged crisis over Krogstad's threat of exposure was driving her towards madness. Several features of the play in its final form were missing in this draft version. The forbidden macaroons eaten by Nora on the sly are not there; there is no tarantella, nor yet the scene where Nora plays the coquette in the attempt to get a loan from Dr Rank. The characters of both Torvald and Nora had to be crucially adjusted to complete the critical anatomy of a marriage that is *A Doll's House*.

In the earlier draft, the Helmer figure has principled reasons for dismissing Krogstad from his job at the bank. He is committed to cleaning up the culture of 'favouritism and jobbery', having got the job of manager 'by opposing the present system ... in a pamphlet, in a series of newspaper articles, and by a pointed speech at the last general meeting' (Ibsen, v, 300–1). He here approximates a Consul Bernick, a man who has built his career on a public reputation for ethical integrity, and by the end of the action, as with Bernick, it would be shown how little he deserved that reputation. In the final play, with its concentration on the domestic interior, Ibsen did away with this public aspect of Helmer's motivation, concentrating instead on the personal. The real reason for his desire to get rid of Krogstad emerges in his conversation with Nora in Act II and has nothing to do with Krogstad's dishonesty:

> [W]e knew each other rather well when we were younger. It was one of those rather rash friendships that prove embarrassing in later life. There's no reason why you shouldn't know we were once on terms of some familiarity. And he, in his tactless way, makes no attempt to hide the fact, particularly when other people are present. On the contrary, he thinks he has every right to treat me as an equal, with his 'Torvald this' and 'Torvald that' every time he opens his mouth. I find it extremely irritating, I can tell you. He would make my position at the Bank absolutely intolerable. (Ibsen, v, 242–43)

Before she can think, Nora reacts to this – 'surely you aren't serious [. . .] it's all so petty' – a charge that so stings Helmer that he demonstrates just such pettiness by insisting on dispatching his letter of dismissal to Krogstad immediately. This becomes a key moment for Nora's ultimate discovery that Torvald is not the person she imagined him to be. It is clinched when he behaves exactly as Krogstad foretold he would when faced with blackmail; he even repeats Krogstad's precise words. Krogstad assures Nora that Helmer will cave in: 'I know him. He'll do it without so much as a whimper' (Ibsen, v, 254). And sure enough, when Torvald realises Krogstad's power over him, he moans, 'I daren't even whimper' (Ibsen, v, 276). The exposure of Helmer is not of a public fraud like Bernick or Stensgard but of a weak private person masquerading as the ideal strong husband.

Many of the changes to Ibsen's first conception of Nora were designed to bring out the corruptness of the Helmers' marriage and the degree to which the marriage has corrupted her also. The macaroons – which show up first in a marginal note in the early draft of Act I (Ibsen, v, 297) – are a case in point. From her first entrance, eating some of her macaroons, then 'stealthily' listening at the door of her husband's study (Ibsen, v, 201), the keynote is that of childish concealment. When Torvald playfully accuses her of indulging her sweet tooth, she becomes ever warmer in her denials: 'I would never dream of doing anything you didn't want me to' (Ibsen, v, 205). The macaroons later provide the occasion to demonstrate how fluently Nora lies. She offers them to a surprised Rank, explaining that they were a gift from Kristine, smothering the latter's protests, 'Now, now, you needn't be alarmed. You weren't to know that Torvald had forbidden them' (Ibsen, v, 219).

The child wife Nora is not only habitually mendacious but equally habitually meretricious. With her flirtatious playacting, she exploits her attractiveness to manipulate Torvald. This was accentuated in the process of composition. In an early draft of Act i, Nora assures Kristine that she will make her husband give her friend a job at the bank: 'You watch me nag him' (Ibsen, v, 294). But in the final text, nagging is not Nora's only method of getting her way with Torvald. Beneath the kittenish charades, at some level, Nora is aware of the source of her power over her husband. This comes out most strikingly when she responds to Kristine's question as to whether she will ever tell Torvald what she did to save his life. She replies 'reflectively, half-smiling':

> Oh yes, some day perhaps . . . in many years time, when I'm no longer as pretty as I am now. You mustn't laugh! What I mean of course is when Torvald isn't quite so much in love with me as he is now, when he's lost interest in watching me dance, or get dressed up, or recite. Then it might be a good thing to have something in reserve. . . (Ibsen, v, 215)

Although she immediately dismisses this thought – 'What nonsense! That day will never come' – the hint of the need for emotional blackmail as a hold over her husband once her sexual power begins to fail gives a measure of how exploitative this relationship is on both sides.

Nora knows, but does not let herself acknowledge she knows, how to get what she wants from men. Another addition to the earlier draft of the play was her fantasy about the rich admirer who would rescue her: 'I used to sit here and pretend that some rich old gentleman had fallen in love with me [. . .] and that now he had died, and when they opened his will, there in big letters were the words: "My entire fortune is to be paid over, immediately and in cash, to charming Mrs Nora Helmer"' (Ibsen, v, 216). The childishness is designed to mask the nature of the 'charm', as we see fully dramatised in the scene with Dr Rank in Act ii, a key development in the final version of the play. There can be little doubt about the erotically suggestive moves Nora makes here, with the notorious flesh-coloured stockings:[20]

NORA. [. . .] Of course, it's dark here now, but tomorrow . . . No, no, no, you can only look at the feet. Oh well, you might as well see a bit higher up, too.
RANK. Hm . . .
NORA. Why are you looking so critical? Don't you think they'll fit?
RANK. I couldn't possibly offer any informed opinion about that.
NORA (*looks at him for a moment*). Shame on you. (*Hits him lightly across the ear with the stockings*)
(Ibsen, v, 247)

However, when this coquettish ploy evokes a downright declaration of love from Rank, the proper bourgeois housewife is back in place, calling the maid to bring in the lamp to dispel the demi-monde half-light: 'Oh, how could you be so clumsy, Dr Rank! When everything was so nice' (Ibsen, v, 249). Ibsen brilliantly exposes here both the sexual realities and the self-deceptions necessary to preserve the proprieties in the Helmer home.

The most striking alteration to the early draft of *A Doll's House* was the introduction of the tarantella. Ibsen had originally envisaged Nora distracting her husband from the letter-box containing the fatal letter from Krogstad by having her play and sing 'Anitra's Song' from *Peer Gynt* (Ibsen, v, 327). This would have been an interesting piece of self recycling, with Nora standing in for the exotically seductive houri Anitra, testifying to the enormous success of the first production of *Peer Gynt* with Grieg's score in 1876, just three years before *A Doll's House* was being written. In the event, Ibsen decided on a different sort of exoticism and seductiveness, the tarantella. Early critics of the play objected to the staginess of this scene. William Archer, Ibsen's main champion in the English-speaking world, dismissed it as 'a last spasmodic effort in the (Gallic) art of keeping up the dramatic tension by means of external devices'.[21] More recent interpreters have viewed it as a key part of the feminist effect of the play. Alisa Solomon, for instance, denies that it is 'stagey effect-hunting [. . .] Rather, it announces itself as a remnant of that old staginess, and then goes it one better. Not a *concession* to the old effect-hunting, Nora's tarantella is an *appropriation* of it.'[22] Toril Moi argues that '[d]ancing the tarantella, Nora's body expresses the state of her soul. Nothing could be more authentic.'[23] It is certainly true that the tarantella is a complex representation onstage, in part an erotic performance for the watching men, in part an expression of Nora's situation inscribed in the supposed origin of the dance itself, 'the dance of the victim of the tarantula spider, and the delirious attempt of the body to rid itself of the poison'.²⁴ As Nora's dancing becomes ever wilder, in spite of Helmer's attempts to control her, she is acting out the conflict between her determination to kill herself and an independent will to live.

Act II ends with this rehearsal of the tarantella in the living room. This sets the stage for the climactic scene in Act III when she returns from the Stenborgs' party in full costume, having danced the tarantella to wild applause. The discordance of the mood of the married couple is embarrassing, painful to watch. Torvald, well-warmed by the party champagne, takes off Nora's shawl and leeringly shows her off to Kristine: '[T]ake a good look at her. I think I can say she's worth looking at. Isn't she lovely, Mrs Linde?' (Ibsen, v, 267). When they are left alone, the urgency of his desire, his proprietorial investment in Nora's beauty, contrasts hideously with her need to prepare herself for what she plans as her imminent death:

HELMER. [...] How irresistibly lovely you are, Nora!
NORA. Don't look at me like that, Torvald!
HELMER. Can't I look at my most treasured possession? At all this loveliness
   that's mine and mine alone, completely and utterly mine.
(Ibsen, v, 269)

The mismatch of feeling is comparable to the final scene of Joyce's 'The Dead', a scene that was in some sense a rewriting of the equivalent moment in *A Doll's House*.²⁵ Where the more sensitive Gabriel Conroy has his sexual urge chilled by the revelation of Gretta's memories of the dead Michael Furey, there is no comparable *éclaircissement* at this point between Torvald and Nora. Indeed, the cross-purposes move perilously close to marital rape before they are interrupted by Dr Rank at the door:

NORA. Go away, Torvald! Leave me alone. I won't have it.
HELMER. What's this? It's just your little game isn't it, my little Nora. Won't!
   Won't! Am I not your husband ...?
(Ibsen, v, 270)

Only the revelation of Rank's imminent death finally puts Torvald off making love. 'This ugly thing has come between us ... thoughts of death and decay. We must try to free ourselves from it. Until then ... we shall go our separate ways' (Ibsen, v, 274).

'The sexual force underlying *A Doll's House* is one of its key elements, all the more difficult to sustain and convey because it is not explicit but deeply imbedded in the dialogue and gestures of the characters.'[26] This is an acute observation of Kirsten Shepherd-Barr. The same feature makes it equally hard to answer the crude question – how good or bad is the Helmers' sex life? We have plenty of opportunities to see the distortions in their sexual attitudes, Nora's willingness to indulge in what Errol Durbach calls her 'dollydom' to gain her own ends,[27] Torvald's voyeuristic fantasies about Nora as his secret young bride – 'quite alone with your young and trembling loveliness' (Ibsen, v, 270). But it is not clear whether there has ever been a full mutuality in their lovemaking. Of this, the absence of the marital bedroom from the implied ground plan of the stage setting may be taken as emblematic. The room off the dining room where Nora changes out of her tarantella costume is specified as the 'spare room' – in the early draft it is the 'side room' (Ibsen, v, 278, 339). Given the specificity with which the nursery, the study, the hall and the kitchen are located in relation to the living room playing area, the lack of any reference to Torvald and Nora's shared bedroom is the more striking. Ibsen never encourages his audience imaginatively to explore this private space.

That physical relationship, however, has a key bearing upon the representation of the breakdown of the marriage in the final scene. The crucial realisation for Nora, when her illusions about Torvald's character are shattered, is the thought of what her past life has really been: 'for eight years I'd been living with a stranger, and had borne him three children'. The thought precipitates a disgust with her own contaminated body: 'Oh, I can't bear to think about it! I could tear myself to shreds' (Ibsen, v, 285). She dismisses out of hand Torvald's by then timid proposal that they might 'go on living here like brother and sister': 'You know very well that wouldn't last' (Ibsen, v, 285). Wouldn't last because of his desire merely, or because of that of both of them? Nora's retrospective diagnosis of their marriage is that she was infantilised by Torvald just as she had been by her father; like a doll plaything, she claims, 'I passed out of Daddy's hands into yours' (Ibsen, v, 280). This image, so powerful a metaphor for patriarchal possession as it is, leaves Nora's own sexual maturation out of account. It is to quite adult purposes, after all, that we see her put on her dolly act through the course of the play. It may be that Ibsen, due to his own temperamental reticence or that of his period, felt unable to deal more explicitly with this dimension to the Helmers' bad marriage. Stage productions and screen adaptations of *A Doll's House* in the later, more direct twentieth and twenty-first centuries were to bring the matter more clearly into focus.

Changing times, changing spaces

The paradox of the naturalist formula is that the individual situation, realistically represented, in its very individuality laid claim to universal significance. The one tastefully decorated living room we see onstage is a theatrical synecdoche for the Helmers' apartment as a whole, which stands in for the class of all other such middle-class apartments. Insofar as the Helmers' model home could be any such home in Germany, France, Russia, or North America, *A Doll's House*, with its deconstruction of marital pieties, struck at a central icon of social faith. But the living room could be extended to take in more of the whole of which it was a part. So, for instance, a 1953 revival of the play at the Lyric Theatre, Hammersmith in London, directed and adapted by Peter Ashmore, 'provided a multiple set that opened up the entire living area of the Helmer household – including the master bedroom'.[28] The introduction of the missing bedroom must necessarily have foregrounded the sexual relationship that Ibsen's text to some degree occludes. Certainly a still from the production is very suggestive, with Mai Zetterling in a white petticoat, holding the tarantella costume she has just taken off, standing with her back to Torvald (Mogens Wieth), who lolls back on the bed in his waistcoat (Figure 1.2).

Cinema and television are almost necessarily bound to move beyond the confines of the theatre's single set. In one sense, these media are the obvious inheritors of naturalism, rendering lifelike images of a recognisable world in which people plausibly interact. So, for example, in Patrick Garland's 1973 film, based as it was on his realistic stage revival of the play (in both cases starring Claire Bloom as Nora), we are taken outside the Helmers' flat. Not only is the winter landscape of the action established in the credits sequence of Nora being driven along in a sledge, but we see Krogstad in the café watching Helmer leave the building in company with Kristine, see Kristine go round to Krogstad's lodgings to plead with him to spare Nora. We are shown, also, the poverty of those lodgings and Krogstad, very sympathetically played by Denholm Elliot, looking after his motherless children. Socioeconomic conditions implied in the plays are brought before us onscreen.

The Joseph Losey film made in the same year as Garland's, starring Jane Fonda, took the tendency towards extended cinematic realisation still further. It was actually shot on location in the small mining town of Røros in Norway. Losey not only extended the setting spatially to include exteriors – we see Dr Rank in his clinic, Nora and Krogstad meet for their

Figure 1.2   Photo of Nora (Mai Zetterling) and Torvald (Mogans Wieth) in *A Doll's House*, Act III, directed by Peter Ashmore, London, 1951.

crucial conversations outside in the snow – but extended the narrative back in time with a precredits sequence showing Nora and Kristine as young friends coming from skating, talking about their relative situations, Nora excited at the prospect of marrying Torvald, Kristine sadly forced to give up Krogstad to marry for money to support her ailing mother and young brothers. As Törnqvist commented on this wider-angle focus of the film, Losey 'replaced the doll's house with a doll town'.[29] Where Ibsen only has Nora rehearse the tarantella in the living room, Losey's film shows the performance itself in the Stenborgs' flat surrounded by a full cast of party-goers in their fancy dresses. Cinema realises what even naturalistic theatre leaves to the audience's imagination.

A Doll's House is a naturalistic play, and most stage productions and film adaptations have sought to follow Ibsen's instructions for lifelike repro-duction of social surfaces. From as early as the beginning of the twentieth century, however, there was a challenge to this tradition from the radical Russian director Vsevolod Meyerhold. Hired by the theatre owner and leading actress Vera Kommisarjevskaya to direct a 1906 revival of *A Doll's House*, he stripped away the realistic Norwegian interior. 'In place of the lovely, soft furnishings that so credibly represented the doll-wife's warm nest', wrote one antagonistic reviewer, 'we are instead shown a cramped corridor passageway with a decrepit piano in one corner'.[30] 'An equally dilapidated three-legged table, two inconspicuous chairs, an arbitrarily suspended window flanked by ballooning, and cranberry-colored drapes that reached the full height of the stage completed the iconography of the doll's house.'[31] A postrevolutionary staging of the play by Meyerhold pushed still further this principle of the 'undressing of the theatre', the set 'consisting of old flats propped back to front against the bare walls of the stage, some gridiron bars, and an odd assortment of old furniture, chests, and the like placed to create playing areas for the actors', intended to represent the 'disintegrating bourgeois milieu against which Nora rebels'.[32]

Few directors followed Meyerhold's antirepresentational lead until the second half of the twentieth century, when at last the standard heavily furnished set of the play was banished from a number of revivals. So, for example, Peter Zadek in the Bremer Kammerspiele 'created a stage space that was hardly a room or even a "setting" at all – a door on either side, a veranda window as background, an old-fashioned sofa at the diagonal mid-point of the stage, and virtually nothing more'.[33] In this deconstructive, minimalising tendency, Ingmar Bergman's production in German in 1981 is often picked out as outstanding. The Munich staging at the

Residenztheater of *Nora* (as the play is generally known in Germany) was part of the epic Bergman *Project for the Theatre*, in which it was mounted as part of a trilogy with *Miss Julie* and Bergman's own *Scenes from a Marriage*, all performed within the one day. Bergman's *A Doll's House* had all its plotted paraphernalia removed, the 'motivating of characters, excusing their absences, providing realistic explanations for everything that happens on stage', and the setting was equivalently stripped down. As Bergman himself said: 'There are always so many *things* lying around everywhere – sofas and chairs and Christmas trees and pianos. [...] You can get lost in all those details.'[34] Bergman therefore avoided altogether any fourth-wall illusion. The playing area was a central raised platform, furnished for each of the scenes by isolated iconic items: 'a heavy, darkly upholstered sofa and chair' at the beginning, with 'an elaborately trimmed Christmas tree, behind it'; this was later replaced by 'a large, round dining table and four stiffly old-fashioned chairs'; and the final scene featured a brass double bed.[35] The cast was reduced to just the five principal characters – the children, maids and porters were all removed. And the actors were continuously present onstage throughout, sitting on the sidelines watching when not involved in the action, stepping up onto the acting platform when required. Most striking of all was the setting, designed by Gunilla Palmstierna-Weiss, within which this was enclosed. 'The entire stage space was a limbo cut off from any contact with the world of reality – a void encompassed by an immense, non-representational box that was uniformly lined with a dark-red, velvetlike fabric. Within this vast, closed space, a smaller enclosure was defined by high, dark walls that suggested both the panelled interior of a courtroom and the wainscoting of a polite mid-Victorian parlor.'[36]

Bergman's drastic recasting of *A Doll's House* is the more remarkable when contrasted with his well-furnished, strongly realistic *Miss Julie* as part of the same *Project*. The intention was to turn the play into something like a Strindbergian dream play in which Nora's is the central dreaming consciousness. Rather than the conventional flighty doll wife who is transformed into the thinking, reasoning liberated person of the last act, it was as though Nora was living through again the chain of actions that led her inevitably to the final parting from Helmer. 'Alone, in the midst of a setting that emphasised its own theatrical nature, she acted out a dream life, from which she was struggling to awaken.'[37] Her difference from the other four characters was accentuated in the costuming. Her 'corseted wine-red dress' picked her out from all the others, who wore clothes in various shades from pale grey to heavy black in the case of Kristine Linde.[38]

The sexual dimension of the Helmers' relationship was accentuated in Bergman's version. The 'laughing, semi-erotic horseplay' between the couple in the opening scene 'ended with a final kiss – which [Rita] Russek [playing Nora] surreptitiously wiped from her mouth with a quick, automatic gesture'.[39] If that suggested a muted sense of distaste, the final confrontation between them played out in the bedroom, which is so signally absent from Ibsen's text, made of Nora's liberation a specifically sexual triumph. 'Naked and asleep in their decorative brass doll-bed, his sexual desire presumably satisfied, [Robert] Atzorn's Helmer awakened suddenly to find himself face to face with a woman in a black travelling dress, a packed overnight bag in her hand. The utter vulnerability of his nakedness, accentuated by a single, piercing shaft of light that turned his figure and the bedclothes into a blaze of white, was confronted by what Bergman's script describes as Nora's "complete ruthlessness and brutality."' Nora's unequivocal victory was accentuated by the coup de théâtre of her exit: 'Without a sound, as if by magic, a hidden aperture in the apparently solid wall swung open, and Nora stepped through it to freedom.'[40]

Ibsen's *A Doll's House* is a drama of the interior. The playwright takes us inside a domestic space as a means of taking us inside a marriage, that most private of relationships. A production such as Bergman's is a further interiorisation, as it becomes a drama played out within the consciousness of Nora, all the other actors reduced to supporting players in her anguished struggle towards liberation. But there is an additional significance in this changed dramaturgical style. Bert O. States contrasts the metonymy, which he identifies as the characteristic mode of naturalism, with earlier metaphoric traditions of scenic illusion.[41] Staging like that of Bergman is a turn back towards metaphor. Instead of the synecdochal metonym by which the Helmers' realistically staged living room stands in for all such living rooms and all such marriages, and by extension the society that places bourgeois marriage at its ideological centre, Bergman's stage design of box within box, with its associations of courtroom and Victorian parlour, becomes a symbolic rendering of the meaning of the play. In this it is typical of much later twentieth-century dramaturgy and Bergman's production of *A Doll's House* characteristic of the reconception of naturalistic drama which it is one of the aims of this book to explore.

The impact of naturalist drama originally depended on its contemporaneity: 'Take our present environment', urged Zola to the would-be naturalist playwright, 'and try to make men live in it.'[42] The aim was the faithful reproduction of lives just like those of the people in the audience. That was exactly what *A Doll's House* achieved with its challenging representation of a supposedly happy marriage in a typical modern apartment, 'tastefully but not expensively furnished' (Ibsen, v, 201). Plays based on that formula, however, of the middle-class audience looking in at people like themselves living in the way they themselves live, are subject to a changed perspective in later periods. Already by the 1920s there was a controversy over whether revivals of Ibsen should be played as period pieces in their own time or updated to make them once again contemporary. There were objections to a 1921 Nora played as a flapper with bobbed hair on the grounds that such a modern woman would never put up with Helmer's patronising pet names.[43] In 1936, one Danish critic declared that Ibsen's plays 'can no longer be performed in modern dress'. To prevent it from appearing dated, *A Doll's House* 'must be presented as a picture from the period (and an image of that period)'. Otherwise, Nora appeared to be 'a modern young woman wrestling in full seriousness with problems and ideas that have been talked out by everyone else almost two generations ago'.[44] The naturalist formula also depends on accepting the implicit assumption of middle-class life as itself normative, with a Nora Helmer representative in her struggle for personal liberation. The strong Marxist perspective of Werner Fassbinder in his 1973 video adaptation *Nora Helmer* made for a vigorous challenge to that assumption. 'In Fassbinder's version the root of the Helmer problem was ultimately the fact that both Nora *and* Torvald were dolls – unwitting puppets manipulated by the strictures and sanctions of their [. . .] repressive bourgeois society.'[45]

Two twenty-first-century productions illustrate the impulse to make the play new for modern audiences and to renew its sense of shock. Thomas Ostermeier's 2002 Berlin Schaubühne production radically updated the setting and sensationally altered the ending.

> The married couple in Mr Ostermeier's 'Nora' [. . .] are flashily nouveau riche German yuppies who live in a chic, multilevel Bauhaus home with Mies van der Rohe furniture and a giant aquarium. They fuss with cellphones and laptops and have a black au pair who keeps the children out of mama's hair, especially when mama shows symptoms of turning into Medea. Occasionally, they burst into fits of hysteria and aggression punctuated with blasts of electronic music. At the end, instead of walking out with the door slamming behind her, Nora turns the groping and psychological violence she has been subjected to into outward rage and she kills.[46]

Ostermeier maintained that his adaptation of the ending was necessary: '[I]t was very shocking to society at the end of the 19th century that a woman should leave her husband and children. We can't nowadays have the same moment of shock when two thirds of families split up.'[47] Ostermeier's version of the tarantella dance was designed to make a point about the limits of contemporary female empowerment.

> He has the actress Anne Tismer dress up as Lara Croft of the 'Tomb Raider' films and video games rather than as the Neapolitan peasant girl that Ibsen had imagined. That is an allusion to the way female pop stars in vehicles like 'Tomb Raider', 'Charlie's Angels' and 'Kill Bill' wield fictional power that women don't truly have.[48]

To offset the sense of *A Doll's House* as a problem play about the long since solved problem of the woman trapped in the space of domesticity, there is this polemic insistence that it is only the forms of patriarchal fantasy and domination that have changed.

Lee Breuer, veteran director of Mabou Mines, considers that 'updating Ibsen is a mistake'.[49] Instead, his coadaptation with Maude Mitchell as *DollHouse* accentuated the play's nineteenth-century origins in melodrama, with a live pianist accompanying the high points of the action with arrangements of Grieg's piano music. The play's title metaphor was literalised; the set was a grand doll's house unpacked by Nora as a Christmas present for the children in the opening scene. The most striking feature of *DollHouse*, however, was the casting of all three male parts with actors of no more than four feet tall, while the women playing Nora, Kristine and the maid Helene were near enough six feet. The point of this contrast in physical scale was obvious: 'At its heart is the image of the doll's house and nursery, where the statuesque Nora (Maude Mitchell, who is superb) must contort her body to fit into the space, while her tiny husband, Torvald (Mark Povinelli), feels perfectly at home.'[50] The conceit of the doll's house was extended down to a miniature version with which the doll-like children play, both dressed like their parents. Human beings from generation to generation were no more than society's mannikins but still within a distorting scale in which small men were in charge. But the style of playing, from the cartoon Norwegian accents in which all the actors spoke, the hammed-up monologues and slapstick business, through to the climactic scene sung as high opera, deconstructed the play's pretensions to realism. 'Breuer shows that what is generally believed to be a modern drama is in fact a nineteenth-century melodrama held together by a rather mechanical plot.'[51]

There is in both Ostermeier and Breuer's versions a felt need to challenge the canonical status of the classic work of nineteenth-century naturalism, to mock the reverence with which it has been treated, to destabilise its representational status with every postmodern device available. Yet at the same time, there is a continuing sense that the play, in its engagement with the space of the family home, can still be made to speak to twenty-first-century audiences. This phenomenon of the directorial impatience with the outdatedness of naturalist home on the stage combined with the desire to return to it is a general one, illustrated again in productions of *The Cherry Orchard*, looked at in the next chapter.

CHAPTER 2

The Cherry Orchard: *all Russia*

A room which is still known as the nursery. One of the doors leads to Anya's room. Half-light, shortly before sunrise. It is May already, and the cherry trees are in blossom, but outside in the orchard it is cold, with a morning frost. The windows are closed.[1]

How different this opening stage direction of *The Cherry Orchard* is from the equivalent setting in *A Doll's House*. Ibsen gives the director and designer a detailed ground plan of the Helmers' apartment: which door leads where, the exact position of each named and described item of furniture. By contrast, Chekhov gestures towards a scene, conjuring it up in impressionistic strokes. 'One of the doors leads to Anya's room' – but what other doors are there? 'The windows are closed' – how many windows are there and where are they placed? The contrast is suggestive of the background of the two writers. Ibsen formed his career in the professional theatre, with thirteen hard years working as a dramaturge and director in Norway before going into exile and concentrating on his own writing. Chekhov made his name in the short story and came to playwriting very uncertainly as a secondary medium. At twenty he wrote a long, more or less unstageable play that has come to be known as *Platonov* (1880–81).[2] He was unhappy with his first staged work, *Ivanov* (1887–89), even though it had a limited success. *The Wood Demon* (1889–90) was sufficiently discouraging that Chekhov swore he would give up the theatre altogether, and the premiere of *The Seagull* in 1896 was even worse. It was with great difficulty that V.I. Nemirovich-Danchenko persuaded him to allow the newly formed Moscow Art Theatre to have another go with *The Seagull* in 1898, thus initiating the extraordinary period of collaboration between playwright and theatre in Chekhov's desperately short final six years of life. Even then, spending most of the time banished to Yalta for his health, he was unable to participate in rehearsals and watch the detailed staging of his plays.

Chekhov seems to have had mixed feelings about Ibsen, or at least his volatile letters include contradictory responses. At one point he called Ibsen his 'favourite writer', but Gordon McVay notes in his edition of the letters that elsewhere Chekhov expressed 'a low opinion of Ibsen as an artificial, insincere writer who lacked knowledge of life and was not a dramatist'.[3] The two are always rightly linked as part of the late nineteenth-century project of theatrical naturalism, the realisation onstage of ordinary people's behaviour as the product of their familial inheritance and social conditioning. Their techniques and dramatic strategies, however, are all but antithetical. Ibsen's art, at least from *A Doll's House* on, is centripetal. All an audience's attention is gathered into that living room of the Helmers; every line, every image, every incident contribute to the one node of Nora and Torvald's marriage that is the play's concern. By contrast, Chekhov's dramaturgy is centrifugal. None of his full-length plays have a single setting; though they may concentrate in and around a house, most often his trademark country house, the several acts shift from inside to outside, from one room to another. If Ibsen cut back the large casts of his earlier plays to spotlight just his chosen principals, Chekhov always works with an ensemble, a group aggregation of characters. Ibsen in *A Doll's House* may have dispensed with the standard stagey contrivances of nineteenth-century theatrical plotting, but his remain well-made plays in the way the action builds relentlessly and inevitably towards its climax. Chekhov is notoriously the dramatist of anticlimax, of indirection and inaction.

In fact, Chekhov had to struggle hard to rid himself of theatrical sensation, what Shaw complained of in Ibsen as the 'the old conventional mortuary ending'.[4] When he completed *The Cherry Orchard*, he congratulated himself on the fact that 'there's not a single pistol shot in the entire play'.[5] But it had taken a long time to get there. This was the playwright who had one of his characters in *Platonov* attempt an onstage suicide by throwing herself under a train and who concluded *Ivanov* with the hero shooting himself on his wedding day. There continued to be a suicide, an attempted murder or death by duel in all three of his other major plays. What Chekhov aimed for, however, was a deliberate dedramatisation of drama, articulated in his well-known dictum: 'On stage everything should be just as complicated and just as simple as in life. People eat, just eat, and at the same time their happiness is being decided or their lives ruined'.[6]

In terms of realising this aesthetic of minimalist theatrical action, what may have been as important as the elimination of the violent pistol shot was a reconception of scenic composition. In all of his plays up to and including *The Wood Demon*, Chekhov followed French practice in demarcating scenes by any exit or entrance: a 'scene' is a specific configuration of characters, whatever the setting might happen to be.[7] The altered scenography is most obvious when *The Wood Demon* is compared with its revised version, *Uncle Vanya* (1897).[8] The action of the earlier play was divided up into a series of separate scenes – no less than sixteen of them in Act III – as the characters come and go, trying to work out their confused destinies. The setting changes at need, with the two middle acts on the Serebryakov estate, as in *Uncle Vanya*, but Act I in the house of a rich neighbour and Act IV in a forest and house by a mill. In *Uncle Vanya*, all the action is set at the Serebryakovs', in the garden, the dining room, the drawing room and Vanya's study, and each act is undivided. Significantly, also, the generic subtitle of the play was changed. *The Wood Demon* was called 'a comedy in four acts', the classification that Chekhov so controversially was to give *The Cherry Orchard*. *Uncle Vanya* instead is subtitled 'scenes from country life', a designation that deliberately avoids the traditional taxonomy of tragedy, comedy or 'drama'. Chekhov here indicates his desire to represent characteristic snapshots of certain sorts of lives, the atmosphere of a given place and situation rather than any shaped dramatic action.

This altered perspective of Chekhovian drama, with its genre scenes and dispersed composition, allows for a different rendering of the home and its significance from that in Ibsen. In *A Doll's House*, exclusive attention is given to the middle-class home, with servants no more than supernumeraries; the one glimpse we are given of the circumstances that forced Anne Marie to give up her child as a working-class unmarried mother is there largely for plot purposes. The Helmers' bourgeois establishment, as it bore a family resemblance to equivalent homes across Europe and North America, was made the site for widely resonant contemporary social issues. The Gayevs, by contrast, are landed gentry. The setting, as Chekhov told his wife, Olga Knipper, is 'an old manor house; once upon a time people lived there in great style, and that must be sensed in the décor. Wealth and comfort.'[9] The well-to-do K.S. Stanislavski 'based the Ranevsky household on his own estate, Lyubimovka, where Chekhov had begun writing the play', with Victor Simov's design for the first production of the play, with its striking high windows, suggested by Stanislavksi's living room.[10] But the extended family and associates that populate the Gayev house make for a full diapason of social class, from the gentry owners through the self-made business man Lopakhin and the radical student Trofimov, down to the resolutely unenfranchised serf Firs. The play offers accordingly something like a cross-section of Russian society, not merely a paradigmatic middle-class couple. *A Doll's House* is set in an implied contemporary present time, and so is *The Cherry Orchard*. But the Russian play is freighted with a sense of the past that has created that present, and the characters repeatedly speculate on the future to come. The home that we see onstage, with all of its embedded history, is about to be demolished, and we are invited to think about what will take its place. The sale of the cherry orchard represents a specific moment not only in the lives of these characters but in the changing social conditions of the whole of Russia. What Chekhov's attitude toward those changes may have been, and the tonal implications for the production of the play, have been the source of endless debate from the beginning. Equally challenging, however, is just how his suggestive, atmospheric settings, with their hints of symbolism, should be realised theatrically. Where Ibsen's quite definitely specified stage decor has to be comprehensively dismantled to yield a metaphoric reconception, as in Bergman's or Breuer's productions, Chekhov's evocative cherry orchard lies open to a continuum of production styles, from the detail-heavy naturalism of a Stanislavski to the emblematic stylisations of Giorgio Strehler or Peter Brook.

Class and gender

Nothing could be less like the confined small-town doll's house of Ibsen than the amorphous, semifeudal country household of *The Cherry Orchard*. To start with, there is the apparent warmth and intimacy across the classes. Ranevskaya kisses the ancient servant Firs according to the custom, thanking him for his attention to her comfort: 'Thank you my dear [. . .] Thank you, my dear old friend' (Chekhov, 291). The first 'dear' in this line translates the word '*rodnoi*', from a root meaning 'kin', and it is significantly the same word that Lopakhin uses when he stresses the depth of his feeling for Ranevskaya: 'I love you like my own flesh and blood . . . more than my own flesh and blood' (Chekhov, 292). There is no doubting the reality of this quasi-familial feeling within the ambience of the group, where Firs clucks around, scolding the fifty-one-year-old Gayev as if he were a careless child in need of protection. And yet, of course, the class gaps are very much in place. Ranevskaya naturally addresses Firs in the informal second-person singular, one of those markers that cannot be rendered in English translation. And her effusion of thanks is rendered comic by the casualness of its conclusion: 'Thank you, Firs, thank you, my dear. I'm so glad to find you still alive' (Chekhov, 291). The paternalism of the masters may be sincere enough, but it hardly represents full recognition of their servants as individual human beings. This seems to be the point of the play's terrible ending, where Firs is left to die in the locked and abandoned house. Again and again through Act IV, we have seen one member of the family after another asking whether Firs has been sent to the hospital. They are concerned – just not quite concerned enough to make sure of it themselves rather than leaving it to the transmission of orders by Chinese whispers to other servants.

Chekhov's country house contains the usual assortment of extras that extends the family outwards. It is one of the features of his work that has made it so attractive for adaptation in Ireland, where it is immediately identifiable with the equivalent Big House with a comparably variegated collection of inhabitants.[11] There is the passportless Charlotta Ivanovna, the ex-circus performer turned governess who continues to be part of the entourage, though the seventeen-year-old Anya no longer needs a governess. Trofimov, the eternal student, former tutor to the drowned Grisha, has come back to pay his respects to Ranevskaya, and stays on for the rest of the summer. Most interesting of all is the figure of Varya. Varya is Ranevskaya's adopted daughter, no less valued than Anya herself, as the mother takes pains to make clear when she greets them tenderly in Act II:

> Here . . . here . . . my own darlings . . . (*Embracing Anya and Varya.*) If only you knew how much I love you both! Sit next to me here – here . . . (Chekhov, 312)

It may in fact be significant that Varya throughout the play uses the diminutive '*Mamochka*', whereas Anya calls her mother simply '*Mama*', as though Varya, by the greater tenderness, seeks to overcompensate for the fact that she is not a daughter by blood.

And she is not actually regarded in the same light as Anya. There is a touch of condescending typecasting in Ranevskaya's recognition of Varya on her return: 'Varya's just the same as before – she looks like a nun' (Chekhov, 286). The negotiations over the always about to be arranged marriage between Varya and Lopakhin bring out the class background. Ranevskaya tries to bring the matter to a boil in Act II with an appeal to Lopakhin: 'She came to me from simple people – she works the whole day long. But the main thing is, she loves you' (Chekov, 311). The order here is significant. Varya's love for Lopakhin may be the 'main thing', but it is very much conditioned by the facts of her humble background and her willingness to work: in marrying her, Lopakhin will be getting a good deal. It is noticeable that, although Anya's marriage to a rich man is mooted a couple of times in the play as a way of solving the family's financial crisis, there is no question of her marrying Lopakhin. He may be a 'good man [. . .] a most [. . .] worthy man' (Chekhov, 296), but he is not conceivable as a son-in-law of the house. In their last abortive conversation, when Lopakhin struggles to force out the proposal that is expected of him, Varya at first tries to put a good face on her future before making its reality explicit. She is going to 'the Ragulins. I've agreed to keep an eye on the running of the house for them. Well, to be housekeeper' (Chekhov, 345). Varya, who for Ranevskaya has been the key-holding 'daughter of the house', will in fact become a paid servant.

Lopakhin himself is the play's central study in class position and class consciousness. Chekhov very much wanted Stanislavski himself to play the part of Lopakhin rather than Gayev, the part the director finally chose. He wrote to his wife, the actress Olga Knipper, when the play was going into rehearsal: 'Lopakhin is the central role. If it's acted badly, the whole piece will fail. Lopakhin mustn't be played as a loudmouth, he doesn't have to be an obvious merchant. He's a gentle person.'[12] Chekhov, himself the grandson of a serf, had an obvious investment in the upwardly mobile Lopakhin, however little the degree of direct autobiographical identification. Very frequently quoted is the moving passage in Chekhov's letter to his friend the newspaper owner A.S. Suvorin, sketching something like his own life:

> Write a story about a young man, the son of a serf, a former shop-minder, chorister, schoolboy and student, who was brought up to fawn upon rank, to kiss priests' hands, and to worship others' thoughts [. . .] playing the hypocrite before God and man through no necessity, but from a sheer awareness of his own insignificance – write how this young man squeezes the slave out of himself drop by drop and then wakes up one fine morning to discover that in his veins flows not the blood of a slave, but of a real human being . . .[13]

That successful trajectory of liberation is what Lopakhin has not achieved in the play, as we can see already in the opening scene. Lopakhin remembers his first encounter with Ranevskaya, when as a fifteen-year-old boy he had been beaten up by his drunken father, and she took him into the house and washed the blood from his face: '"Don't cry, my little peasant", she says. "It'll heal in time for your wedding"' (Chekhov, 284). Lopakhin is recalling this as an example of Ranevskaya's kindness, the gentle graciousness he has never met with before, and in Russian the unselfconscious diminutive '*muzhichok*', 'little peasant', might be less slighting than it appears in English translation. Yet it has stuck with Lopakhin, as he goes on to muse after a pause:

> My little peasant . . . it's true, my father was a peasant – and here am I in a white waistcoat and yellow shoes. Like a pig in a pastry-cook's . . . The only difference is I'm a rich man, plenty of money, but look twice and I'm a peasant, a real peasant . . .

Awareness of his social status is so introjected in Lopakhin that he has never been able to manage that spiritual and psychological independence that Chekhov celebrates in his letter. One sign of it is his insistence on maintaining class hierarchy in others, reproving the maid Dunyasha for her aping of the manners of her betters: 'Not the way, is it? You want to remember who you are' (Chekhov, 284).[14]

Lopakhin is drawn with sympathy throughout the play. The irony is that when he first produces his scheme for the leasing out of the cherry orchard land for summer cottages, it is with the intention of raising the spirits of the beleaguered family: 'I want to tell you some very pleasant and cheering news' (Chekhov, 292), he says before outlining his plan. It is a case of cross-purposes. He has no inkling of why Ranevskaya and Gayev might resist what seems to him a brilliant commercial alternative to the selling of the estate. He waxes lyrical on its possibilities:

> [C]ongratulations, you're saved. It's a marvellous position with this deep river. The only thing, of course, is that you need to tidy it up a bit. Remove all the old buildings, for example – like this house, which won't have any use now – and cut down the old cherry orchard. (Chekhov, 293)

Lopakhin is the very opposite of the villain of so many nineteenth-century melodramas, foreclosing on the mortgage of the impoverished upper-class heroes, forcing them out into the cold: he truly believes what he proposes is the happy ending for them. He does not begin to understand what the house, the cherry orchard and the deep river – where Ranevskaya's son was drowned – with all their deep roots and emotional associations, mean to the family.

Lopakhin's genuine goodwill and his equally genuine incomprehension of the aristocrats' attitudes make for the running comedy of his attempts to get them to see sense. We can feel for his frustration in Act ii: 'Forgive me for saying this, but such frivolous people as you, such strange unbusiness-like people, I have never come across. You are told in plain language that your estate is being sold, and you simply do not understand' (Chekhov, 309). Lopakhin's class background and the conflicted nature of his relationship with the family lie beneath the superb climax of the play in Act III, with his long speech of triumph at having bought the cherry orchard. It is the ultimate, all but unbelievable proof of his success:

> If my father and grandfather could rise from their graves and see it all happening – if they could see me, their Yermolay, their half-beaten, half-literate Yermolay, who ran barefoot in winter – if they could see this same Yermolay buying the estate ... The most beautiful thing in the entire world!

But if the cherry orchard stands for 'the most beautiful thing in the entire world', then class triumphalism expresses itself in the prospect of destroying it:

> Everyone come and watch Yermolay Lopakhin set about the cherry orchard with his axe! Watch the trees come down! Summer cottages, we'll build summer cottages, and our grandchildren and our great-grandchildren will see a new life here ...

Yet he cannot sustain this mood of class revenge and he turns in remorseful reaction to the weeping Ranevskaya:

> Why, why, why didn't you listen to me? My poor dear love, you won't bring it back now. (*In tears.*) Oh, if only it were all over. If only we could somehow change this miserable, muddled life of ours. (Chekhov, 334)

The speech expresses the whole range of emotions generated by a socially conditioned life together with a wretched feeling of their cross-grained fatedness.

Chekhov considered the understanding of Lopakhin the key to the success or failure of *The Cherry Orchard*, but of course Ranevskaya is the play's star role and raises issues of gender as well as class. The starting point for *A Doll's House* was Ibsen's acute awareness of women's unequal position in law, their complete dependence on husbands or fathers in financial dealings. Up until the Married Women's Property Acts of 1870 and 1882, under British common law, women automatically lost all separate rights to property upon marriage, and in many other western European countries, the tradition of male primogeniture limited women's rights to inheritance. This was not the case in Russia, where, since before the eighteenth century, testators were free to bequeath and women to inherit and own property.[15] Ranevskaya is unequivocally the 'landowner' of the estate in *The Cherry Orchard*, heading the cast list as such, while Gayev appears only as 'brother of Ranevskaya'. In the opening stage direction of Act II, it is referred to as 'the Gayev estate' (Chekhov, 304), presumably because that is the family name, but at no point is it thought necessary to explain why it was inherited by the daughter Liubov rather than the son Leonid. Leonid, indeed, in the play is very much a sidelined figure, the powerless bachelor uncle, talking too much and doing too little, playing his imaginary billiards, popping sweets into his mouth, laughed at even by the valet Yasha. It is Ranevskaya who is in control – insofar as anyone is in control – and if she is a spendthrift, as Nora is accused of being in *A Doll's House*, she has a whole lot more to spend.

Chekhov originally planned to make Ranevskaya an old woman and was even doubtful if the play could be mounted by the Moscow Art Theatre because they did not have an actor of a suitable age to play the part.[16] In the event, he rewrote the role, and it was eventually created by Olga Knipper, who had already played the middle-aged Arkadina in *The Seagull*. The result is a character who is at once a *grande dame*, a mother figure and a sexually alluring, even flirtatious woman. All the available men in the play are under her spell. To Firs, she is his adored mistress whose return he has awaited as the *Nunc dimittis* that will allow her servant to depart in peace: 'My lady has come home! I waited for her! I can die happy . . .' (Chekhov, 290). For Lopakhin, seeing her for the first time in five years, she is 'still as magnificent as ever', and the chronically impecunious visiting neighbour Pishchik 'breathes hard' as he goes one better: 'You've grown even more lovely . . .' (Chekhov, 292). There is real feeling behind Trofimov's attempts in Act III to persuade her of the worthlessness of her lover in Paris, however misguided the effort. Ranevskaya always, inevitably, wins everyone over by the charm and authority of her presence.

In the patriarchal triad of female iconography, Ranevskaya contrives to be both mother and whore simultaneously. Leonid voices the negative stereotype of his sister:

> She married a commoner, and the way she's behaved – well, you couldn't say it was very virtuously. She's good, she's kind, she's a splendid woman, I love her dearly, but however many extenuating circumstances you think up, the fact has to be faced: she is depraved. You can sense it in her slightest movement. (Chekhov, 300)

Realising he has been overheard by Anya, he is deeply embarrassed and retracts, or at least regrets, what he has said: 'Really that was terrible!' (Chekhov, 301). Ranevskaya herself has sufficiently accepted such a view of her misbehaviour that among the sins she confesses in Act II are her marriage and her love affair. She even sees the death of her son as a providential judgement on her for such 'sins'. And yet, when she admits to her continuing attachment to her worthless lover to Trofimov in Act III, she manages to downface his disapproval with one of her characteristic emotional U-turns:

> It's time you were a man. At your age you must understand people who know what it is to love. You must know what it is yourself! You must fall in love! (*Angrily.*) Yes, yes! You're no more pure than I am! You're just a prig, a ridiculous freak, a monster . . . ! (Chekhov, 327)

The uptight Trofimov is completely routed by this mature, sexually self-confident woman.

Ranevskaya as mother of her family and owner of the estate reanimates her house when she returns to it. She is no matriarch, if that word suggests a maternal ruler who directs the affairs of her tribe. Ranevskaya, by her own admission, is a hopelessly irresponsible person, constantly seeking advice and support from those around her: Lopakhin, Anya, Varya – everyone except the even more useless Leonid. But she is integrally identified with the estate and it with her: 'I love this house. Without the cherry orchard I can't make sense of my life, and if it really has to be sold, then sell me along with it . . .' (Chekhov, 325). When it is sold in Act III, hers is the central tragedy; it is her life that is unmade, her role as mother of the family, genius of the place, that is lost.

The Cherry Orchard puts Ranevskaya as a woman and a landowner on trial and, with Chekhov's characteristic impartiality, delivers no decisive judgement. The original Stanislavski production, it is generally agreed, tipped audience sympathies towards her and the about to be dispossessed aristocracy: 'Knipper established Ranevskaya as the play's centre, positioned between two trends in Russian life: Lopakhin's practical materialism and Trofimov's idealistic reforms.'[17] Later directors have sought to change this emphasis, reducing Ranevskaya's charm, making her emotional effusiveness suspect. Judi Dench, for example, in Sam Mendes's production in London in 1989, after demonstratively tearing up the telegrams from her lover in Act I, was seen to put the pieces carefully away for later consideration.[18] The text allows for any number of such interpretive adjustments, directing an audience's view of the character one way or another. But however she is played, and whatever we think of her, she is no doll wife trapped in a doll's house of her husband's making. The house, the orchard and the estate are hers and embody the class to which she belongs. The life she herself has lived in the house, and those of her ancestors, are written into it, and open out into the history of the surrounding country.

Time and history

A Doll's House takes place over three days. Ibsen builds his family crisis around the family holiday, the joyous anticipation of Christmas Eve, the anxious suspense of Christmas Day, and the bitter aftermath of Boxing Day. In Chekhov, a whole turn of the seasons gives the play its temporal rhythm: from the spring sunrise of Act I, the action dawdles through the early summer of Act II and reaches its August climax in Act III before the autumn finale of Act IV. In Russia, however, the weather does not always do what it should. 'I can't give our climate my seal of approval' (Chekhov, 284), says the absurdly pontificating clerk Yepikhodov, about the three degrees of frost that so unseasonably accompanies the dawn sunshine on the cherry trees in full blossom. And there is again that same three degrees of frost in the sunny October of Act IV, when in other years there would already have been snow on the ground. The contrariness of the weather works with the shifting and volatile movement of the human moods that know no due season through the play. The action is concerned with change as it is experienced in time by people who live as much in the past and the future as in the present.

'A room which is *still* known as the nursery': that 'still' suggests a setting frozen in time. It is bound to evoke nostalgia from the two generations of family who have spent their childhood there. The theatre director Michel Saint-Denis reported Anya's first entrance in a Moscow Art Theatre performance in Paris in 1922:

> Anya . . . who has been brought up in that nursery, jumps on to a sofa and, crouching on it, is caught up by a fit of that high-pitched laughter which is induced by a combination of tiredness and emotion. And on that piece of wordless acting the audience of two thousand five hundred people burst into applause.[19]

For Ranevskaya, too, the excitement of return produces a regression into childhood, as she is unable to keep still, kissing the bookcase, saluting the table. It is customary to stock the ex-nursery with period rocking horses and the like, but the original production brilliantly included child-sized furniture within the otherwise imposing space: 'The great height of the room created a comic contrast with the miniature furniture on which the characters sat awkwardly.'[20] A still from Act I is very suggestive of the effect. The adult characters sit like Brobdingnagians on the children's chairs, but they are Lilliputians when measured by the windows, even the more-than-Gayev-high bookcase (see Figure 2.1). The sheer grandeur

Figure 2.1   Scene from *The Cherry Orchard*, Act I, directed by K.S. Stanislavski,
Moscow, 1904.

of the house rebukes the pettiness of its occupants – 'we ought properly to
be giants', says Lopakhin in Act II (Chekhov, 314) – while these infantilised grown-ups look grotesquely out of place amid the diminutive nursery
surroundings that they used to fit.

The nursery setting at a moment of return must necessarily be an
occasion for memory, and not only for the family who grew up in the
house. When Lopakhin recalls his first meeting with Ranevskaya, it was 'in
this room, in the nursery' (Chekhov, 284) that he remembers her bringing
him with his bloodied nose. For Ranevskaya herself, the vision of the
cherry trees in bloom brings the past flooding back:

> Oh, my childhood, my innocence! In this nursery I slept, from this room
> I looked out at the orchard, and happiness woke with me every morning.
> The orchard was just the same then, nothing has changed. (*Laughs with
> joy.*) All, all in white! Oh, my orchard! After dark foul autumn and cold cold
> winter, again you're young and filled with happiness, and not abandoned by
> the angels.

So intense is this feeling that it generates a spectral vision of the mother
who would have been visible from the window in that past childhood:

'Look – there's Mama, our own dead Mama, walking through the orchard ... in a white dress!' (Chekhov 297). But within seconds, she has relinquished that delusion: 'There's no one there. It just looked like it for a moment. To the right, on the turning to the summer-house – a tree bending under its blossom like the figure of a woman.' And at this exact point, there appears, as unlike that lyrical vision as possible, 'Trofimov, in a shabby student's uniform and spectacle' (Chekhov, 298), Trofimov, the dead Grisha's tutor, to remind Ranevskaya of the bitterest of her adult memories, the very reason why she has been away from the house for the last five years. The house is a palimpsest of the past, with the remembered childhood life of the nursery overwritten by all that has happened since.

Nostalgia is almost by definition a sentimental feeling, in excess of its object because its object, the absent past, is not there. And when it is actually there as an object, the sentimentality is made all the more obvious. So it is with Gayev's address to the bookcase. Ranevskaya's kissing the bookcase is a measure of her childlike joy, but her brother's solemn apostrophe is something else again.

> Dear bookcase! Most esteemed bookcase! I salute your existence, which for more than a hundred years now has been directed towards the shining ideals of goodness and of truth. For a hundred years your unspoken summons to fruitful labour has never faltered, upholding, (*on the verge of tears*) through all the generations of our family, wisdom and faith in a better future, and fostering within us ideals of goodness and of social consciousness. (Chekhov, 295)

What makes this so funny is the very evident failure of the bookcase in summoning the likes of Gayev to fruitful labour, or indeed any sort of labour at all. But what embarrasses everyone present about the effusion is the fact that it does express something of what they feel about this inanimate surviving witness to an imagined past, yet is appallingly wrong in the way it is expressed or perhaps that it is expressed at all. The deepest feelings of memory are unspeakable.

The house in the play is suffused with recollections of the lives that have been lived there: Ranevskaya has her vision of her dead mother walking in the orchard; Gayev remembers 'when I was six years old, sitting up on this windowsill [in the nursery] on Trinity Sunday and watching my father go to church' (Chekhov, 347); Firs, rejoicing in his mistress's return from Paris, thinks of her father – or possibly grandfather – 'The master went to Paris once ... by post-chaise ...' (Chekhov, 290). The stage space is tremulous with the feeling of the past. But those who project forward into the future fill it with a comparable overspill of emotion. Lopakhin has his Utopian vision of the 'new class' of 'summer countrymen' whose dachas will be built on the estate: 'Now he merely sits on his verandah and drinks tea, but you know it may come to pass that he'll put his couple of acres to some use, and start to cultivate them. And then this old cherry orchard of yours will become happy and rich and luxuriant . . .' (Chekhov, 294). Anya too tries to reconcile her mother to the loss of the property at the end of Act III after it has been sold:

> We'll go away, love, you and me, we'll go away from here, we'll go away. We'll plant a new orchard, lovelier still, and when you see it you'll understand. And your heart will be visited by joy, a quiet, deep, joy like evening sunlight, and you'll smile again, Mama! (Chekhov, 335).

The speech is moving and deeply felt, but as so often with the lyrical prophecies with which Chekhov endows his characters, this is a consolatory fiction. And in Ranevskaya's sudden and unexpected rebuke to Lopakhin, who has been chuckling over a play he has seen recently, it is as though Chekhov rounds on his own audience, who might be disposed to revel in the characters' self-indulgent emotions: 'People shouldn't watch plays. They should look at their own selves a little more often. What grey lives they all lead. How much they say that should never be said at all' (Chekhov, 311).

Act I of *The Cherry Orchard* solidly establishes the house with all its memories for the returning family, while for the younger generation that very return brings hope for seasonal renewal. The act ends with Trofimov's ecstatic salute to his vision of Anya: 'My sunshine! My springtime!' (Chekhov, 303). Act II opens out spatially with its vista of the countryside and locates the representative lives of the characters in the history of their country. Firs's reminiscences, addressed to Ranevskaya, take an audience back to the most important single event in nineteenth-century Russia:

> I've lived a long life. They were marrying me off before your Papa even arrived in the world. (*Laughs*.) And when the Freedom came, in sixty-one, I was already head valet. I didn't agree to have the Freedom – I stayed with the masters . . .
>   *Pause.*
>   And I remember, everyone was glad. But what they were glad about they didn't know themselves.

The date has been added in Michael Frayn's translated text here; it is not in the original Russian.[21] For a Russian audience in 1904 would not have needed to be reminded that in 1861 – two years before Lincoln abolished slavery in the United States – Tsar Alexander II promulgated the legislation emancipating the serfs, who had been bound to the land under the reign of Peter the Great in the early eighteenth century. The absurdity of Firs's feudal nostalgia for the pre-Emancipation days is swiftly under-lined by Lopakhin's sarcastic retort: 'Lovely it was before. At least they flogged you' (Chekhov, 312). But there would have been some point, also, in the gloomy scepticism of Firs about the joy greeting Emancipation. In the light of the forty years of Russian history since that time, the Act had not proved the dawn of a new era hoped for at the time. Freeing the serfs had brought economic problems not only for the landowners but for the freed peasants themselves. There was a rise in radical opposition to Alexander's initially reformist government, which grew correspondingly more reactionary. And then in 1881, just twenty years after Emancipation, the tsar was assassinated, to be succeeded by his draconian son Alexander III.

It is to this latter time that Gayev refers ruefully, as he is bundled off to bed by his nieces in Act 1.

> I am a man of the eighties. Not a period they speak well of these days, but I can tell you that I have suffered not a little in this life for my convictions. It is no accident that your ordinary peasant loves me.

In the stop-go dialectic of liberalism and repression that shaped so much of Russian political history from the Tsarist to the Soviet era, Alexander III's reign (1881–94) was one of the most autocratic. Gayev here positions himself as one of those liberals who tried to maintain populist political principles through this strongly reactionary period: hence his conviction that he is loved by the peasants. However little we may trust Gayev's posturings – Anya and Varya hear them as more of his effusive rhapsodies ('Uncle you're off again!' [Chekhov, 302]) – the realities of the remem-bered 1880s would have been vivid to the original audience, and indeed to the playwright. This was the time when Chekhov began his literary career, when every line he wrote, even the most lighthearted of his comic sketches for the newspapers, had to be submitted to the government censor. And that position had not changed by 1903, when he was writing *The Cherry Orchard*.

It was Trofimov that caused most problems, because it was impossible to make explicit why he was the 'eternal student' he is teased for being throughout: '[Y]ou have to understand', Chekhov explained to his wife, 'that Trofimov is continually being sent into exile, and continually expelled from university – but how can such things be depicted?'[22] As it was, two key passages of Trofimov's speeches were struck out by the censor. One was in his denunciation of the intelligentsia for ignoring the social realities of the time: '[E]veryone knows the workers are abominably fed and sleep without proper bedding, thirty or forty to a room – with bed-bugs everywhere, to say nothing of the stench, the damp, the moral degradation.' The other came in Trofimov's stirring political manifesto addressed to Anya at the end of Act II, beginning 'All Russia is our orchard': 'Owning living souls, that's what has changed you all so completely, those who went before and those alive today, so that your mother, you yourself, your uncle – you don't realize that you're actually living on credit. You're living on other people, the very people you won't even let inside your own front door.'[23] Within such conditions of censorship, political meanings needed to be coded or suggested rather than stated outright. The 'passer-by' who so frightens the company in Act II mutters snatches of poetry that may mean little to Western audiences. Michael Frayn accordingly fills in more of the lines from the nineteenth-century Russian poet Nikolai Nekrasov that bring out an element of protest against current social conditions:

> Go to the Volga. Hear again
> The song it sings, the song of groans –
> The litany of hauling men,
> Groaned from weary hearts and bones.

(Chekhov, 316)[24]

Frayn notes that 'the word for "Passer-by", *prokhozhy*, meant in Siberian usage at that time someone who was tramping the road to escape from prison or exile' (Chekhov, 368) and speculates that Chekhov might have had this political significance in mind.

Trofimov speaks against a backdrop of 'a row of telegraph poles, and a long way away on the horizon a large town' (Chekhov, 304). The view itself bespeaks the period of rapid modernisation that Russia was undergoing at the time. It is the proximity of the town and the convenience of the railway that allowed the family party to drop into town for lunch in Act II, which also lends itself to Lopakhin's scheme for summer cottages. His vision for the future is that of a prosperous middle class, expanding suburbia out into the country estates previously owned by the about to be dispossessed landed gentry. Trofimov, by contrast, is sceptical, looking forward as he does to a more radical redistribution of property. 'Don't keep waving your arms about', he advises Lopakhin as they are about to part in Act IV. 'Break yourself of this habit of gesticulating. And all this business of building summer cottages, then calculating that eventually people who rent them will turn into landlords themselves – that's also a form of arm-waving' (Chekhov, 338). If Lopakhin represents the capitalist business entrepreneur driving the industrial revolution that was coming late but rapidly to Russia in the first decade of the twentieth century, Trofimov is regularly seen as a prophet of the political revolutions of 1905 and 1917.

This was to become a standard interpretation of *The Cherry Orchard* in years to come, even though, as Laurence Senelick points out, no one in Moscow or Petersburg saw it like that in 1904.[25] The political emphasis would repeatedly shift, depending on whether the play was read as a sympathetic treatment of the ousted aristocrats or an apocalyptic prevision of the Revolution, with Trofimov as its prophet. What is crucial is that the action of the play is inscribed in time, both in the lived time of the characters and in the history of their society. In this it is different from *A Doll's House*. What was crucial about Ibsen's 'modern tragedy' was its contemporaneity. The Helmers' small-town apartment was a model of all such middle-class family dwellings, transferable to any other such space. The details of Torvald's and Nora's past lives are important only insofar as they offer a case study in a certain sort of marriage; the fact that they are Norwegian affords a local colour but no defining condition. *The Cherry Orchard*, by contrast, is so much of its place and time that Chekhov himself thought it more or less untranslatable. He was incredulous at the idea of a French version: '[W]hat's the point of translating my play into French? Why, it's a mad idea. The French won't understand anything about Yermolay [Lopakhin] or about the sale of the estate and will only be bored.'[26] Chekhov's plays were indeed slow to make an impact in western Europe, but since then they have become some of the most universally translated and revived of stage classics. *The Cherry Orchard* speaks across cultures and periods, for all the specificity of its historically located situation, because of the evocative nature of the theatrical images with which it is expressed.

Sights, sounds and symbols

From the beginning, the vision of the cherry orchard itself was essential to Chekhov's conception of the play. In February 1903 he wrote to Stanislavski, saying that his play was 'already completed in my head. It's called *The Cherry Orchard*, it has four acts and in Act One cherry trees can be seen in bloom through the windows, the whole orchard a mass of white. And ladies in white dresses.'[27] Stanislavski worked hard to realise Chekhov's conception, writing in November 1903, when the play was in rehearsal, 'I seem to have found the set for the first act. It's been very difficult. The window has to be down-stage so that the cherry orchard is visible both from the upper and lower parts of the auditorium.'[28] Later productions, such as Peter Stein's neorealist staging in 1989, emphasised the need for the audience 'to see the orchard and believe that nothing is more beautiful'.[29] Other directors have preferred to rely on the audience's imagination in creating an orchard that is not actually visible. So, for instance, in the minimalist production of Peter Brook in Paris in 1981, where the stripped-back bare Bouffes du Nord theatre itself represented the Gayev house, Natasha Parry, playing Ranevskaya, was instructed to 'look out front, into the audience' when gazing at the orchard.[30] Similarly, in the 1981 television broadcast version of Richard Eyre's 1977 Nottingham staging of the play, the characters at the end of Act I stood looking out through the windows bathed in white light, but neither then, nor in Act IV, did the viewers catch a glimpse of the trees. Whether actually realised or not, the sense of the loveliness of the cherry trees in blossom is an aesthetic effect built into the play.

The Russian word *sad* in the play's title, *Vishnevii Sad*, is the ordinary term for a garden as well as an orchard. It is startling to take in, therefore, just how extensive the cherry orchard is: in English usage it might be more appropriate to talk about 'the cherry plantation'. Lopakhin does the sums for the bemused Ranevskaya and Gayev in Act I:

> [I]f the cherry orchard and the land along the river are broken up into building lots and leased out as sites for summer cottages, then you will possess an income of – at the very least – twenty-five thousand rubles a year. [...] You will get from your lease-holders at the very minimum ten rubles a year per acre. (Chekhov, 293)

The cherry orchard extends over 2,500 acres of land – and it only constitutes one part of the estate. This is an enormous building development that Lopakhin proposes, but then he is used to doing things on this sort of scale: 'I planted nearly three thousand acres of poppy this spring', he tells Trofimov in Act IV, 'and I've made a clear forty thousand rubles on it' (Chekhov, 339). For those of us used to western European acreage, the sheer amounts involved in Russia are staggering. Chekhov was by no means a rich man; when he bought the estate of Melikhovo in 1892, it was as a modest country retreat for himself and his large dependent family. But it was almost 600 acres.[31]

After the concentration on the interior of the house with its view out to the cherry orchard in Act I, the design of Act II was to provide some sense of the expansiveness of the landscape beyond. 'The open fields. A wayside shrine – old, crooked, and long neglected. Beside it – a well, large slabs which were evidently once tombstones and an old bench. A path can be seen leading to the Gayev estate. At one side rise the dark shades of poplars; this is where the cherry orchard begins' (Chekhov, 304). Stanislavski elaborated on this in his plan for the set:

> A little chapel, a small gully, a neglected cemetery in an oasis of trees amid the Steppes. The left part of the stage and the centre without masking flats – just the distant horizon. This will be done with a continuous semi-circular backdrop with supports to take it into the distance. In one place a stream glistens, on a hillock a country house can be seen. Telegraph poles and a railway bridge. Allow us, during one of the pauses, to bring a train with little puffs of smoke across. That could work splendidly. Before the sunset the town is briefly visible. Towards the end of the act, mist; it will rise especially thick from the canal downstage. The concert of frogs and the corncrake at the end of the act likewise.[32]

Chekhov had to restrain his director's enthusiasm for proliferating detail – no corncrakes, no frogs; neither of them would be heard at haymaking season in June – and agreed to the train only if it 'can make its appearance without any noise, not a sound'.[33] In the event, the designer Victor Simov's device of the 'continuous semi-circular backdrop' was an early innovative use of the cyclorama. And Giorgio Strehler's wholly non-naturalistic 1974 production at the Piccolo Theatre, Milan, would eventually feature a train, if only a toy train passing at the front of the stage.[34]

'Lord, you gave us immense forests, boundless plains, broad horizons – living in it all we ought properly to be giants' (Chekhov, 314). The vista we see in Act II provides an ironic context for Lopakhin's effusion of Russian self-reproach. The sense of immensity is certainly there, but without any of the Edenic promise. Instead, the landscape demonstrates a country at an identifiable point of human development. The slabs of stone that were once tombstones – 'No churchyard', Chekhov corrected Stanislavski, 'there *was* one a very long time ago'[35] – speak of a forgotten past. The neglected shrine suggests the secularisation of a once-devout society. And of course the telegraph poles and the distant prospect of the city tell of the modernising forces that are in the process of changing the land that the likes of the Gayevs used to own. The point was heavily underlined at the beginning of Act II in Andrei Serban's 1977 New York production, where the 'image of telegraph poles towering over labourers dragging an ancient plough was visible through the scrim', while later as a backdrop to

Trofimov's revolutionary speech, 'the skyline changes once again, this time to overwhelm us with factory chimneys beneath a soot-stained red sky'.[36]

Chekhov's sets speak their meanings: the nursery of the old landowner's house with its accumulation of memories and its view out onto the cherry orchard in Act I, the vista over the changing Russian countryside in Act II. What later directors have sought to do is to conceptualise those means scenically. In this process, images from the play are often recycled, dislocated from context. So, even the minimalist Peter Brook, whose basic decor for the play consisted of nothing but Oriental rugs spread on the floor of the stage, retained the apostrophised bookcase. For the iconoclastic 1975 production at the Taganka Theatre in Moscow by Anatoly Efros, the designer Valery Levental created a single set for all four acts 'dominated by a large central mound covered with gravestones', but also containing 'pieces of furniture and cherry trees; on the back wall hung family portraits; white curtains blew at the sides of the stage; and a single cherry branch hung out over the audience'.[37] Serban's New York designer Santo Loquasto similarly placed a scatter of the key pieces of furniture – bookcase, sofa, toy rocking horse and train to conjure up the nursery – in an unwalled open space that included the blossoming cherry trees (Figure 2.2). Behind such conceptualising there is an impulse of impatience with naturalism that amounts to polemic aggression, comparable to that seen in Ostermeier's or Breuer's versions of *A Doll's House*. Efros was unapologetic for directing *The Cherry Orchard* 'not as a museum piece, or an anthology piece, but so as to knock the corners off it and shove your face in it'.[38] Serban came to Chekhov with a reputation as 'the director who destroys the classics'.[39] But, aside from this desire to make it new, there is also the basic drive to translate Chekhov's images into a different dramaturgical notation.

Chekhov himself, for all his recurrent captious criticism of Stanislavski's interpretation of his work, was at times prepared to trust the director's theatrical instinct for its visual realisation. So, for example, he was happy to go along with Stanislavski's desire to keep the same set for Act IV as Act III.

> Of course you can use the same set for Acts Three and Four, the one with a hall and staircase. In general don't stint yourself with the scenery – I defer to you. [. . .] Whatever you do will be splendid, a hundred times better than anything I could think of.[40]

He had not planned Act IV to be set back in the nursery, as in the final version, but in a different room in the house altogether. For Chekhov, who spent so much of his career writing short fiction, certain key details were

Figure 2.2   Scene from *The Cherry Orchard*, Act II, directed by Andrei Serban, New York, 1977.

absolutely crucial in creating the imaginative impression he wanted. But he did not conceive the *tout ensemble* that was to be realised in the theatre. This is true of his soundscape as of his visual settings. He sometimes could supply minute aural directions that crystallised meaning by their net-worked resonances and associations. So, for instance, in Act II, when Varya fetches the telegrams that have come for Ranevskaya, she 'selects a key which clinks in the lock as she opens the antique bookcase' (Chekhov, 294). The bunch of keys that hangs at her waist is the token of Varya's ambiguous status as daughter/housekeeper. In immediate reaction to Lopakhin's announcement that he has bought the estate in Act III, she wordlessly 'takes the keys off her belt, throws them on the floor in the middle of the room, and goes out' (Chekhov, 333). When Lopakhin eventually picks them up, he voices her meaning: 'she wants to demon-strate she's no longer mistress here' (Chekhov, 334). Varya is the locker-up, the constricted would-be economist in this hopelessly improvident house-hold. But the bookcase she unlocks in Act I is the piece of antique furniture that Ranevskaya has kissed and Gayev has effusively addressed, and those telegrams are from the lover in Paris who is the other major pull in Ranevskaya's life. All these magnetic fields of dramatic significance gather for an instant around the clink in the bookcase lock.

Chekhov was impatient with Stanislavski's superfluous croaking frogs and calling corncrakes and would tolerate a train only if it could be completely silent. His sounds were not designed to create wraparound illusion but to support the sense of character and mood. So, for example, the moony Yepikhodov sings his song at the beginning of Act II to the accompaniment of a guitar he insists on calling a mandoline: 'For a madman who's in love it's a mandoline' (Chekhov, 305). The mood music and the absurd joke coexist. In Act III, 'there is the sound of billiards being played in the next room' (Chekhov, 321), to be followed up sometime later by Yasha's laughing entrance, derisively announcing that 'Yepikhodov's broken the billiard cue' (Chekhov, 324). It is symptomatic of the moment that the pretentious clerk is ineptly playing billiards in the absence of the billiard-obsessed gentleman Gayev – a subversion of hierarchy at which Varya furiously protests. The approaching destruction of the cherry orchard is signalled tactlessly early when the thud of the axe is heard from outside even before the family has left in Act IV, an occasion of embarrassment to the awkwardly well-wishing Lopakhin. We are being prepared for sound to start once again when the stage has – apparently – emptied at the end: 'Through the silence comes the dull thudding of the axe. It sounds lonely and sad' (Chekhov, 348).

Directors have sought to amplify the intended effect here – literally in the case of Michael Bogdanov's 1992 production at the Gate Theatre, Dublin, where it was the violent noise of chainsaws biting into wood that was heard at this point. Stein's coup de théâtre in 1989 was to have 'one of the bare cherry trees' come 'crashing through the tall shuttered windows, scattering broken glass and splintered wood across the stage'.[41] The audience were intended to reel back from the full impact of the old regime under demolition. But Chekhov set his directors and sound designers their hardest problem with the repeated sound of the snapping string, first heard as it falls into the sunset silence of Act II: 'Suddenly there is a distant sound, as if from the sky: the sound of a breaking string – dying away, sad' (Chekhov, 315). The sound, apparently based on something Chekhov had actually heard on the steppe, was used first in the 1887 short story 'Fortune', where it is an 'ominous mine shaft catastrophe deep beneath a doomed landscape'.[42] That, of course, is Lopakhin's conjecture as to the source of the sound in the play: 'Somewhere a long way off, in the mines, a winding cable has parted. But a long, long way off' (Chekhov, 315). The sound becomes a sort of Rorschach test for all the characters as they produce alternative explanations, Gayev fatuously suggesting 'a bird of some sort ... something like a heron'; Trofimov, like Hamlet with Polonius and the whale/camel-shaped cloud, egging him on by proposing an 'owl'; Ranevskaya with a shiver hearing it as 'horrible, I don't know why'. A pause prepares the way for the comic conclusion, when the mumbling and superstitious Firs declares that 'it was the same before the troubles. The owl screeched, and the samovar moaned without stop.' 'Before what troubles?' asks Gayev. 'Before the Freedom', comes the lugubrious reply (Chekhov, 315). The incident is a triumph of Chekhov's tragicomic art; the sound *is* ominous, and the audience feel it to be so, even as we smile at the characteristically different ways in which the characters onstage deal with it.

The repetition of the sound and the exact repetition of the stage direction at the very end of the play, when there is no one present to hear it but the now-inert Firs, change its status. It is at this point manifestly a theatrical sign extrinsic to the diagetic realisation of any actual environment. And it is not easy to make it work. Chekhov, during the first run of the play, wrote impatiently to say 'that the sound [. . .] must be shorter, a lot shorter, and must be felt as coming from a great distance. What a lot of fuss about nothing – not being able to cope with a trifle like this, a mere noise, although it's so clearly described in the play.'[43] Is it, though? The sound is heard '*as if* from the sky': from what direction is a sound to be generated to make it appear as if it comes from the sky? The aim seems to be simultaneously to evoke something musical, with the resonance of a concluding chord 'dying away, sad', and a catastrophic single moment of fracture like the snapping of a mine shaft cable. It is a tonally complex symbol that has no place in the concretised environment of sights and sounds of *The Cherry Orchard*.

Chekhov has been called 'a Symbolist playwright trapped in a Naturalist theatre'.[44] The different traditions of *The Cherry Orchard* are often traced back to Stanislavski, on the one hand, with his comprehensive system of realization, and Meyerhold, on the other, an early protester against that system. 'Your play is abstract, like a Tchaikovsky symphony', he wrote to Chekhov. 'The stage director must feel it above all with his ear.'[45] The question of whether Chekhov should be classified as a symbolist or a naturalist is not directly relevant to the argument of this book, any more than that other long-running debate as to whether *The Cherry Orchard* is, as the playwright maintained, 'a comedy, at places even a farce', or the deeply tragic drama of mood that it has often been taken to be.[46] What is evident is that Chekhov's stage impressionism, with its lacunae in scenic conception, makes possible various sorts of imagistic or symbolic reinterpretation as alternatives to Stanislavskian naturalism. He literally opened out and loosened up the confined focus on the middle-class home devised by Ibsen in *A Doll's House*. The house, the cherry orchard and the estate belonging to Ranevskaya are figured in a specific continuum of time and space, gesturing towards past and future, expanding into the whole vast country and its history. But at the same time, Chekhov's associative and indirect dramaturgy provides meanings that go well beyond the local and historical. If the Russian country house of *The Cherry Orchard* can be contrasted with the doll's house of the Helmers, it was to prove very different also when re-created in Sussex by Shaw in *Heartbreak House*, his 'fantasia in the Russian manner', which is the subject of the next chapter.

CHAPTER 3

Heartbreak House: *waiting for the Zeppelin*

'Most of my plays are independent of scenery, but the scenery described in the book is an integral part of Heartbreak House. The Captain's house and garden are not only a place but an atmosphere.'[1] Shaw here pinpoints one of the ways in which *Heartbreak House* differs significantly from his earlier plays. Playwriting came easily to Shaw. He boasted in the preface to *Plays Unpleasant*, his first published collection in 1898, that 'I have encountered no limit but my own laziness to my power of conjuring up imaginary people in imaginary places, and finding pretexts for theatrical scenes between them.'[2] But the places remained imaginary or undefined until late on in the process. For example, in the wake of the first production of *Arms and the Man*, he asserted with his usual brazen panache that it was 'written without the slightest reference to Bulgaria. [. . .] My own historical information being rather confused, I asked Mr. Sidney Webb to find out a good war for my purpose' (Shaw, I, 481). Even when the Serbo-Bulgarian War of 1885 had been chosen, the opponents were initially the other way round, and Shaw switched his original Bulgarians into Serbs and vice versa.[3] The writing of the dialogue always came first for Shaw. It was only after it was complete that he wrote in the setting, the blocking and the emotional choreography of the characters. This is true even of *Heartbreak House*, for all the importance of its scenery. A revised typescript of the play shows the detailed opening description and all the stage directions indicating movement and mood added into an already complete draft of the dialogue.[4]

Shaw would often make use of places where he happened to have visited to provide him with locations for his work. A 1915 stay with Lady Gregory in Coole Park, for instance, yielded ad hoc settings for the playlet *O'Flaherty VC* and the section of *Back to Methuselah* entitled 'Tragedy of an Elderly Gentleman', two of his very few Irish-based works.[5] *Heartbreak House* came together topographically from similar sorts of personal happenstance. The main starting point was the story told Shaw by his actress friend Lena Ashwell, of her father, the seafaring Commander Pocock. During her childhood, Pocock was in command of the training vessel the *Wellesley*, moored on the river Tyne.[6] 'The ship became the family home and was fitted out with a nursery, a drawing room, and even (on the upper deck) a greenhouse.'[7] The eccentric Pocock (who called for cheese to go with the Communion wafer when he was thought to be dying) evidently gave Shaw his initial inspiration for the ship house of the play.[8] But Windham Croft, the country house in Sussex where he stayed with his friends the Webbs in June 1916, provided a crucial additional dimension. It was here that Shaw met Virginia and Leonard Woolf, and it was apparently the garden of this house that provided the basis for the scene glimpsed through the windows in Act I of *Heartbreak House* and realised in Act III. It 'had a lamp post on the terrace which cast its circle of light like "a moon on its opal globe"; and a quarry beyond the gardener's cottage', and from it 'could be heard the guns of the Somme offensive'.[9] The Bloomsbury association of the Woolfs and the prospect of the garden, with the awareness of the war far off, all contributed to the ambiance of Heartbreak House as conceived in the play.

However, if the setting of *Heartbreak House* was to become something more than merely the scenic backdrop for the clash of characters and ideas, it was largely because the play represented Shaw's self-conscious attempt to write in the style of Chekhov. This is the reason it became so exceptionally 'not merely a place but an atmosphere'. All through the 1890s, Shaw had been the high-profile advocate of Ibsen in England, publishing his *The Quintessence of Ibsenism* (1891) to advance the cause of the then avant-garde Norwegian playwright. He had sought to do something similar for Chekhov in the first decade of the twentieth century but with limited success. When the pioneering Stage Society did eventually mount a one-off performance of *The Cherry Orchard* in 1911, the audience were baffled, walked out, 'actually hissed', as Shaw reported with disgust.[10] As though in defiance of such Philistinism, *Heartbreak House* was subtitled 'A Fantasia in the Russian Manner on English Themes'. Although Shaw also mentions Tolstoy's *Fruits of the Enlightenment* as one of his models in the preface to the play, it was specifically Chekhov that inspired the free-form movement of the country house group, which he thought of as a musical fantasia. In May 1916, when just started on *Heartbreak House*, he told Hesketh Pearson: 'In my spare moments I've been working on a play in the Chekhov manner. It's one of the best things I've done. Do you know Chekhov's plays? There's a dramatist for you! . . . He makes me feel like a beginner!'[11] The country house of *The Cherry Orchard*, with its feckless landowners about to be dispossessed, provided the template for Heartbreak House and its occupants, who are equally oblivious to the much greater catastrophe that is all but upon them.

And yet, for all its point-by-point parallels with Chekhov, *Heartbreak House* is fundamentally un-Chekhovian, and not only because Shaw has picked out 'English themes' as the basis for his Russian fantasia. The cherry orchard estate is owned by Ranevskaya and the house is imbued with her distinctively feminine presence. By contrast, Shotover's nautical living quarters are starkly masculine; a 'small but stout table of teak', we are told in the opening description, 'is the only article in the room that suggests (not at all convincingly) a woman's hand in the furnishing' (Shaw, v, 60). Heartbreak House is a contested site of gender politics: 'I keep this house: she upsets it', declares the Captain about his daughter Hesione (Shaw, v, 63). The naturalistic house in *The Cherry Orchard* is plausibly representative of its social type, an unsustainably large and wasteful country house of the gentry. Heartbreak House, with its idiosyncratic nautical form, and its name supplied by Ellie Dunn in the course of the action, necessarily prompts allegorical interpretation. Trofimov's ringing speech 'All Russia is our orchard' may or may not be a prophecy of the Revolution to come. But, even though *Heartbreak House* never overtly mentions the war, the play, written in 1916–17 and ending with a Zeppelin raid, is governed by the awareness of immediate cosmic crisis. In terms of the theatrical representation of domestic space that is the concern of this book, *Heartbreak House* is distinctive in its beleaguered masculinism, its metaphorical suggestiveness and its attempt to respond to the terrible context of the Great War.

The Captain's house

Committed Ibsenite though Shaw was, *Candida* (composed in 1894) was written by way of a counter to *A Doll's House*; he declared that the effect of the play was to show that 'domestically' the husband 'is the pet and the doll' (Shaw, I, 601). On the face of it, the plot of *Candida* features a standard love triangle, the staple of so many nineteenth-century dramas that Shaw abhorred. The young poet Eugene Marchbanks is infatuated with Candida, wife of the strong and upright clergyman Morell. A confrontation between the two men builds to a denouement in Act III, where Candida is forced to choose between them. Predictably, the honourable wife elects to stay with her husband – but not for predictable reasons. 'I give myself to the weaker of the two', she declares and, in a conscious echo of *A Doll's House*, demands that the men sit down and listen to her explanation (Shaw, I, 591). She proceeds to show how completely dependent the hardworking, successful public man Morell is on her, as he is brought to confess: 'What I am you have made me with the labor of your hands and the love of your heart.' By contrast, the timid, effeminate Marchbanks recoils 'with a fierce gesture of disgust' at the prospect of such all-enveloping love: 'Ah, never. Out, then, into the night with me!' (Shaw, I, 593). The play ends conventionally with the married couple embracing, but, Shaw adds in a famous final stage direction, 'they do not know the secret in the poet's heart' (Shaw, I, 595).

Candida in the play is identified with a picture that hangs onstage, given her by Marchbanks, 'a large autotype of the chief figure in Titian's Assumption of the Virgin' (Shaw I, 517). Margery Morgan discusses the play, finally subtitled 'A Mystery' in place of the original 'A Domestic Play in Three Acts', in relation to Shaw's characterization of Candida as the Virgin Mother.[12] While Marchbanks may worship her from afar, at the point of glorious assumption into heaven, the prospect of a more earthly relationship with Candida, such as that enjoyed by Morell, has the ardent lover scurrying out into the night. Shaw's own peculiar relations with women as a young man have a bearing on this pattern. This was the man who, famously, did not lose his virginity until his twenty-ninth birthday and then, as he confided in his diary, 'I did not take the initiative in the matter.'[13] Shaw through his twenties and thirties had a series of passionate love relationships with women in which consummation was ruled out for one reason or another: he was 'Sunday husband' to women like Kate Salt and Edith Bland (the writer E. Nesbitt), who were married and/or lesbian; he took care never to meet Ellen Terry, the great actress with whom he conducted his most intense epistolary affair. Women who fell in love with him, such as the painter Bertha Newcombe or William Morris's daughter May, found him always elusive. Shaw was conscious of his own amorous peculiarities and created a critical self-portrait in *The Philanderer* (written in 1893), where the enigmatic Charteris, caught between the counterparts of Shaw's real-life lovers Jenny Patterson and Florence Farr, is unable finally to commit to either. When Shaw did eventually marry Charlotte Payne-Townshend in 1898, it was at least in part to make it possible for her to nurse him back to health after a crippling illness, and it appears that their marriage, though long and happy, was never physically consummated.[14]

Shaw's plays rarely show sexual attraction and romantic passion leading on to happy-ever-after marriage. In the *Candida* version of *Doll's*

House, it is Marchbanks who must escape from what is seen as the trap of marital attachment. In *Man and Superman* (written in 1903), Shaw's perverse reinterpretation of the Don Juan myth, Ann Whitefield is not like Mozart's Donna Anna the victim of attempted rape, but the predatory pursuer of her Don Giovanni, John Tanner, who drives frantically across Europe in the hope of escaping marriage to her. He fails in the end because, in Shaw's version of the battle of the sexes, the female in the grip of the Life Force must have her way with the reluctant man of genius to fulfil her need for a 'father for the Superman' (Shaw, II, 689). In his later discussion plays *Getting Married* (1908) and *Misalliance* (1910), Shaw further developed his sceptical vision of the institutions of marriage and the family. 'Marriage', declares the *raisonneur* of *Getting Married*, the wise greengrocer Collins, 'is tolerable enough in its way if youre easygoing and dont expect too much from it. But it doesnt bear thinking about' (Shaw, III, 603).[15] And the restless Hypatia in *Misalliance* inveighs against the domestic institutions in which she feels trapped: 'Oh, home! home! parents! family! duty! how I loathe them! How I'd like to see them all blown to bits!' (Shaw, IV, 182). Hypatia duly finds a suitably vital partner in Joey Percival, but it is the admired aviator Lina Szczepanowksa, who has literally crashed into the Tarletons' house, who most authoritatively expresses her verdict on it as she prepares to leave:

> [T]his is a stuffy house. You seem to think of nothing but making love. All the conversation here is about love-making. All the pictures are about love-making. The eyes of all of you are sheep's eyes. You are steeped in it, soaked in it: the very texts on the walls of your bedrooms are the ones about love. It is disgusting. It is not healthy. (Shaw, IV, 248)

This claustrophobic space, in which the vital business of life is stifled by the all-absorbing pursuit of desire, is re-created in *Heartbreak House*.

Shaw relatively rarely set his plays in the sort of enclosed, exclusively domestic interior of *A Doll's House*. Even *Candida*, so taken up with a marital drama, is actually placed in the Rev. Morell's study in the north-east of London, with a view out onto Victoria Park. This tended to be Shaw's preferred location for his plays: professional or semiprofessional spaces – studies and libraries (*Man and Superman*), consulting rooms (*The Doctor's Dilemma*), Higgins's linguistic laboratory (*Pygmalion*) and often, as in *Candida*, rooms with a view. In one sense, therefore, there is nothing out of the way about the setting of *Heartbreak House*, the living room that doubles as the Captain's workshop with its garden visible through the big windows at the back. What is unusual is the thoroughness with which Shaw carried through the concept of the 'room which has been built so as to resemble the after part of an old-fashioned high-pooped ship' (Shaw, v, 59). The initial description of the space refers to 'port' and 'starboard' throughout for left and right. Every detail is in place, down to 'a ship's fire bucket'; 'the uncarpeted floor of narrow boards is caulked and holystoned like a deck' (Shaw, v, 60). The replication of a ship reflects Shotover's determination to control the house as his captain's quarters, while the carpenter's bench on one side of the stage and the drawing table near the centre mark this out as an austere male workplace.

However, he is not by any means in sole command of his ship; if he 'keeps' the house, Hesione is there to 'upset it'. And it is not only Hesione. In the opening sequence of the play alone, Shotover's male preserve is invaded by Ellie, an invited but unexpected guest; Nurse Guinness, who brings unwelcome pots of Indian tea; and Ariadne, Shotover's long-gone daughter whom he claims not to recognise. Rather than presiding in firm control at the helm of his vessel, Shotover is forced to move distractedly in and out in search of reviving alcohol in the pantry or fresh air and exercise in the garden. The house is his insofar as its design reflects his nautical life and his masculinity, but Hesione Hushabye is its mistress, inviting the guests, responsible for its economy. The conventional businessman Boss Mangan, attacked by the strange and unknown Captain at his first entrance, tries to sort out where he is: 'I dont quite understand my position here. I came here on your daughter's invitation. Am I in her house or yours?' (Shaw, v, 88). The answer to Mangan's question is never clear. At the end of Act 1, Hesione exclaims rhetorically: 'What do men want? They have their food, their firesides, their clothes mended, and our love at the end of the day. Why are they not satisfied?' (Shaw, v, 104–5). The play suggests that men are not satisfied because they want something more and other than this mothering, housekeeping love, which is felt as both a temptation and a trap.

The most obvious example of this is Hector Hushabye, Hesione's husband whom she has kept at home, away from any useful occupation: 'I might as well be your lapdog', he says 'bitterly' (Shaw, v, 103). His philandering and his fantasies of adventure are all the idle diversions of Hesione's 'household pet' (Shaw, v, 125). 'It's a dangerous thing to be married right up to the hilt, like my daughter's husband', the Captain tells Ellie. 'The man is at home all day, like a damned soul in hell' (Shaw, v, 142). The exchange between Hector and Shotover about the Hushabyes' marriage is suggestive of an underlying misogyny that is one vein of the play's feeling:

> CAPTAIN SHOTOVER. [. . .] She has used you up, and left you nothing but dreams, as some women do.
> HECTOR. Vampire women, demon women.
> CAPTAIN SHOTOVER. Men think the world well lost for them, and lose it accordingly. Who are the men that do things? The husbands of the shrew and of the drunkard, the men with the thorn in the flesh.
> (Shaw, v, 102)

The lulling love of sexual attraction is a disabling emasculation, suggested in the very name of Hushabye, a Hector whose wife successfully keeps him from the battlefield. It takes a Xantippe to make a Socrates. Shotover dreams of an all-male Utopia: '[W]hen you have found the land where there is happiness and no women', he says to Mangan, 'send me its latitude and longitude; and I will join you there' (Shaw, v, 131).

Both of Shotover's daughters, different as they are from one another, are just such 'vampire women, demon women'. It is noticeable that though Hesione and Ariadne are mothers, almost no reference is made to their presumably grown-up children or to their mothering. One exception is itself telling. After Ariadne has reduced her permanently unrequited lover Randall to tears, she explains her tactics to Hector:

> It's quite simple. When the children got nerves and were naughty, I smacked them just enough to give them a good cry and a healthy nervous shock. They went to sleep and were quite good afterwards. Well, I cant smack Randall: he is too big; so when he gets nerves and is naughty, I just rag him til he cries. (Shaw, v, 155)

Female sexuality is thus tyrannical and infantilising. It is such castrating maternalism that provokes the apocalyptic apostrophe of Hector that ends Act II: 'Oh women! women! women! (*He lifts his fists in invocation to heaven*) Fall. Fall and crush' (Shaw, v, 157).

The echo of *King Lear* is almost certainly deliberate.[16] When Lear enters with Cordelia dead in his arms, the bystanders can only take it for the end of the world:

> KENT. Is this the promised end?
> EDGAR. Or image of that horror.
> ALBANY. Fall and cease.
> (5.3.238–39)[17]

Shaw was conscious of the parallels between *Heartbreak House* and Shakespeare's tragedy. In *Shakes versus Shav*, his spoof puppet-play contest with Shakespeare, Shav answers the challenge of Shakes: 'Couldst thou write King Lear?' with the positive affirmation: 'Aye, with his daughters all complete. Couldst thou / Have written Heartbreak House? Behold my Lear' (Shaw, VII, 475). Shaw plays games with the intertextual comparisons. Where Goneril complains of the disruptive presence of Lear's hundred knights in her house, it is the Lear-like Shotover whose home is disturbed by the comings and goings of Hesione's guests. Ellie is spiritual daughter to the Captain, no actual kin to Hesione and Ariadne. The misogynistic diatribes against women's predatory sexuality in *King Lear* appear later in the play, most notably in the king's mad speeches:

> Down from the waist
> They're centaurs, though women all above.
> But to the girdle do the gods inherit;
> The rest is all the fiend's.
>
> (4.5.121–24)

From the beginning, Hesione and Ariadne are characterised by their dangerous sexual allure, though in a much more attractive and less moralised form than Goneril and Regan. It is in this that they are most obviously different from Ellie. 'In contrast' with the older women, Shaw told a Swedish director of the play, 'the girl Ellie must be perfectly virginal: her spiritual marriage with the old captain must be like the marriage by which a nun is made the bride of Christ'.[18] The alternative to the essentially nonreproductive sexuality of Hesione and Ariadne (for all their offstage children) is this Platonic marriage of souls between the old sea captain whose 'last shot was fired years ago' and the celibate young woman.

The union between Shotover and Ellie in Act III was a late addition to the play, appearing as a manuscript insertion on the typescript draft.[19] But the affinities between the two are apparent from the beginning, even in stage positioning. When Ellie, with the new self-command born of disillusionment, prepares to deal with the matter of her engagement to Mangan, we see her 'settling into the draughtsman's seat' (Shaw, V, 106) that is Shotover's. Later on in the scene, the association is strengthened when 'propping her elbows on the drawing-board and her chin on her hands, she composes herself to listen' (Shaw, V, 108). Ellie's dominance here, with the aura of authority given by the Captain's working table, is contrasted with the attitude of Mangan, who 'sits down in the wicker chair; and resigns himself to allow her to lead the conversation' (Shaw, V, 107). If Ellie is aligned with the Captain by her occupation of his male workstation, the alluringly feminine Hesione habitually sits on the sofa. When she wants to persuade her young friend to confide in her, 'she snatches at Ellie's waist, and makes her sit down on the sofa beside her' (Shaw, v, 74), and similarly, we see her 'laying Ellie down at the end of the sofa' to soothe her after the shock of discovering that her adored Marcus Darnley is in reality Hesione's husband Hector. Ellie, however, refuses thus to recline in hysterics and 'have a good cry', but 'raising her head' exclaims, 'Damn!' (Shaw, v, 84). When Hesione fails to get the better of Mazzini Dunn in Act II, she 'retires to the sofa' in the sulks (Shaw, v, 117). Shotover's middle-aged daughters, his Goneril and Regan, with their tempting attractions, belong to the comfort zones of the stage; Ellie must come through the bracing experience of heartbreak to join the Captain in his strenuous resistance to such temptations.

The Captain is assertive in his proprietorship of his ship/house, indignant at the notion that the 'numskull', Sir Hastings Utterword, should have criticised it: 'Whats wrong with my house?' (Shaw, v, 160). Yet this is a Lear who positively wants to be out on the heath, or at least is always conscious of the expanse of space outside the house. In answer to Mangan's affronted question as to whether he is in Shotover's house or Hesione's, the Captain retorts, 'You are beneath the dome of heaven, in the house of God' (Shaw, v, 88). When Mangan, driven beyond endurance by repeated humiliations in Act III, announces his intention of getting 'to hell out of this house', Shotover assures him, 'You were welcome to come: you are free to go. The wide earth, the high seas, the spacious skies are waiting for you outside' (Shaw, v, 130). Heartbreak House is Shotover's insofar as it is the ship of which he is captain, but as it is a closeted hothouse of lovemaking, intrigue and battles for dominance, he disdains its significance. But, if at one level the house dramatises the conflict between male independence and purposeful control against a distracting and debilitating female sexuality, the Captain's ship also affords a vision that transcends such gendered oppositions.

Ship of state, ship of fools

In a letter to Lee Simonson, the designer for the first production of *Heartbreak House* by the Theatre Guild in New York, Shaw evoked the windows he imagined for the back of the set: 'The XVII century Dutch marine pictures shew us lovely stern windows in brown woodwork with magnificent gilt framing, tall and handsome, with a balcony or stern gallery, gold in the framing, gold in the water, gold in the brown paint'.[20]

Figure 3.1　Sketch by G.B. Shaw of set design for *Heartbreak House*, c. 1920.

On sketches of the stage made at about the same time, he made his theatrical concept clear (Figure 3.1).[21] The three windows were set into the back wall, representing the stern of the ship, looking out onto the garden. An arrow on the drawing is marked 'Astern'/'Ahead' to show the orientation of the ship. The effect that Shaw evidently intended was that the ship-shaped house should be felt by the audience to be sailing away from land in their direction. It was a novel application of the fourth-wall convention. Not only are the spectators to be allowed to look in at the play's staged interior, but that space itself could be imagined advancing towards them. That was part of the monitory effect built into the metaphor of the ship in the play.

In the creation of the play it has been suggested that Shaw may have 'remembered Thomas Carlyle, for whom a dominant metaphor of England was the ship which must round Cape Horn and keep off the rocks'.[22] The trope of the ship of state is of course a generic one, but certainly the exchanges between Shotover and Hector in Act III are explicit in their denunciatory application:

HECTOR. And this ship we are all in? This soul's prison we call England?
CAPTAIN SHOTOVER. The captain is in his bunk, drinking bottled ditch-water; and the crew is gambling in the forecastle. She will strike and sink and split.

Do you think the laws of God will be suspended in favor of England
because you were born in it?

HECTOR. Well, I dont mean to be drowned like a rat in a trap. I still have the will
to live. What am I to do?

CAPTAIN SHOTOVER. Do? Nothing simpler. Learn your business as an
Englishman.

HECTOR. And what may my business as an Englishman be, pray?

CAPTAIN SHOTOVER. Navigation. Learn it and live; or leave it and be damned.

(Shaw, v, 177)

What, though, are the chances of Hector, the posing adventurer, learning
the art of navigation? The play represented England as a drifting ship
sailing aimlessly out towards the audience, with those who should be
steering temperamentally incapable of doing so.

As a Fabian activist, Shaw had always urged political engagement on the
liberal intelligentsia. The burden of *Major Barbara* (1905) was the need for
professors of Greek like Adolphus Cusins to become armament manufac-
turers like Andrew Undershaft, to take literal control of the means of
production as the means to power. At the end of the action, Cusins and
Undershaft form a tripartite alliance with Barbara, the ex–Salvation Army
major, who will give moral and spiritual purpose to this Utopian union.
But in the years since 1905, the skies had darkened. The appalling catastrophe of the war made it impossible to think in these positive conceptual
terms. The actual involvement of a business tycoon in government, very
unlike the admired Undershaft, had left Shaw disgusted with the experiment. Lord Devonport, originally the self-made grocer Hudson Kearley,
was appointed Minister of Food Control by Lloyd George in his war cabinet
in December 1916. Devonport would have been notorious to socialists as
the past administrator of the Port of London who had ruthlessly broken
the dockers' strike in 1912. But Shaw's real outrage against his appointment
was the assumption that his experience as 'a practical business man' (Shaw,
v, 163) would make him a competent government minister. In point of
fact, Devonport lasted less than six months, resigning in May 1917.
Devonport was the model for Boss Mangan in the play, the most vituperative portrait of a capitalist in all of Shaw's work, as is apparent even in
the opening description of him: 'Mangan, carefully frock-coated as for
church or for a directors' meeting, is about fiftyfive, with a careworn,
mistrustful expression, standing a little on an entirely imaginary dignity,
with a dull complexion, straight, lustreless hair, and features so entirely
commonplace that it is impossible to describe them' (Shaw, v, 86). Shaw
seems to have recognised the degree to which his animus against the

character and his real-life counterpart unbalanced the play. When sending the first proof of *Heartbreak House* to his Swedish translator Hugo Vallentin, Shaw said that 'it seems to me a fine opening spoilt by the war and by Lord Devonport (Mangan)'.[23]

Mangan, the loathed businessman turned incompetent politician, is the outsider in Heartbreak House. But what about the actual occupants of the house? They are summed up well by Mazzini Dunn as 'a favorable specimen of what is best in our English culture. [...] very charming people, most advanced, unprejudiced, frank, humane, unconventional, democratic, free-thinking, and everything that is delightful to thoughtful people' (Shaw, v, 173). Dunn intends to be complimentary, but this is in fact Shaw's indictment of the Heartbreak Householders. In the preface, Shaw gives a sweeping significance to the house: 'Heartbreak House is not merely the name of the play which follows this preface. It is cultured, leisured Europe before the war' (Shaw, v, 12). Chekhov is there invoked as his model. Chekhov, though, had represented with the neutrality of an observer a feckless landowning class in the historically inevitable process of being replaced. By contrast, the abdication of responsibility of Shaw's Heartbreakers is castigated for its consequences:

> They took the only part of our society in which there was leisure for high culture, and made it an economic, political, and, as far as practicable, a moral vacuum; and as Nature, abhorring the vacuum, immediately filled it up with sex and with all sorts of refined pleasures, it was a very delightful place at its best for moments of relaxation. In other moments it was disastrous. For prime ministers and their like, it was a veritable Capua. (Shaw, v, 14)

Given the encounter with the Woolfs at Windham Croft at the early stages of the play's conception, it seems likely that Shaw had the ethos of Bloomsbury specifically in mind. Certainly it is suggestive that he classifies sex with other sorts of 'refined pleasures'. In the typescript draft of the play, Ariadne's liaison with Randall Utterword is made much more obvious. Hesione tells Ariadne, 'I have given him the room next to yours' and introduces Randall to Dunn as 'my sister's young man'.[24] The lovemaking of the characters is placed by Shaw along with Randall's flute playing as a mere diversion of the idle. But the reference to Capua, where the Emperor Tiberius went for his debauchery – 'for prime ministers and their like, it was a veritable Capua' – makes country-house flirtation into something much more reprehensible. The cultured, thinking upper-middle classes, who should have been giving guidance to the politicians, provided them instead only with escapist sexual R and R. This is the more culpable because, as Shaw argues in the preface, the only alternative to Heartbreak House is Horseback Hall, the seat of Philistines like Ariadne and her numskull husband Sir Hastings Utterword. Ariadne's solution to the problem of steering the ship of state is straightforward: 'Get rid of your ridiculous sham democracy; and give Hastings the necessary powers, and a good supply of bamboo to bring the British native to his senses: he will save the country with the greatest of ease' (Shaw, v, 165). Shaw so berates the people of Bloomsbury/Heartbreak House because they *ought* to be offering an enlightened other way to this brutal know-nothing imperialism and they are not.

In the array of characters that makes up the cast of *Heartbreak House*, there are radical moral and political oppositions. Shaw may be critical of the lack of engagement of the house's inhabitants, their unwillingness to learn the art of navigation, but the Utterwords have nothing to recommend them. The Captain's reply to Ariadne's panacea – the dictatorship of Hastings with 'a good supply of bamboo' – is definitive: 'Any fool can govern with a stick in his hand. *I* could govern that way. It is not God's way' (Shaw, v, 165). Figures such as the capitalist 'boss' are even more stigmatised; when Hector asks the Captain what he stores his dynamite for, he says 'to kill fellows like Mangan' (Shaw, v, 100). And even though Hector claims he would spare such 'human vermin' out of 'simple magnanimous pity', he makes an absolute moral distinction between them and himself: 'I must believe that my spark, small as it is, is divine, and that the red light over their door is hell fire' (Shaw, v, 101). Yet when Hesione mocks Mangan to Ellie – 'Isnt he a fool, pettikins?' – Hector retorts 'fiercely': 'Do not scorn the man. We are all fools' (Shaw, v, 170). Shaw uses a Biblical language of reprobation to an unparalleled degree in *Heartbreak House* in his denunciation of the sins of the people, his call of the backsliding heartbreakers to service. But he draws also on a levelling perspective in which all his characters alike are embarked together on a ship of fools.

The ship of fools was a common emblem in medieval and Renaissance iconography, the most famous example being the painting by Hieronymous Bosch now in the Louvre. Bosch features an assortment of grotesque figures eating and drinking and making merry on a ship that is going nowhere incongruously in the midst of a landscape, their only oar a ladle, their sailless mast adorned with a bouquet of flowers. Painted at the time of the Reformation, with the central figures a monk and a nun, it may have been intended as a reproach to the church for failing to provide the steering leadership it should have done, in this like Shaw's critique of the people of Heartbreak House. But the ship of fools is a figure for all humanity, drifting purposelessly through life, caught up in their pleasures, indifferent to their long-term destination. It is in these terms that Hector utters his Act III prophecy: 'I tell you, one of two things much happen. Either out of that darkness some new creation will come to supplant us as we have supplanted the animals, or the heavens will fall and destroy us' (Shaw, v, 159). Coded into the first of Hector's alternatives is Shaw's creed of creative evolution, by which *Homo sapiens* is only a stage in a divinely guided development that will bring beings ever greater self-reflective intelligence. But, like his prewar hopes of a political alliance of culture with economic power and moral purpose, this now seems a doomed aspiration. Instead, his ship of fools appears to be threatened by an apocalyptic cataclysm of which they remain completely oblivious.

The unseen war

Shaw claims in his preface that 'when the play was begun not a shot had been fired; and only the professional diplomatists and the very few amateurs whose hobby is foreign policy even knew that the guns were loaded' (Shaw, v, 12). There may have been here an attempt to endow himself with more foresight than he actually had, because there is clear evidence that composition of the play actually began in March 1916 and was completed in May 1917.[25] This was an unusually long time for Shaw, and in a letter to Mrs Patrick Campbell he explained why:

> I cant write: nothing comes off but screeds for the papers, mostly about this blasted war. I am old and finished. I, who once wrote whole plays *d'un seul trait*, am creeping through a new one (to prevent myself crying) at odd moments, two or three speeches at a time. I dont know what its about.[26]

The letter makes clear Shaw's degree of self-identification with Shotover. He was only just sixty at the time, and Shotover was eighty-eight, but the added years reflected Shaw's mood of being 'old and finished'. He had indeed written 'screeds' on the war situation, including his enormous pamphlet *Common Sense about the War*, published as a supplement to the *New Statesman* within months of the war's outbreak, which made him deeply unpopular. Nobody seemed to listen to him; nobody seemed aware of the depths of his frustration and despair. The mad old sea captain in his ship-shaped house with its indifferent inhabitants seemed a fit metaphor for his mood. The strategy Shaw adopted as a means of expressing this sense of alienation was to show a group of people going about their country-house entertainments of love and proposals wholly unaware of the war. The Zeppelin attack in Act III comes as a complete surprise, and even then it is never identified as such. At no point in *Heartbreak House*, in fact, is there any indication that there is a war going on.

In Act III the characters move out of the house, and Shaw fills the stage with the garden only glimpsed through the windows in Acts I and II. In the dialogue and the grouping of the characters, this makes for the loosest and most flexible version of the fantasia form.[27] In the nighttime garden, lit by 'the circle of light cast by the electric arc' (Shaw, V, 158), Ariadne is stretched in the hammock and Ellie is leaning up against the sleeping Shotover; other characters – Hector, Hesione, Mangan – appear from the house or the darkness around. Randall plays his flute inside; Mazzini, awakened by the talk, comes out to join them 'in pyjamas and a richly coloured dressing-gown' (Shaw, V, 170). It seems a romantic and relaxed scene after all the emotional entanglements of the earlier action, fit background for the 'life with a blessing' that Ellie seeks in her 'marriage' to Shotover (Shaw, V, 169). In terms of the stage design, it is as though the ship of the house had sailed off into the auditorium, leaving the characters beached in the garden. This, though, renders them all the more vulnerable and exposed to what comes next.

It is Hesione who first hears it: 'There was a sort of splendid drumming in the sky. Did none of you hear it? It came from a distance and then died away' (Shaw, V, 159). Michael Holroyd points to the similarity between this and Chekhov's snapping string in *The Cherry Orchard*;[28] indeed, the wording here exactly echoes that in Chekhov, where the sound 'is heard in the distance [. . .] dying away, sad' (Chekhov, 315, 349). In Shaw, too, there is the guessing game as to what the sound might be, and the different interpretations reflect the mood and temperament of the interpreters. Mangan, the practical man – like Lopakhin before him – insists on a pragmatic explanation: 'I tell you it was a train'. Hector, full of world-weary self-loathing, pronounces it 'Heaven's threatening growl of disgust at us useless futile creatures'. As in Chekhov, it is associated with ill omen, but ironically here it is Mangan – Mangan the down-to-earth businessman – who has 'the presentiment that he is going to die' (Shaw, V, 159) and is merely mocked for his belief. Shaw's 'splendid drumming', however, has none of the plangent melancholy of Chekhov's snapping string. It is given a very real explanation with the advent of the Zeppelin raid in which Mangan does indeed die.

It is well known that the ending of the play was based on the incident of a Zeppelin that crossed right over Shaw's house in Hertfordshire on

1 October 1916 and was shot down only ten miles away.[29] He rode his motorbike to see the wreckage the following day, and described his emotions in a letter to Beatrice and Sidney Webb:

> What is hardly credible, but true, is that the sound of the Zepp's engines was so fine, and its voyage through the stars so enchanting, that I positively caught myself hoping next night that there would be another raid. I grieve to add that after seeing the Zepp fall like a burning newspaper, with its human contents roasting for some minutes (it was frightfully slow) I went to bed and was comfortably asleep in ten minutes. One is so pleased to have seen the show that the destruction of a dozen people or so in hideous terror and torment does not count. 'I didnt half cheer, I tell you' said a damsel at the wreck. Pretty lot of animals we are![30]

Shaw's sense of excitement at the spectacle of the Zeppelin, which he gives to his characters in the play, was apparently not all that unusual for civilian onlookers in the war. Ariela Freedman cites, among other examples of the sense of the 'Zeppelin sublime', an eyewitness account by Katherine Mansfield in Paris: '[T]he Ultimate Fish passed by, flying high, with fins of silky grey. It is absurd to say that romance is dead when things like this happen.'[31] Freedman places this reaction as characteristic of an early stage of awed wonder at the sight of the Zeppelins, which was followed by 'Zeppelin fatigue', and finally a sense that the attacks brought awareness of the war to the home front in new ways. Within such a pattern of development, the effect of Shaw's play and its final scene is a complicated one.

There is no doubt of the reality of Shaw's anguish, the depth of his revulsion at the war, expressed repeatedly in letters like that to Mrs Patrick Campbell, quoted earlier, where his writing of the play was an inadequate distraction to prevent him from crying. He emphatically turned down an invitation from Lady Gregory to lecture on behalf of the Irish national theatre: 'NO. The very words nation, nationality, our country, patriotism fill me with loathing. Why do you want to stimulate a self-consciousness which is already morbidly excussive in our wretched island, and is deluging Europe with blood?'[32] The measure of the change brought about in him can be seen in the difference between the commandingly self-assured armaments manufacturer Undershaft, who acts as something like a Shavian spokesman in *Major Barbara*, and the mad old Shotover, seeking to invent a mind-ray to explode dynamite in his campaign against 'fellows like Mangan'. A cancelled draft line in his Act 1 colloquy with Hector is suggestive: 'Remember, we are no longer free as we were. They have made hell and cast us into the cauldron. I will fight for my own soul and yours.'[33]

It was all very well for Undershaft to score debating points about the need for the professors of Greek to become makers of arms, but the technology of mass destruction that the Great War had shown in action made for a quite new urgency and a new desperation in Shaw's attitude towards the issue of power. The crazed Shotover and the apocalyptic mood that runs through the whole of *Heartbreak House* are the result.

Yet Shaw was temperamentally resistant to the full apprehension of tragedy.[34] He lent his own sense of exhilaration at the Zeppelin raid to the people of Heartbreak House, who thrill to its excitement:

MRS HUSHABYE. [. . .] the sound in the sky: it's splendid: it's like an orchestra: it's like Beethoven.
ELLIE. By thunder, Hesione: it *is* Beethoven.
She and Hesione throw themselves into one another's arms in wild excitement.
(Shaw, v, 178)

Even Hector's bravado in turning on all the lights in defiance of the blackout has a heroic grandeur to it, at least by contrast with the miserable cowardice of the burglar, Billie Dunn, and Mangan, both of whom are killed when they seek shelter in the gravel pit/dynamite store. There is a degree of moral satisfaction, even wish fulfilment, in this destruction of 'the two burglars – the two practical men of business' (Shaw, v, 181). By contrast, the survivors win audience identification by their fearlessness. As Shotover puts it: 'The judgement has come. Courage will not save you; but it will shew your souls are still alive' (Shaw, v, 179). And it is hard not to see the final exchange between Hesione and Ellie as an upbeat ending:

MRS HUSHABYE. But what a glorious experience! I hope theyll come again tomorrow night.
ELLIE (*radiant at the prospect*) Oh, I *hope* so.
(Shaw, v, 181)

Against this there is the irony of Randall Utterword's final flute-playing – the tune he plays is 'Keep the Home Fires Burning', the 1914 Ivor Novello song that was so hugely popular in the early years of the war – but it is a fairly muted irony. By way of contrast, taken from a different medium in reaction against a much later war, one might compare the terrible scene in Francis Ford Coppola's 1979 film *Apocalypse Now* where the American helicopters bomb a Vietnamese village to the accompaniment of 'The Ride of the Valkyries'.

Shaw withheld the play for the duration of the war, only finally publishing it in 1919, when it became, as he explained in the preface, the first time in nearly twenty years that he was 'obliged to introduce a play in the form of a book for lack of an opportunity of presenting it in its proper mode by a performance in a theatre' (Shaw, v, 45). As so often with Shaw's prefaces, written as they always were some years after the plays themselves, it reinterprets the dramatic text in the light of the later situation. Heartbreak House, a complex and ambivalent image in the play, becomes unequivocally 'cultured, leisured Europe before the war' (Shaw, v, 12). The political analysis is notably extended and historically contextualised. Ariadne's celebration of the conventional life of the hunting, shooting, fishing country house, only introduced in the play in one speech of Act III, provides the basis for the symmetrically alliterative Horseback Hall, the Philistine alternative to the cultured Bohemianism of Heartbreak House. Shaw indicts not only the governing classes of England, divided between the ignorant riding classes and the educated, uninvolved, flute-playing classes, but what he calls 'the wicked half century' of political Darwinism, which had resulted in 'the banishment of conscience from human affairs' (Shaw, v, 20). By 1919, compounding Shaw's sense of the massive misguidedness that had led to the war in the first place (anatomised in *Common Sense*) was the accumulated anger against the rhetoric of the 1918 general election, the vengefulness of the Allies at Versailles, and above all his horror at the tragic waste of so many young lives, including sons of close friends like Mrs Patrick Campbell and Lady Gregory. He wrote sympathetically and consolingly to Gregory, but to Campbell he vented his feeling of appalled frustration: 'It is no use: I cant be sympathetic: these things simply make me furious. I want to swear. I *do* swear. Killed just because people are blasted fools.'[35] It is such feelings that made for the Old Testament ferocity of the preface: 'Thus were the firstborn of Heartbreak House smitten; and the young, the innocent, the hopeful expiated the folly and worthlessness of their elders' (Shaw, v, 22).

Heartbreak House was given a critical mauling when it was first published in 1919, in a collection with a number of other 'playlets' of the war. J.C. Squire was only the most extreme of its detractors when he said of it that 'a worse volume [. . .] has never appeared under the name of a man of reputation, and seldom under any sort of name at all'.[36] With a playing time of over three and a half hours, it looked as though it might never be produced. In spite of the critical success of the brave New York production by the Theatre Guild, its London premiere, codirected by Shaw himself with the producer J.B. Fagan, was a disastrous failure. However, in the second half of the twentieth century it came to be viewed as one of Shaw's most important plays and was frequently revived as such. This was in part for theatrical reasons – it affords a major starring role for a veteran actor in the part of Shotover and two outstanding opportunities for mature women actors in Hesione and Ariadne – but also because it was by then interpreted as one of the major works of the modernist imagination inspired by the war, to be compared with *Women in Love* or *The Waste Land*.[37]

Increasingly, the retrospective view of the war, already initiated by Shaw in his 1919 preface, was made visible in the realisation of the play. So, for example, in Cedric Messina's 1977 BBC television production, the broadcast opened with a grainy black-and-white image of Zeppelins cutting through the clouds, as in a period newsreel, and it was against this background that the play title appeared. The first image of Ellie sitting in the window seat was in black and white before mutating into colour. Each entr'acte was punctuated with a return to the newsreel Zeppelins. The surprise effect of the attack, coming from nowhere in the play, was replaced by the constant framing awareness of the audience of the historical situation viewed from the distance of seventy years. A similar postwar consciousness of the war and its terrible consequences was embedded in Patrick Mason's 1986 Dublin production at the Gate Theatre. A mysterious veiled woman in mourning crossed the stage at the beginning and end of the action, and a coup de théâtre at the last moment revealed a war memorial from behind a curtain at the back of the set.

In some productions, Shaw's image of the ship/house sailing to disaster was emphasised. Jocelyn Herbert's design for the 1983 West End revival of the play directed by John Dexter, with a cast led by Rex Harrison, removed much of the detailed furnishings of the set 'to present the simple and bare environment of a lofty ship's poop'. Irving Wardle's *Times* review went on to describe the effect:

> What comes over is the sense of a luxury cruise for a group of people who are free to lounge about and talk on the way to some fatal destination. This image that becomes even more pronounced in the third act, [is] played on the likeness of a ship's deck against an impenetrable black sky from which the airship arrives to gratify the liberal English death-wish by delivering its cargo of bombs.[38]

But other stagings moved away from the ship concept to other methods of rendering the play's metaphoric meaning. For Christopher Newton's 1985 Shaw Festival production, 'Michael Levine created a set that allowed Captain Shotover's [...] antiquarian mansion to grow or shrink, as in a kind of *Alice in Wonderland* dream. [...] And then at the end, as the bombs began to fall, the dream turned into the nightmare of a world bent on destroying itself.'[39] There was what appears to have been an eclectic design for a premillennial Shaw Festival revival directed by Tadeusz Bradecki in 1999.

> Bradecki used Mahler and Stravinsky for mood and context, complementing the discordant geometric angularity of Peter Hartwell's set (more Japanese than the traditional nautical atmosphere), full of wood and canvas frames suggesting early, yet threatening airplane wings, or, more ominously, Zeppelins. [...] And jerky projections from silent movies increased the sense of clumsiness and lack of communication on this ship of vainglorious fools.[40]

With its postmodern collage of images and associations, this is a long way from the theatrical style of Shaw's original text. That distance, though, is used only to enforce an understanding of Shaw's play as an early twentieth-century precursor to later imaginations of disaster.

In *Heartbreak House*, there is a mixture of modes and moods. The Chekhovian 'fantasia' provided the country house setting, the ensemble cast of highly individuated characters and the loose, all but plotless plot. But Shaw's dramaturgical bent resulted in something very different from Chekhov. Chekhov's action dawdles and drifts along, making its impact through its constantly modulating tone and atmosphere. Shaw's technique is to move forward by a series of galvanic shocks, each entrance yielding another surprise, one more disorienting clash of characters.[41] *The Cherry Orchard*, Chekhov's wry tragicomedy, is transformed in *Heartbreak House* into something like tragic farce.

Shaw's play reflects also its author's own ambivalent attitude towards women. Committed political feminist though he was and strong supporter of the suffragist cause, he oscillated between a passionate flirtatiousness and an underlying distaste for a fully consummated and domesticated love relationship. The alluring attractiveness of Hesione Hushabye owes much to Mrs Patrick Campbell, on whom she was modelled and with whom Shaw had come closest to an extramarital affair. Hesione and her sister disrupt the would-be masculine enclave of the Captain's house with their Circe-like enchantments. A comparable instability of feeling extends to the Bloomsbury-like atmosphere of Heartbreak House. In the preface, Shaw is stern in his condemnation of the frivolity and irresponsibility of the Heartbreakers. Yet in a letter to Virginia Woolf, written years later, he recalled his meeting with her at Windham Croft with characteristic

Shavian gallantry: 'There is a play of mine called Heartbreak House which I always connect with you because I conceived it in that house somewhere in Sussex where I first met you and, of course, fell in love with you.'[42] Shaw might disapprove of the atmosphere of the Bloomsbury group, with their high culture, tangled emotional relationships and lack of the right – from his point of view – political engagement. But he endowed them with considerable charm, and in contrast with the unspeakable capitalist Mangans and the Philistine Utterwords, there was no question as to which side Shaw supported.

Composition of *Heartbreak House* did not begin before the war, as the preface asserts, but the play is expressive at once of prewar anxiety, the excitement of its early years and the terrible realisation brought about by its later phases. The semi-allegorical treatment of the country house as a ship was conditioned by the global crisis of the war during which the play was actually written. The blood-drenched period of the Battle of the Somme and beyond, 1916 to 1917, informs Shotover's imagination of imminent apocalypse. And yet the mood of the play's ending more resembles the atmosphere of the early years of the war, the sense of relief and release felt by those who had lived through so many years of uneasy peace. If it has none of the providentialist assurance of Brooke's sonnets – 'Now God be thanked / Who has matched us with His hour' – it has something of the death-delighted consciousness of Julian Grenfell's extra-ordinary poem 'Into Battle'.[43] The Zeppelins provoke in the people of Heartbreak House, as they did in Katherine Mansfield, a sense that it is 'absurd to say that romance is dead when things like this happen'. The dateless setting of *Heartbreak House*, the lack of any direct reference to the war, allowed it simultaneously to represent the know-nothing oblivi-ousness of the house's inhabitants in the midst of Armageddon, and the bracing amazement of facing into it for the first time. A second world war, the threat of nuclear annihilation, and electronic media alerting us continually to disasters near and far have conditioned productions of the play in which Heartbreak House and its occupants waiting for the Zeppelin speak unequivocally to our latter-day terrors.

CHAPTER 4

Long Day's Journey into Night: *the Tyrones at home in America*

Shaw wrote *Heartbreak House* in immediate reaction to the war in 1916–17, though he masked that immediacy by disguising the play as a monitory image of prewar complacency. In the period after the war, it was received with incomprehension and disgust; it had to wait for another, more globally threatened time to find an audience for what was then perceived as its apocalyptic warning of catastrophe. Writing in 1940–41 during the Second World War, O'Neill prepared a time capsule of private life: he meticulously re-created a specific milieu and period, an Irish-American family in 1912 with all the inheritance of its history. And in putting the play under embargo for twenty-five years after his death, he set up his time capsule to be opened long after the period of composition. Had his widow, Carlotta, not decided to disregard the embargo, it would have been in 1978, not 1956, that *Journey* was first seen – its 1912 action viewed down the telescope of the years.[1] The original naturalistic model of home on the stage depended on its contemporaneity, the audience recognizing the living space in the theatre as one that might be their own. O'Neill's play, by contrast, is multiply distanced from its later twentieth-century audiences not only by its period setting but by the fact of its autobiographical origins. This is not just any representative family but O'Neill's own: star actor father, morphine-addicted mother, drunkard older brother and consumptive would-be writer. What is the effect of the domestic space rendered with such retrospective particularity?

O'Neill reflected with satisfaction on the completion of *Journey*: I 'like this play better than any I have ever written – does most with the least – a quiet play! – and a great one, I believe'.[2] It is a just self-assessment. By O'Neill's standards, *Journey* is indeed a 'quiet play'. O'Neill had not, like Chekhov, sought through his career to write a play without a pistol shot; on the contrary, violent death, suicide and infanticide had been his stock in trade. A play in which the whole stage action consists of conversations between the four family members in the living room of their home was unlike anything he had written before. The observation that the play 'does most with the least' is also striking in relation to the playwright's past practice. O'Neill's impulse had always been to seek big theatrical effects and not to count the cost. There were his outsize plays, the nine-act *Strange Interlude* (1927), which had to be played over two evenings, and *Mourning Becomes Electra* (1931), his re-creation of Aeschylus's *Oresteia* trilogy. He was notably extravagant in the demands he made of producers and theatrical resources. So, for example, even his one low-key domestic comedy, *Ah, Wilderness!* (1933), has fifteen speaking parts, including the prostitute Belle, who appears in only one scene, and Richard's girlfriend Muriel, who figures in just another. In it O'Neill used the same setting as for *Journey*, both based on the O'Neills' own New London home, but in *Ah, Wilderness!*, besides the sitting room of the Millers, all but identical to the Tyrones' living room, we are shown their dining room, the 'back room of a bar in a small hotel', and 'a strip of beach along the harbour'.[3] O'Neill's early work was well served by the avant-garde Provincetown Players; his middle plays were staged by the enormously adventurous Theatre Guild, who had been prepared to produce *Heartbreak House* (1920) and even Shaw's 'metabiological pentateuch' *Back to Methuselah* (1922). But *Lazarus Laughed* (written in 1926), O'Neill's masked 'play for an imaginative theatre' with its 'Chorus of 159 persons, doubling in approximately 420 roles', was too much for even the most experimental of professional companies and was eventually staged by the largely amateur Pasadena Community Players (O'Neill, II, 1090).

Even in plays where O'Neill did limit himself to a single family and a domestic setting, more or less realistically represented, there was a schematic design to his dramaturgy. In his first full-length Broadway play, *Beyond the Horizon* (1920), the scenes alternate between an open road and the interior of the Mayos' farmhouse, which, over the eight-year span of the play's action, markedly degenerates to reflect the disastrous misman- agement of the poetic brother Robert. Similarly, the two acts of *Diff'rent* (1920) show the same room, first as an old-fashioned 1890 parlour, then thirty years on, with 'an obstreperous newness about everything' to go with the heroine Emma's grotesque attempt to make herself look young and modern (O'Neill, II, 27). Most famously, the elms in the Freudian *Desire Under the Elms* (1924) 'brood oppressively over the house. They are like exhausted women resting their sagging breasts and hands and hair on its roof, and when it rains their tears trickle down monotonously and rot on the shingles' (O'Neill, II, 318). O'Neill wished to give theatrical expression to the deep structures of human experience – hence the spoken asides of unspoken thoughts in *Strange Interlude* and the split persona of John Loving played by two actors in *Days Without End* (1933). One of his most ambitious efforts to come at the ancestral traumas underpinning the individual psyche was *The Emperor Jones* (1920), where the self-appointed emperor on his island lives through memory, not only of his own past as a Pullman porter and escaped convict but of the prehistory of his African American race.

Given such ambitions, it is no wonder that O'Neill should have sneered at the limited and outdated mode of naturalism: 'It represents our father's daring aspirations toward self-recognition by holding the family Kodak up to ill-nature.'[4] For him it was Strindberg, not Ibsen, who was the maker of modern drama, the proto-expressionist Strindberg of *The Dance of Death* (written in 1900) and *The Ghost Sonata* (1908), not the naturalistic drama- tist of *The Father* (written in 1887) and *Miss Julie*. It is the more remarkable that in *Long Day's Journey* he should have chosen to return to this long- rejected mode. Yet in writing it, O'Neill retained much of his previous style and the amplitude of its reach. So, in *Long Day's Journey* there is the characteristically symmetrical progression through the day act by act, from early morning sunlight through increasing fog to dark midnight as the family members probe ever further into their shared past. What is more, that past is shown to be conditioned by contexts beyond the lives of the Tyrones themselves; *Long Day's Journey*, as much as *The Emperor Jones*, is about the historical formation of ethnic identity in its characters. The aim of this chapter is to show how ethnicity, class and period shape the play's staging of home and family and how these have been realised in the theatre.

No place like home

> **Home** [...] In N. America and Australasia (and increasingly elsewhere), freq. used to designate a private house or residence merely as a building.
> *OED*, *Supplement* (1987)

It is probably not accidental that this meaning of home should have developed first in English-speaking countries settled by immigrants. One of the first *OED* citations is from *Harper's Magazine* in 1882: 'A lovely drive [...] is bordered with homes, many of which make pretensions to much more than comfort.' One of the pretensions of such 'homes' is to be a home before anyone has even moved in. For English-speakers not familiar with the usage, it feels like semantic overheating, preinvesting the material construction of the house with all the emotional loading that its inhabitants will bring to it. It is easy to see where such a tendency might come from in the immigrant imaginary. With a homeland left behind, there is an urgency in the need to transfer the sense of belonging to the new country. 'Home', shorn of its associations with neighbourhood, history and ethnic origins, must be carried by the family and vested in the place where it comes to rest, whether temporarily or permanently: hence the linguistically premature designation of the house as home. The status of the Tyrones' house in *Long Day's Journey*, Mary's insistence that it is not a real 'home', are freighted with this sort of diasporic insecurity.

The very first line sets the scene: 'Living room of James Tyrone's summer home on a morning in August, 1912' (O'Neill, III, 717). It is not just by virtue of patriarchal ownership that the 'summer home' is attributed to James Tyrone the householder rather than the family as a whole. The real-life counterpart in New London was constructed by James O'Neill out of the proceeds of his great touring success, *The Count of Monte Cristo*.[5] In the play, the house is a home to Tyrone, not to the others. The grown-up sons Jamie and Edmund are temporary residents, and Mary Tyrone insists that 'I've never felt it was my home. It was wrong from the start'. 'I've always hated this town', she declares to Edmund in Act I, 'and everyone in it. [...] I never wanted to live here in the first place, but your father liked it and insisted on building this house, and I've had to come here every summer' (O'Neill, III, 738). This becomes her theme song as the play goes on, one of her key accusations against Tyrone: 'He thinks money spent on a home is money wasted. [...] He doesn't understand a home. He doesn't feel at home in it. And yet, he wants a home. He's even proud of having this shabby place' (O'Neill, III, 749–50). With the maddening detachment that comes to her when she has begun to take morphine again, she repeats her litany of complaints to Tyrone himself:

> It was never a home. You've always preferred the Club or a barroom. And for me it's always been as lonely as a dirty room in a one-night stand hotel. In a real home one is never lonely. You forget I know from experience what a home is like. I gave up one to marry you – my father's home. (O'Neill, III, 756)

Mary's memories of her father's home provide the settled norm of happiness against which the misery of her peripatetic life as a touring actor's wife is measured and found wanting.

Mary's idyllic nostalgia for her old home and the contrast with her life as the wife of James Tyrone have as background two different versions of the

Irish immigrant experience. Although the parents of James O'Neill and Ella Quinlan, the originals of James and Mary Tyrone, were both poor post-Famine emigrants, the Quinlans had done much better than the O'Neills. The marriage between James O'Neill and Ella Quinlan in real life, like that of the Tyrones in the play, did originate in a friendship between the young Irish actor and the middle-aged businessman. But, given their class difference, O'Neill's biographer Louis Sheaffer comments: '[I]t is doubtful that [Quinlan] would have allowed a romance to develop between [Ella] and James O'Neill, still less have given his blessing to their marriage, no matter how much he liked James himself. But [he] died when she was still at school.'[6] Tyrone/O'Neill was still only aspiring to the success represented by the solid middle-class home and the convent-educated daughter. For him and his family, the immigrant story had been tougher and more traumatic.

Tyrone tells a version of this story to Edmund in Act IV of the play, evidently an oft-told tale that his sons have heard repeated many times. Still, it is the formative experience that has made him what he is:

> When I was ten my father deserted my mother and went back to Ireland to die. Which he did soon enough, and deserved to, and I hope he's roasting in hell. [. . .] My mother was left, a stranger in a strange land, with four small children [. . .] There was no damned romance in our poverty. Twice we were evicted from the miserable hovel we called home, with my mother's few sticks of furniture thrown out in the street, and my mother and sisters crying. (O'Neill, III, 807)

The father's return to the homeland associates Ireland with death and despair, though out of Catholic piety Tyrone attempts to deny he committed suicide. In the strange land where the mother and children are left, there are evictions, not an eviction from the family homestead that was a standard icon of oppression in Ireland, but from 'the miserable hovel *we called* home'. There followed for Tyrone a descent into a Dickensian abyss of child labour, working twelve hours a day in a machine shop at the age of ten, while 'my poor mother washed and scrubbed for the Yanks' (O'Neill, III, 807–8). It was out of this situation of profound alienation that Tyrone remade himself as an actor. 'I was wild with ambition. I read all the plays ever written. I studied Shakespeare as you'd study the Bible. I educated myself. I got rid of an Irish brogue you could cut with a knife' (O'Neill, III, 809). These are the origins of the older Tyrone's performative self, a specific subtype of the immigrant made good.

For all his staunch Irish patriotism and his stubborn defence of the proposition that Shakespeare was an Irish Catholic, Tyrone is a product of his family's colonial conditioning: his ideal of success is to become a classical actor in the plays of the great canonical English dramatist, and it is to this end that he works so hard to lose his Irish accent. But he is doomed instead to become a matinée idol, forced for thirty years to re-create the one melodramatic part on tour across the country. He is always lecturing his sons on the need to learn 'the value of a dollar', the lessons he learned the hard way in the poverty of his childhood. But he finally confesses to Edmund that 'maybe life overdid the lesson for me, and made a dollar worth too much, and the time came when that mistake ruined my career as a fine actor. [. . .] That God-damned play I bought for a song and made such a great success in – a great money success – it ruined me with its promise of an easy fortune' (O'Neill, III, 809). The heady excitement of the always shifting, constantly re-created stage self and the drunken bar-room aftermath can never do away with the underlying anxiety:

> It was at home that I first learned the value of a dollar and the fear of the poorhouse. I've never been able to believe in my luck since. I've always feared it would change and everything I had would be taken away. But still, the more property you own, the safer you think you are. That may not be logical, but it's the way I have to feel. Banks fail, and your money's gone, but you think you can keep the land beneath your feet. (O'Neill, III, 806)

The psychopathology manifested in Tyrone involves the compulsive, atavistic need to own land, so endemic in his Irish ancestors, combined with the immigrant's inability to find a home for the settled self.

The significance of the Tyrones' Irish American Catholic identity in the dramatisation of their home situation is made more obvious by *Ah, Wilderness!*, an idealising twin to *Long Day's Journey*. The two plays use exactly the same opening setting, in both cases based on the O'Neills' living room in New London, but the tone with which the 'sitting-room of the Miller home' is described is totally different: 'The room is fairly large, homely looking and cheerful in the morning sunlight' (O'Neill, III, 5). O'Neill declared that *Ah, Wilderness!* was 'a sort of wishing out loud. That's the way I would have *liked* my boyhood to have been.'[7] The Millers are your average prosperous American family, at the time of the action celebrating the Fourth of July national holiday: six children – though two are grown-up and unseen – a wise father with a solid job as editor/owner of the local paper, a good mother who is conventional in her attitudes but kindly to all and a comic drunken uncle and prim spinster aunt for good measure. Above all, the Millers appear to be white Anglo-Saxon Protest-ants.[8] They have an uncouth Irish maid, Norah, a first sketch for Cathleen in *Long Day's Journey*, but the family can afford to treat her with mere amusement, having no connection to this gauche Irish girl. The Millers have exactly the sort of stable family and settled home to which all good Americans aspire, and which the Tyrones with their ethnic background can never achieve.

Class, creed, ethnicity

Florence Eldredge, who created the part of Mary in the play's New York premiere, was taken aback when the cast went on a background trip to New London as part of the preparation for the production, 'to see the O'Neill house that is the scene of the play and the cause of Mary Tyrone's lamentations for a decent home. I was surprised to find it full of attractive possibilities and charmingly situated looking out on the sound.'[9] The house at 325 Pequot Avenue is indeed attractive-looking, set back from the road on a slight hill, even if its view over Long Island Sound is by now impeded by a row of houses that would not have been there in 1912 (Figure 4.1). Such things, however, are always relative. For a vacation home it might well have been delightful, but as the only permanent residence of the O'Neill parents and their two grown-up sons, it must have felt fairly cramped. The living room, where the play's action is set, is quite small, and the three other main downstairs rooms, back and front parlour and dining room, are even smaller. Upstairs, the four bedrooms are low-ceilinged and the corridor off which they open is extremely narrow. Every sound would have been audible, and it is easy to imagine the claustrophobia of an Ella O'Neill/Mary Tyrone constantly scrutinised by her menfolk for signs that she was returning to her drug use. Much more than the modesty of the house's internal dimensions was the social situation it represented. This is well caught in the 1982 television broadcast based on the 1981 New York theatre production, where the camera pans over the much grander summer homes of New London before coming to rest on the humbler Pequot Avenue house. In *Long Day's Journey*, we are always conscious of the placing of the Tyrones in a social geography of the town and of their own ethnic background.

In an early and influential essay on *Long Day's Journey*, John Henry Raleigh commented that the play 'shows the Irish in the process of assimilation, or, rather – for none of the characters can be called assimilated – in the process of breaking away from the culture of the "Old Country"'.[10] Everywhere through the text there are the gradations and distinctions that mark the class consciousness involved in that

Figure 4.1 O'Neill family home, 325 Pequot Ave., New London.

assimilation. Mary complains that because Tyrone is too mean to pay decent wages for servants each summer, 'I have stupid, lazy greenhorns to deal with' (O'Neill, III, 749). The greenhorns are girls more or less straight off the boat from Ireland, like Cathleen, the 'second girl', with her rough ways and her unselfconscious Irish dialect. Offstage is the bad-tempered cook Bridget, for whom a second cousin on the police force in St Louis is an occasion for boasting. Tyrone's tenant Shaughnessy, who as Phil Hogan becomes a central character in *A Moon for the Misbegotten* (1947), is described by his landlord in stereotypical and class contemptuous terms: 'He's a wily Shanty Mick, that one. He could hide behind a corkscrew' (O'Neill, III, 724). Tyrone's sons lure him into amused identification with the triumph of the 'Shanty Mick' over the Standard Oil millionaire Harker, but Tyrone reverts immediately to his position of class superiority over his fellow countryman: lace curtain Irish looking down on shanty Irish.

For Mary, the Irish American Catholic actor's wife, there is the social anxiety represented by WASP neighbours like the 'Chatfields in their new Mercedes'. For her, 'the Chatfields and people like them stand for something. I mean they have decent, presentable homes they don't have to be ashamed of. They have friends who entertain them and whom they entertain' (O'Neill, III, 738). The actual family on whom the Chatfields were based were the Chapells, who did indeed look down on the O'Neills. As the Chapell daughter later recalled: 'We considered the O'Neills shanty Irish, and we associated the Irish, almost automatic-ally with the servant class.'[11] In the play, Edmund is dismissive of his mother's aspiration to join the circle of the Chatfields: '[W]ho ever heard of them outside this hick burg?' (O'Neill, III, 738). Though there is an egalitarian socialist slant to Edmund's attacks on the rich and powerful throughout *Long Day's Journey*, the keynote here is the contempt for the provincial standards of 'this hick burg'. While Edmund does not share Jamie's addiction to the Great White Way, measuring everything by the standards of New York, he can have no respect for the community of the small seaside town in itself. For Irish American immigrants, real success had to be metropolitan success. Behind Mary's dissatisfaction with her 'home' in *Long Day's Journey* lay Ella O'Neill's feeling that 325 Pequot Avenue was 'below their means and the station in life they should maintain', that what she was owed, and always denied by her wealthy, miserly husband, was a permanent residence of appropriate style in New York.[12]

The ethnic identity of the Tyrones is evident in the play even in their transparent pseudonym: the hereditary lands of the O'Neill clan were in Tyrone, and the Elizabethan Hugh O'Neill was created Earl of Tyrone. In the introductory description of each of the four characters, O'Neill picks out one or another feature of their Irishness in essentialist terms. Mary's voice has a 'touch of Irish lilt in it'; Tyrone's inclinations are close to those of 'his Irish farmer forebears'; Jamie has 'the remnant of a humorous, romantic, irresponsible Irish charm'; and Edmund has a 'long, narrow Irish face' (O'Neill, III, 718, 722–23). Their Irish origins are a flashpoint in the continuing war between Tyrone and Jamie:

JAMIE. I know it's an Irish peasant idea consumption is fatal. It probably is when
     you live in a hovel on a bog, but over here, with modern treatment –
TYRONE. Don't I know that! What are you gabbing about, anyway? And keep
     your dirty tongue off Ireland, with your sneers about peasants and bogs and
     hovels!
(O'Neill, III, 732)

For Tyrone, Ireland is a sacred place: James O'Neill christened his second son, Edmund Burke, after the eighteenth-century Irish patriot; his third,

Eugene Gladstone, in tribute to the British prime minister who in the 1880s had espoused the cause of Irish Home Rule.[13] Jamie regards Ireland with the contempt of the New York man about town, a Godforsaken country of poverty and superstition. Tyrone points out to him that he too is unmistakably Irish: '[K]eep your dirty tongue off Ireland! You're a fine one to sneer, with the map of it on your face!' Jamie scoffs back: 'Not after I wash my face' (O'Neill, iii, 761).

Most productions have made the Irishness of the characters more or less audible. It is a requirement of the text that Cathleen should speak with a thick accent, while Tyrone has been given more or less of a brogue by different performers. Frederic March, creating the part in New York in 1956, spoke with an Irish accent throughout.[14] Laurence Olivier, playing Tyrone in a National Theatre production in 1971, spoke an actorly received standard English except for occasional lapses into a brogue.[15] In Jonathan Miller's 1986 staging, the brogue was used only for mimicry, as when an otherwise completely American Jack Lemon as Tyrone illustrated his original 'Irish brogue you could cut with a knife' or Kevin Spacey playing Jamie contemptuously derided his father's 'Irish peasant idea consumption is fatal' (O'Neill, iii, 809, 732).[16] The apparently essential Irishness of the Tyrones made the 1981 New York production with an all–African American cast the more interesting.

Originally produced in the Theatre at St Peter's Church with a transfer to the Public Theatre, it was directed by Geraldine Fitzgerald, who had herself played a notable Mary Tyrone in 1971.[17] All the references to Irishness in the text were removed with surprising ease. So the story of Shaughnessy and his pigs remained intact except for Edmund's line about Tyrone being 'tickled to death over the great Irish victory' (O'Neill, iii, 726). The story of Tyrone's father having gone back to Ireland to die is cut – he merely deserted the family – and Mary's reminder to Edmund that his father's 'people were the most ignorant kind of poverty-stricken Irish' became merely the 'worst kind of ignorant poor folks' (O'Neill, iii, 782). Rhetta Hughes, the African American actor playing Cathleen in the television version, was darker skinned than the Tyrones and spoke a more obviously 'black' English; the class differential of the original text remained the same. Only the Tyrones' Irish American Catholicism could not be changed. 'Church' was substituted for 'Mass' in the exchanges between Jamie and Tyrone about the supposedly devout father not practising his religion, but Mary had to be convent-educated and pray to the Virgin. The Irishness of the characters could be edited out, but their Catholic faith could not.

For Tyrone, it is the betrayal of their Catholicism that has made his dissolute sons what they are. For him, Edmund's socialism and his freethinking, just like Jamie's free living, are all of a piece:

> There's little choice between the philosophy you learned from Broadway loafers, and the one Edmund got from his books. They're both rotten to the core. You've both flouted the faith you were born and brought up in – the one true faith of the Catholic Church – and your denial has brought nothing but self-destruction.

However, Jamie is quick to respond to this accusation: 'I don't notice you've worn any holes in the knees of your pants going to Mass' (O'Neill, III, 759). In fact, neither of the older Tyrones is a practising Catholic, though both are still believers. Cathleen is astonished that Mary should ever have thought of becoming a nun: 'Sure, you never darken the door of a church, God forgive you' (O'Neill, III, 775). Edward L. Shaughnessy interestingly points out that in O'Neill's hypermeticulous description of the set of this Catholic home, there is no mention of any icons or religious images.[18] In *Long Day's Journey*, we are shown an Irish American family who are not yet fully lapsed Catholics but are in the painful process of lapsing.

Tyrone struggles to keep together his beliefs against the sardonic onslaughts of his sons. He protests vehemently against the charge that he does not go to Mass. 'It's true I'm a bad Catholic in the observance, God forgive me. But I believe! [. . .] I may not go to church but every night and morning of my life I get on my knees and pray.' 'Did you pray for Mama?' Edmund retorts.

TYRONE. I did. I've prayed to God these many years for her.
EDMUND. Then Nietzsche must be right. (*He quotes from Thus Spake Zarathustra.*) 'God is dead: of his pity for man hath God died'.
(O'Neill, III, 759)

In the moments when she has fullest self-awareness, the anguish of Mary's situation is compounded by her simultaneous failure of faith and conviction of sin:

> If I could only find the faith I lost, so I could pray again! (*She pauses – then begins to recite the Hail Mary in a flat empty tone.*) 'Hail, Mary, full of grace! The Lord is with Thee; blessed art Thou among women'. (*sneeringly.*) You expect the Blessed Virgin to be fooled by a lying dope fiend reciting words! You can't hide from Her! (O'Neill, III, 779)

Mary's idealising memories of young girlhood, the convent and her father's home are based on a sanctioned idea of the self from which she feels herself estranged. At times she can look forward to finding her soul again, as she tells Edmund: '[S]ome day when the Blessed Virgin Mary forgives me and gives me back the faith in Her love and pity I used to have in my convent days, and I can pray to Her again' (O'Neill, III, 770). But at other times, unconsoled by morphine or religion, she voices her despair in the terms of a secular fatalism:

> None of us can help the things life has done to us. They're done before you realize it, and once they're done they make you do other things until at last everything comes between you and what you'd like to be, and you've lost your true self for ever. (O'Neill, III, 749)

While the older Tyrones feel themselves abandoned within a faith in which they still believe, the sons rebel against it with an ostentatious defiance that testifies to its continuing threat to them. Spiritual dislocation is part of the homelessness they share.

Period piece

As an aide-mémoire when writing *Long Day's Journey*, O'Neill drew a detailed sketch of the ground floor of his New London family home.[19] It was on the memory of twenty-five years before that he was drawing, because he had never once reentered the house since he left in 1915. The set description in the play recalled in detail the Pequot Avenue living room as he remembered it, down to the title of the books in bookcases that no one beyond the second row of a theatre was going to be able to read. The furnishings are evoked in just as much detail:

> The hardwood floor is nearly covered by a rug, inoffensive in design and color. At centre is a round table with a green shaded reading lamp, the cord plugged in one of the four sockets in the chandelier above. Around the table within reading-light range are four chairs, three of them wicker armchairs, the fourth (at right front of table) a varnished oak rocker with leather bottom. (O'Neill, III, 717)

This was already for O'Neill himself a period piece at the time of writing, a re-creation of the home of his childhood and young manhood. That period effect of the set has varied in the many productions since.

David Hays, designer of the set for the New York premiere in 1956, created a mise-en-scène quite independent of the New London house, which he, unlike the cast members, never visited.[20] Many reviewers commented on its dated shabbiness. 'A masterpiece of drab discomfort' was the reaction of one critic at the Boston tryout; 'a cheerless living room with dingy furniture and hideous little touches of unimaginative decor' was the view of Brooks Atkinson at the New York opening.[21] The *New Yorker* review made it clear how much this was 1956 recoiling from the tastes of 1912: 'David Hays' set, a living room hideous even by suburban 1912 standards, is a fitting graveyard for all mortal hopes.'[22] The 1962 Sidney Lumet film also sought with its interior set 'to produce a realistic replica of the period that would plunge the audience into the Tyrones' world'. Accordingly, it 'included many small touches that dated the house as 1912, such as the inglenook under the stairs, a vase with cigar bands pasted around it, wicker planters, shell-beaded curtains, Tiffany lamps, and oriental rugs'.[23] In later productions, an element of nostalgia came into this sort of period decor. The television broadcast version of the 1971 Olivier production, which had modelled its set closely on the O'Neill home, opened with a black-and-white photograph of the actual New London house, and authentic-looking miniatures of each family member being polished by the maid as focus for the introductory voiceover.

Whether regarded with the distaste of the 1950s for the styles of two generations back or the more benign enjoyment of its picturesque 'period' style as it was further distanced in time, the detailed setting that O'Neill demands is essential to the play's dramatic imagery, not mere historical colouring. One example will do by way of illustration: 'the green shaded reading lamp, the cord plugged in one of the four sockets in the chandelier above' that sits on the table in the centre of the living room. The use of electricity is one of the recurring instances of Tyrone's meanness. Both his sons complain about his refusal to keep a light on in the entrance hall; both have to stumble into the house in the dark. In the play's chiaroscuro economy, with its steady progression from sunlight to fog-bound darkness, the lighting of Act IV is particularly important. When the act opens, 'only the reading lamp on the table is lighted' in the living room (O'Neill, III, 792). After a furious confrontation with Edmund over his refusal to turn off the light in the hall, Tyrone makes a histrionic gesture of contrition:

> No, stay where you are. Let it burn. (*He stands up abruptly – and a bit drunkenly – and begins turning on the three bulbs in the chandelier, with a childish, bitterly dramatic self-pity.*) We'll have them all on! Let them burn! To hell with them! The poorhouse is the end of the road, and it might as well be sooner as later! (*He finishes turning on the lights.*) (O'Neill, III, 794)

This was a period before there were regular wall outlets for electric appliances, so that the reading light has to be plugged into one of the light sockets of the chandelier overhead.[24] That is what requires the stage business here, as Tyrone must stand to switch on each light bulb by turning it in its socket. That image has its comic reprise, of course, later in the act, when

Figure 4.2   Ronald Pickup (Edmund) and Laurence Olivier (Tyrone) in *Long Day's Journey into Night*, Act IV, National Theatre, London, 1971.

(more relaxed with Edmund) Tyrone reverts to type – 'The glare from those extra lights hurts my eyes. You don't mind if I turn them out, do you?' (O'Neill, III, 810) – and we see the process reversed. Olivier made this a virtuoso piece of stage business, climbing up onto the table to turn on and off the light bulbs, with different acrobatic descents each time (Figure 4.2).

The staged lighting and dimming of the intimate conversation between Tyrone and Edmund, the relighting of the bulbs by Jamie for his tête-à-tête with his brother, sets up the scene for the moment when 'all five bulbs in the chandelier in the front parlour are turned on from a wall switch', heralding the climactic final entrance of Mary (O'Neill, III, 823). The theatrical lighting of the play's action in all its suggestiveness is embedded in the living space onstage with its 1912 forms of electric wiring.

The books in the bookcases, listed in the opening stage directions in what may seem from a stage designer's point of view such a supererogatory degree of detail, are nonetheless just as integral to the play's pinpointedly period meaning. The Oedipal war between father and sons in the play is fought out with literary allusions. Tyrone's Shakespeare, high-sounding Victorian source of wisdom and morality, is used to berate his good-for-nothing offspring: '"How sharper than a serpent's tooth it is—"' he starts up, but Edmund has heard it so often that he interrupts to complete the quotation, '"to have a thankless child"' (O'Neill, III, 767). Jamie deflates his father with a wittily apropos line from *Othello* on his snoring: '"The Moor, I know his trumpet"' (O'Neill, III, 724). Faced with Edmund's troubling pessimism, Tyrone insists that for this too Shakespeare had a word: '"We are such stuff as dreams are made on, and our little life is rounded with a sleep."' But Edmund replies that, however fine and beautiful these lines may be, 'I wasn't trying to say that. We are such stuff as manure is made on, so let's drink up and forget it. That's more my idea' (O'Neill, III, 796). The listed authors in the bookcase make it clear that Edmund has read all the nineteenth-century heresiarchs – Schopenhauer, Nietzsche, Marx – but it is the poetry of the 1890s that is quoted most extensively in the play as the expression of the sons' rebellion.

'Then in 1900', said Yeats, 'everybody got down off his stilts; henceforth nobody drank absinthe with his black coffee; nobody went mad; nobody committed suicide.'[25] In 1912 New England, however, no one had told the young Tyrones that the fin de siècle had ended. Edmund and Jamie are still declaiming with relish the poetry of Wilde, Dowson, Swinburne and Arthur Symons's versions of Baudelaire. O'Neill, re-creating in 1940–41 his literary tastes of thirty years before, brings out in the play both their datedness and importedness. Edmund satirises the grotesque incongruity of Jamie's decadent posing. Baudelaire's 'Epilogue', he tells his father, 'is a good likeness of Jamie [. . .] hunted by himself and whiskey, hiding in a Broadway hotel room with some fat tart [. . .] reciting Dowson's Cynara to her' (O'Neill, III, 798). Later in Act IV, Jamie himself quotes Wilde's 'The Harlot's House' when recounting his encounter with Fat Violet in the local whorehouse (O'Neill, III, 815). There is a full sense of the absurdity of these borrowings, downgraded from their literary origins in Paris or London to the seaside New England town.

And yet O'Neill can use the poetry of the Nineties with perfect dramatic appropriateness and full pathos when, as the three men look on helplessly at Mary high on morphine, Jamie recites from Swinburne's 'A Leavetaking', 'simply but with a bitter sadness':

> 'Let us rise up and part; she will not know.
> Let us go seaward as the great winds go,
> Full of blown sand and foam; what help is here?
> There is no help, for all these things are so,
> And all the world is bitter as a tear.
> And how these things are, though ye strove to show,
> She would not know.'
>
> (O'Neill, III, 825–26).

O'Neill's tone, here and throughout, is poised between irony and tragic feeling.[26] The fatedness of the family is bound up with the faded and derivative literary styles with which it is expressed.

O'Neill chose 1912 as the time for his autobiographical play because that was the year that he, like Edmund, was diagnosed as suffering from tuberculosis and had to go into a sanatorium. It is an open question whether Edmund, deeply disenchanted, death-haunted, will survive to become the Nobel Prize–winning playwright that O'Neill did, just as no one can be sure if the Stephen Dedalus of *A Portrait of the Artist as a Young Man* – or indeed the Stephen of *Ulysses* – will emerge as the great novelist who wrote those books. In both cases, the fictional stand-in remains at a moment of arrested development. Stephen Dedalus is the poet of the mawkish, ninetyish villanelle; Edmund Tyrone is conscious of the fact that he does not have the 'makings of a poet [...] I'm like the guy who is always panhandling for a smoke. He hasn't even got the makings' (O'Neill, III, 812). But it is not really relevant to speculate on whether Edmund can live on as a writer. As a dramatic character, he is sealed into his period moment, the product of his family and its deformations.

The mad woman in the spare room

The Edmund of the play may or may not be cured by his stay in the sanatorium, as Eugene O'Neill was by the summer of 1913. There is no hint in the play, though, that Mary Tyrone is to be cured of her morphine addiction as Ella O'Neill apparently was in 1914.[27] The implication of Mary's return to addiction after a temporary cure, the climactic effect of her drug-induced reverie with which the play ends, is that she is irrecoverable. All four Tyrones suffer from what we would now call substance abuse or substance dependence. Jamie is a classifiable alcoholic, well on the road to the death that claimed his real-life counterpart James O'Neill Jr at the age of forty-five. Although Tyrone claims to be only a social drinker, with his constant boast that he never missed a performance through drunkenness, Mary paints a different picture: 'I would never have married you if I'd known you drank so much. I remember the first night your barroom friends had to help you up to the door of our hotel room [...] I didn't know how often that was to happen in the years to come' (O'Neill, III, 783). If Edmund does not drink as heavily as his brother Jamie, he seems nearly as dependent and physically much less well able to cope with it. But Mary's morphine addiction is treated as something quite different from the men's abuse of alcohol; it is the family's disgraceful, heavily guarded secret, represented in theatrical terms by the retreat into the unseen spare room above the staged living room.

The terms for referring to the use of drink or drugs are strikingly different. Drunkenness is often conveyed through emollient, euphemistic slang. So, for example, Shaughnessy, when Edmund meets him in the pub, has 'a beautiful bun on' (O'Neill, III, 724). The attributive adjective is positively admiring, as in the case of Edmund's later comment that the night-returning Jamie 'must have a peach of a bun on' (O'Neill, III, 813). When Tyrone defends his idol Shakespeare from Edmund's charge that he was a 'souse' – itself a mildly depreciative term – it is in significant terms: 'I don't doubt he liked his glass – it's a good man's failing – but he knew how to drink so it didn't poison his brain with morbidness and filth' (O'Neill, III, 799). Heavy drinking is quite compatible with morally upright manliness. Indeed, it may even be a required part of being such a man; it is the right 'failing' for a good man to have, hardly regarded as a failing at all. This sort of tolerance for excessive drinking is associated specifically with the Irish by Cathleen, who herself drinks the whiskey Mary offers her 'without bothering about a chaser', and repeats Tyrone's exculpatory bromide: 'Well, it's a good man's failing. I wouldn't give a trauneen for a teetotaler' (O'Neill, III, 774). Drinking is manly, high-spirited, scarcely something to be ashamed about because it is socially convivial.

By contrast, drug taking is a secret vice, a scandalous activity in anyone, much less in a respectable middle-class woman. It is Mary herself who first uses the extreme derogatory term: 'You expect the Blessed Virgin to be fooled by a lying dope fiend' (O'Neill, III, 779). The phrase would have still been relatively new in 1912. *OED*, defining 'dope-fiend, *n*. slang (orig. U.S.)' as 'a drug-addict', gives as its first citation from the *Sun* (NY) in December 1896: '"A dope fiend" . . . a victim of the opium habit'. Though at this moment of self-castigation Mary refers to herself as such, Edmund's line in Act III, spoken 'staring condemningly at her – bitterly', must be one of the cruellest in the play: 'It's pretty hard to take at times, having a dope fiend for a mother!' (O'Neill, III, 788). For both sons, what is intolerable is the appalling stigma associated with drug taking. Jamie recalls his sense of trauma at the discovery: 'Never forget the first time I got wise. Caught her in the act with a hypo. Christ, I'd never dreamed before than any women but whores took dope!' (O'Neill, III, 818). Underlying the brutality of Jamie's even more cynical language – 'Another shot in the arm!' 'Where's the hophead?' (O'Neill, III, 758, 818) – is the intolerable feeling of betrayal at having his mother degraded to the level of a whore.

Drinking is normalised in the play; drug taking is demonised. Mary accuses Tyrone of being responsible for Jamie's alcoholism: 'You brought him up to be a boozer. Since he first opened his eyes, he's seen you drinking. Always a bottle on the bureau in the cheap hotel rooms!' Tyrone is 'stung' by the accusation but maintains it is merely the drug talking. 'When you have the poison in you, you want to blame everyone but yourself' (O'Neill, III, 782). Morphine is a 'poison' turning Mary into someone other than herself. By contrast, Edmund at this point calls his father back to normality by 'changing the subject': 'Are we going to have this drink, or aren't we?' 'You're right', Tyrone agrees, 'I'm a fool to take notice. (*He picks up his glass listlessly.*) Drink hearty, lad' (O'Neill, III, 782). Drink brings the men closer together, precipitating the confessions of Act IV, 'not drunken bull', as Jamie puts it, 'but "in vino veritas" stuff' (O'Neill, III, 820). Against that, Mary becomes the unseen incommunicable mad woman up in the spare room, whose descent Edmund and Tyrone dread: '[S]he moves above and beyond us, a ghost haunting the past, and here we sit pretending to forget' (O'Neill, III, 811).

Tyrone charges Mary with wanting to 'blame everyone but yourself'. This blame game of relieving guilt by shifting responsibility is one in which all four characters engage. Jamie is blamed for leading Edmund astray, and even more seriously, for causing the death of his infant brother Eugene by infecting him with measles. Edmund is blamed for the very fact of his birth because it was in her postpartum illness that Mary first began to take morphine. Most of the lines of accusation, however, lead back to Tyrone. He started both sons on drink with his belief that 'whiskey is the healthiest medicine for a child who is sick or frightened' (O'Neill, III, 782). It was Tyrone's miserliness that made him hire the cheap doctor who treated Mary with morphine in the first place. It was that same miserliness that made him reluctant to have her hospitalised to cure her addiction early on. And only the indignant protests of both Jamie and Edmund stop him from sending Edmund to a 'state farm' sanatorium when he is diagnosed with TB. But the gendered difference of the play's treatment of Mary skews the characters' blame game and the way it is perceived by an audience.

For all their mutual recriminations and fractious aggressiveness, the men are united by bonds that isolate Mary. This pattern is read by Michael Manheim as a positive affirmation of the 'language of kinship', which the men share and she does not. 'Fathers and sons in *Long Day's Journey* establish links which none of them can ever establish with Mary Tyrone, much as each one tries, simply and solely because of Mary's uncontrollable withdrawal. *Withdrawal* is the great enemy of kinship and therefore of life.'[28] Laurin Porter looks at the same phenomenon from an opposite, feminist perspective:

> While Mary occupies the centre of the Tyrone family and, in many ways, the centre of the play, her husband and sons persistently try to marginalize her. Although they love her, as the focus of their constant and watchful gaze she is important to them primarily for what they need from her as wife and lover (James), cured addict (Jamie), and mother and comforter (Edmund). Her own needs – for acceptance, for forgiveness, for agency – go unmet.[29]

A still more hostile view of the play as an illustration of the patriarchal male gaze is that of Johan Callens, discussing it in connection with the Wooster Group's deconstructive appropriation of the text in the 1979 show *Point Judith*: 'O'Neill's men either idealize women or denigrate them when the reality strays from the projection. In both cases the men turn the women into fascinating objects, whether of piety as with Mary or perversion with the character of Fat Violet.'[30] The interpretation in performance depends a great deal on the extent to which we as spectators in the audience find ourselves aligned with the men as watchers of Mary in the play. Do we watch her as they watch her? In our sharing of the stage space where the men drink together, is she relegated for an audience to the stigmatised spare room above?

In early productions of the play, Mary seems to have been played largely as a creature of her circumstances, at least primarily an object of pathos. Geraldine Fitzgerald, cast for the part in an off-Broadway production in

1971, challenged that view, maintaining that Mary 'is really not a victim of her family at all: she is a victim of her own neurosis'. Fitzgerald went on to elaborate: 'She is what she is because of her sense of guilt. She feels deeply guilty about her relationship with her mother, whom she didn't like, and about her father, whom she adored but who died young. Many of O'Neill's characters are based on ancient prototypes, and Mary Tyrone was a kind of Electra.'[31] Later productions also portrayed Mary in negative terms, and the comments by (male) reviewers are significant. So, for instance, Brendan Gill commented on how Jonathan Miller's 1986 staging, in which Bethel Leslie played Mary, reversed 'the seeming intention of the plot, which might be coarsely summed up as "That poor woman! With a houseful of drunken, no-good men to look after, no wonder she's a drug addict." [In this production], on the contrary, and despite the plot, the theme is that women are murderously destructive by nature and men are in constant peril of not surviving their machinations.'[32] Colleen Dewhurst, playing opposite Jason Robards in a 1988 revival directed by Jose Quintero, was 'an extraordinarily, almost shockingly unsentimentalized Mary. One sees just how little the author forgave his mother [...] this Mary, for all her ethereal beauty and maternal silver hair ... [is] a killer, forever twisting the knife in old familial wounds.'[33]

'One sees just how little the author forgave his mother.' There is no doubt that the discovery of his mother's drug taking was a traumatic event in Eugene O'Neill's life, apparently responsible for his loss of religious faith.[34] As Edmund puts it in the play, '[I]t made everything in life seem rotten!' (O'Neill, III, 787). In his initial scenario for *Long Day's Journey*, O'Neill planned a harsher version of the drugged Mary: 'very hipped up now, her manner strange – at the moment a vain happy, chattering girlishness – then changing to a hard cynical sneering bitterness with a bitter biting cruelty and with a coarse vulgarity in it – the last as if suddenly poisoned by an alive demon'.[35] This is very much the language of poison and possession used by Tyrone in the play. But in the development of the play from scenario to full text, O'Neill came to soften the view of Mary, removing the emphasis on 'the dual-natured mother as the betrayer, "the guilty one"'.[36] As a result, the character of Mary remains open to very different performances. It is possible to foreground the hostility, the cynicism and the bitterness in her harangues of her husband, in the manner of Bethel Leslie in the part. Alternatively, a much greater degree of empathy can be conveyed, for instance, by playing key speeches of Mary in voiceover, as Constance Cummings did in the television version of the 1971 National Theatre production, and by using images of her standing alone at a window inside the house, emphasising her loneliness and isolation as a prisoner within the house and the self.

No doubt there was anger against his mother in the emotions inspiring O'Neill to write *Long Day's Journey* as well as the tangle of feelings of guilt and resentment about his dead father and brother. What he created from that in the play was the shared psychopathologies of the four characters. Mary is indeed the object of the male gaze of the three men, as the lost love of Tyrone, the once-adored, now-degraded mother of the two sons. With their idolised mother fallen from grace, it is symptomatic of the sons' condition that the only women they seem capable of having relationships with are whores. (It has been pointed out that one of the facts that O'Neill suppressed about his own life in creating Edmund in the play was that by 1912 he had married and was the father of a son.)[37] Mary herself has sufficiently introjected the patriarchal view of herself that her neurotic anxiety under the men's suspicious scrutiny is expressed in self-conscious awareness of what had been the 'points' of her attractiveness, her hair, her eyes and her hands. 'Why do you look at me like that? (*Her hands flutter up to pat her hair.*) Is it my hair coming down? [. . .] I couldn't find my glasses' (O'Neill, III, 754). The psychological attitudes and the gender dynamics are just as convincingly of their time and place as the period house in which the characters live.

It was in favour of the Royal Dramatic Theatre in Stockholm (Dramaten) that Carlotta O'Neill decided to override the author's ban on production, or rather, she claimed O'Neill on his deathbed had 'willed' the play to the theatre.[38] Sweden in general and Dramaten in particular had remained loyal to O'Neill, producing and admiring his plays through the long years from the mid-1930s, when he was very much out of favour in his own country. The four-and-a-half-hour-long premiere of the play in February 1956 proved a triumph, a production that was to stay in the company's repertoire for six years. It was a meticulously naturalistic staging, appropriately following in the tradition of Strindberg and Ibsen. Indeed, the director, Bengt Ekerot, saw it as 'the end of an epoch, the end of the Ibsen-Chekhov line', making it impossible to 'proceed further within this style. It seems consummated with O'Neill's play.'[39] *Journey*, in its concentrated attention on the one nuclear family in the single living space, certainly does seem some sort of ultimate example of the naturalistic home on the stage as originally conceived. Though Ingmar Bergman, who was to take over as artistic director of Dramaten, did mount a non-naturalistic production of the play, it has on the whole proved more resistant to stylised reconception than earlier texts such as *A Doll's House* and *The Cherry Orchard*.[40]

The period detail of *Journey*, so definitely specified in the text, appears to be essential to its meaning. As one reviewer of the 1986 Jonathan Miller production put it, 'As with any great naturalistic work, O'Neill's play turns out to have achieved the general only by clutching obdurately at the particular.'[41] However, *Journey* is different from other naturalistic works in the gap between the time of its action, its composition and its reception. The characters in the play conform perfectly to the very principles of naturalism as products of their history, heredity and environment, second-generation Irish American Catholics with characteristic attitudes to house and home, class, religion and culture, drink and drugs, men and women. But for audiences looking on at that scene from an ever-increasing distance of time, it does not appear as a mere historical re-creation of a long-gone period; rather, it seems as though we are trapped in the eternally recurring present of this dysfunctional family. It may well be that Ekerot was right about O'Neill's play being the consummation of the naturalistic style. At least, all of the plays considered in the rest of this book more or less modify that style, not least *A Streetcar Named Desire*, written after *Journey* but produced nine years before it, the subject of the next chapter.

CHAPTER 5

A Streetcar Named Desire: *see-through representation*

In an early draft of the play that was to become *A Streetcar Named Desire*, the Stanley Kowalski figure was Irish. 'You folks are pretty refined compared to my folks, I guess', he said to the equivalents of Blanche and Stella. 'We're just old shanty Irish. You know – pigs in the parlor and all that sort of thing. Never had a lace-curtain in the home!'[1] Originally of Italian immigrant origins, eventually Polish, the central male character of the play in all its metamorphoses belongs to an emergent American working class. Where the characters and action of *Long Day's Journey* are confined within the ethos of a second-generation Irish American family, in Williams's play the clash is between an older, settled culture and its aggressively lower-class alternative. And unlike O'Neill's self-conscious re-creation of a period setting in *Long Day's Journey*, *Streetcar* is very much of its own postwar time. Stanley and Mitch are both returning World War II vets who served together in the same unit of the American army. In the play's final scene, Stanley attributes his luck to his self-belief: 'Take at Salerno. I believed I was lucky. I figured that four out of five would not come through but I would ... and I did.'[2] Stanley is remembering the fiercely fought Battle of Salerno during the Allied invasion of Italy in September 1943.[3] It is the photo of Stanley as decorated Master Sergeant of the Engineer Corps that Stella DuBois, formerly of Belle Reve, proudly displays to her sister.

Tennessee Williams, like O'Neill, was resistant to conventional naturalism from the start of his career. In his 'Production Notes' for *The Glass Menagerie* (1944), his first hugely successful play, he set out his aesthetic:

> The straight realistic play with its genuine frigidaire and authentic ice-cubes, its characters that speak exactly as its audience speaks, corresponds to the academic landscape and has the same virtue of a photographic likeness. Everyone should know nowadays the unimportance of the photographic in art: that truth, life or reality is an organic thing which the poetic imagination can represent or suggest, in essence, only through

transformation, through changing into other forms those which were merely present in appearance.[4]

The impatience with mere surfaces – the 'genuine frigidaire and authentic ice-cubes' – is very much in the spirit of O'Neill's praise of Strindberg's 'behind-life' plays. Both playwrights wanted to come at essences, to penetrate below what could be represented as photographic likeness. However, O'Neill in *Long Day's Journey* found the means within the naturalistic framework of representation to create a stage situation in which all the past history of his characters was an immanent present; the deep truths of their lives could be spoken in the casual interchanges of conversation. For *The Glass Menagerie*, Williams developed instead the distinctive dramaturgy of the memory play. As the narrator Tom puts it in his opening address to the audience: 'I am the opposite of a stage magician. He gives you illusion that has the appearance of truth. I give you truth in the pleasant disguise of illusion' (Williams, 1, 400).

The strategy here was to find a stage design to render the texture of the remembered past as it is projected in the mind. The solidity and stability of the well-made, convincingly real set was therefore inappropriate, as Williams explained in his opening stage description:

> The scene is memory and is therefore nonrealistic. Memory takes a lot of poetic licence. It omits some details; others are exaggerated, according to the emotional value of the articles it touches, for memory is seated predominantly in the heart. The interior is therefore rather dim and poetic. (Williams, 1, 399)

This dim, poetic interior was realised onstage with a set of gauze transparencies. The conventionally invisible fourth wall of naturalism was actually represented as the exterior of the building but in the form of a scrim through which the audience could look into the Wingfield apartment when it was lit. Within the apartment itself, the portieres dividing the downstage living room from the upstage dining room were figured on another scrim. Hence, 'the audience hears and sees the opening scene in the dining room through both the transparent fourth wall of the building and the transparent gauze portieres of the dining-room arch' (Williams, 1, 400). This simultaneous set makes possible the rendering of both inner and outer, past and present, in a stage device that acknowledges its own illusoriness.[5]

The representation of the one confined space in *A Doll's House* makes its impact by a principle of indexical referral from the living room of the Helmers' flat to the rest of the flat, the building, and the wider world into which Nora enters when she slams the door so dramatically. The opening stage direction of *The Glass Menagerie* shows how Williams seeks to reverse this sequence by moving from the general to the particular, from exterior to interior.

> The Wingfield apartment is in the rear of the building, one of those vast hive-like conglomerations of cellular living-units that flower as warty growths in overcrowded urban centres of lower middle-class population and are symptomatic of the impulse of this largest and fundamentally enslaved section of American society to avoid fluidity and differentiation and to exist and function as one interfused mass of automatism. (Williams, 1, 399)

Yet, having got this piece of sociological protest poetry off his chest, Williams goes on to show the lives of the Wingfields in their distinctive individuality, in no way part of an 'interfused mass of automatism'. And he does so by means of the very 'fluidity and differentiation' that these urban conglomerations are said to suppress. The principle of see-through representation first devised by Williams for *The Glass Menagerie* allows for the inclusion of more of the outside world of the city, more of the sense of the society that surrounds the home on the stage. But in the end, its purpose is to take an audience within the individual mindscapes of the characters rather than merely the interior of their homes.

One of the techniques of Williams's 'new, plastic theatre which must take the place of the exhausted theatre of realistic conventions' was the 'screen device' involving projected slides of images or titles (Williams, 1, 395). Although he claimed not to regret the omission of this device from the Broadway production of *The Glass Menagerie*, he included it in the published text to illustrate his original conception. As a result, the acting version of the play is quite different from the reading version, a difference that becomes even more marked with the texts of *Streetcar*. *Streetcar* went into rehearsals in October 1947, and the first edition of the play, published by New Directions at the end of that year, was largely based on the preproduction script.[6] The revised 1953 acting text is based instead on the promptbook used in the Broadway production that opened in December 1947 and ran through until December 1949.[7] Recast as a 'play in three acts' from the original eleven scenes, it reflects the collaboration between the playwright, the director Elia Kazan, the designer Jo Mielzener and the composer Alex North to realise the script in the theatre.[8] I have used that text as my primary reference point through this chapter, not because I regard the original production as definitive, but because the acting version illustrates most fully the effect of the play in taking an audience into an urban scene, a domestic interior and the emotional life of the protagonist, and it is that theatrical interiorisation which is my principal concern here.

City choreography

In *Streetcar*, as in *The Glass Menagerie*, Williams planned to show both interior and exterior. As in the earlier play, the audience was to be transported from an initial view of the outside of the building, with the scrim on which it was represented lifted during the first scene, into the apartment where the action was to take place. In *Streetcar* there was to be a further revelation of the street outside during Scene 10, when Blanche is about to be raped. 'Through the back wall of the rooms, which have become transparent, can be seen the sidewalk. A prostitute has rolled a drunkard. He pursues her along the walk, overtakes her and there is a struggle. A policeman's whistle breaks it up. The figures disappear' (Williams, 1, 553). Clearly, Williams wanted to show a routine vignette of sordid urban life that is almost a parody of the horrific scene we are watching inside the apartment. This was in line with his strategy throughout the play to use external figures and actions as occasional counterpoints to the drama: the street cries of the tamale vendor, 'Red hot! Red hots!' that so frighten Blanche at the end of Scene 2 (Williams, 1, 492); the Young Man collecting for the *Evening Star* at the conclusion of Scene 5; the blind Mexican woman selling tin funeral flowers, whom Williams originally planned to have meeting Blanche on her first arrival, 'foreshadowing Blanche's fears of death and the destructive forces she is facing'.[9] In place of this, the acting text worked out in production made for a much more continuous, less pointedly symbolic sense of the city environment.

Mielzener's design was an important part of achieving that sense. Instead of moving an audience from an exterior view into the apartment, as Williams had originally planned with his lifted scrim, Mielzener contrived to suggest a receding cityscape beyond the interior we see in the foreground. In his setting, the street

> runs across stage behind the two rooms of the Kowalski apartment, and can be seen, when lighted, through back walls of apartment, these being constructed of gauze on which the outlines of windows are appliquéd. Beyond [the] drop that falls immediately behind the street – this drop also being of gauze – one can see a backdrop suggesting railroad tracks, which pass close by. (*Streetcar*, 5)

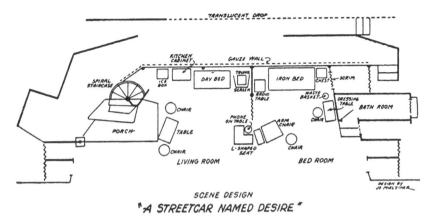

SCENE DESIGN
"A STREETCAR NAMED DESIRE"

Figure 5.1   Scene design by Jo Mielziner for *A Streetcar Named Desire*, directed by
Elia Kazan, New York, 1947.

The scene design reproduced in the acting text (Figure 5.1) indicates the layout (*Streetcar*, 104). The effect, as Mielzener himself put it, is of an 'impressionistic X-ray'.[10] The street scene behind the apartment in this design is not just lit at a moment of high drama, as in Williams's original Scene 10. It is where we see ordinary passersby, such as the 'woman carrying a shopping-bag full of parcels [who] passes wearily across the stage' in the opening moment, where Stanley appears for the first time with Mitch, significantly loping behind, trying to keep pace (*Streetcar*, 6). In place of the symbolic blind street vendor, it is a sailor Blanche encounters in this street scene, an encounter played in dumb show because their words are covered by the music (*Streetcar*, 7). As in the establishing shots of a film, a whole social landscape is suggested, with the comings and goings of the city dwellers, the urban sights and sounds that include the Louisville and Nashville railroad to be glimpsed on the stage backdrop.

The realisation of the urban setting is of course intended to highlight the incongruity of Blanche's appearance in it. 'She looks as if she were arriving at a summer tea or cocktail party in the garden district' – that is, the fashionable part of New Orleans, at the opposite social extreme from the French Quarter (*Streetcar*, 7).[11] As a refugee from the plantation elegance of Belle Reve, Blanche is appalled at what she finds in the ironically named Elysian Fields. 'Never, never, never in my worst dreams', she says to Stella, 'could I picture – Only Poe! Only Mr Edgar Allen Poe – could do it justice! Out there, I suppose is the ghoul-haunted woodland of Weir!' 'No', replies her sister with literalist irony, 'those are the L. & N. tracks' (*Streetcar*, 11). The designed contrast is between the representative of the decaying old culture of Southern landed gentry and the urban modernity of railroads and streetcars. Elia Kazan, when preparing to direct the play, was in no doubt as to the message conveyed by that contrast:

> *Theme* – this is a message from the dark interior. This little twisted, pathetic, confused bit of light and culture puts out a cry. It is snuffed out by the crude forces of violence, insensibility and vulgarity which exist in our South – and this cry is the play.[12]

But, as Stella says, 'New Orleans isn't like other cities' (*Streetcar*, 11), and the difference complicates the unequivocal vision suggested by Kazan's note.

Williams lived a number of times in New Orleans, as a struggling writer in 1938–39 in the house on Toulouse Street that he was to re-create in his late play *Vieux Carré* (1977), and again in 1946–47 when he was writing *Streetcar*.[13] For him the French Quarter was immensely attractive, bohemian, multicultural and tolerant: when Blanche apologises to Mitch for not being 'properly dressed' on the porch, he reassures her – 'That don't make no difference in the Quarter' (*Streetcar*, 43). We can see the difference for Williams between St Louis, the setting of *The Glass Menagerie*, and New Orleans in the way he introduces the setting in the two plays. The St Louis of *The Glass Menagerie* is a grim urban landscape consisting of those 'vast hive-like conglomerations of cellular living-units' of which the Wingfield apartment building is one. Nothing could be less like the setting of *Streetcar* as Williams evokes it in the play's reading text:

> The exterior of a two-story corner building on a street in New Orleans which is named Elysian Fields and runs between the L&N tracks and the river. The section is poor but, unlike corresponding sections in other American cities, it has a raffish charm. The houses are mostly white frame, weathered grey, with rickety outside stairs and galleries and quaintly ornamented gables. [...]
>
> It is first dark of an evening early in May. The sky that shows around the dim white building is a peculiarly tender blue, almost a turquoise, which invests the scene with a kind of lyricism and gracefully attenuates the atmosphere of decay.

And this romanticising glamour continues with the references to the sounds of jazz – the 'Blue Piano' that 'expresses the spirit of life which goes on here' – and the 'relatively warm and easy intermingling of the races' (Williams, 1, 469). What the production realised, reflected in the eventual acting text of the play, was a marriage of this Romantic Southern writer's vision of the city and the Northern director's view of it as representative of 'the crude forces of violence, insensibility and vulgarity which exist in our South'.

One detail of Mielzener's work on the set catches the spirit of that compromise. 'In *A Streetcar Named Desire* I took a fine, rather ornate door and worked over it to show the smudged handprints of the no longer genteel and careful Stella, the scuffed heel marks of her angry and temperamental husband. The door became a symbol of the fall of Stella's family from elegance to seediness.'[14] The sense of Stella's slovenliness was underlined in the play's opening minutes by added stage directions. She puts the package of meat on the table, not in the icebox, and 'steps over a broom lying on floor inside front door' in her eagerness to go watch Stanley bowl (*Streetcar*, 6). Yet it is still a 'fine, rather ornate door' that the audience see onstage, however scuffed and abused, and like the wrought-iron spiral staircase running up to the Hubbells' apartment, it is expressive of the down-at-heel elegance of the city. The play, with the mode of 'stylised realism' that Kazan brought to the direction, could create the poetic texture of urban life that Williams wanted while yet conveying the stressful pressure that it exerted on someone of Blanche's temperament and condition.[15]

In many cases, this involved the theatrical elaboration of what was suggested in Williams's script. So, for example, the opening stage direction to Scene 4, the morning after the poker night with its violent ending, indicates that '[t]here is a confusion of street cries like a choral chant' (Williams, 1, 504). In the acting text, the street criers are heard through the scene change from behind the curtain, and they are given specific lines:

> Street cries: 1 (Man) – Young fryers! 2 (Man) – Blackberries, 10 cents a quart. 3 (Woman) – Nice fresh roas'n ears. 4. (Man) – Watermelons! 5 (Man) – Irish potatoes! 6 (Woman) – Tender young snap beans! 7 (Man) – Fresh country eggs! (*Streetcar*, 43)

Brenda Murphy shows how precisely these voices were worked up for musical effect: 'As carefully recorded by the sound manager, the rhythm and pitch of each cry and the order of the cries were encoded to evoke the spirit of the French Quarter aurally.'[16] For Blanche, the events of the night before, Stanley's assault on Stella and her return to the marital bedroom, constituted a shocking emergency. By contrast with that high drama, this continuo of city sounds represents an ongoing normality of life.

In Scene 10 of the original script, as rape threatens and Blanche desperately tries to telephone for help, the stage directions call for the projection of an expressionist theatre of terror:

Lurid reflections appear on the walls around Blanche. The shadows are of a grotesque and menacing form. [...] The night is filled with inhuman cries like cries in a jungle. The shadows and lurid reflections move sinuously as flames along the wall spaces. (Williams, 1, 553)

It is only after this series of nightmarish hallucinations that the street scene of the prostitute and the drunkard was to appear through the scrim. In the acting text, shadows, lurid reflections and inhuman cries are all removed, and instead there is an extended sequence of incidents outside, none of them so obviously paralleling the action within. In the first episode, 'A woman laughs insanely, and runs into street from U.L. with a purse. A man in a tuxedo follows, protesting. Woman strikes him. He falls. Babel offstage U.R. increases. Another man rushes on from U.R., attacks first man from behind. Sound of police whistles and a siren in the distance, groans from the felled man, as his assailants vanish R. and L.' (*Streetcar*, 92–93). There is a second quite separate set of events involving a mugging, and when Blanche tries to run from the apartment, she 'comes face to face with the muggers' (*Streetcar*, 93). The violence that threatens her inside the apartment has an all-too-actual counterpart outside in the city. And yet, significantly, this backstage pantomime was referred to as a 'ballet', and the effect, according to one observer of the New York production, was just what Williams intended, a theatrical reflection of Blanche's experience: 'This movement behind the main set parallels the hysterical break-up of the principal character and adds mightily to the force of the scene.'[17]

Streetcar is often read as a conflict between the old South, the colonial plantation class of Belle Reve, and the new South of urban modernity, much as Kazan initially interpreted it. Harry Smith, however, points to the social hybridity of that new South:

> The specific location of *A Streetcar Named Desire* is interesting for its curious blend of the old and the new elements which contribute to the shape of the modern South. Desire and Elysian Fields are real New Orleans streets. The neighborhood in which the Kowalski apartment is located is newer than the Old Quarter familiar to tourists, older than the more elegant, more 'modern', suburban areas. Its people belong neither to the Creole culture of old New Orleans nor to the American aristocracy of suburban 'middle' and professional classes. It is a near-slum neighborhood, a nether-land of railroad tracks, warehouses, and other shabby elements of a commercial culture. Such a juxtaposition of aesthetic values is a major element in this play's formal unity.[18]

As realised in the play, it is a place of street cries and street crime, an urban jungle, but one in which the fresh produce of the land is daily brought into the city. It may not quite be the Old Quarter, the Vieux Carré visited by the tourists, but the blues that drew the tourists to that district is heard throughout. Williams's scripted solo 'Blue Piano' was extended to a 'small jazz band' consisting of piano, clarinet, trumpet and drums (*Streetcar*, 5).[19] Alex North's music was through-scored to point and counterpoint the action, now echoing Blanche's emotions, now mocking them by its strident vitality. The achievement of the production, as expressed in the acting text, was to render onstage the experience of a city, not just as a backdrop to the drama of the interior but as an interpenetrating texture of life.

Close quarters

Felicia Londré picks out one of the more unusual claims of the play to innovation: 'It was not until 1947, when Tennessee Williams's *A Streetcar Named Desire* opened, that Broadway saw a play in which the bathroom figured so prominently in the setting, in the plot, and in the dialogue.'[20] The bathroom is of importance in *Streetcar* in part because of the way it highlights the confined living space of the Kowalskis' apartment. Although Synge and O'Casey had dramatised the cramped conditions of the poor, the naturalistic home on the stage had been largely a middle-class milieu. However stifling Nora Helmer may ultimately find the doll's house Torvald has created for her, there are plenty of other rooms – nursery, study, spare room – off the well-appointed living room where she spends her time. The house in *The Cherry Orchard* is so large that Ranevskaya has to be prompted to remember the function of the old nursery. However many stray guests show up in Captain Shotover's Heartbreak House, there seems always to be another bedroom in which to put them. And though Mary Tyrone may complain that their summer house is not a real home, it has that luxury of genteel living, an all-but-unused 'front parlour' kept for best. Blanche, used to the scale of Belle Reve, is appalled to realise that Stella and Stanley have just two rooms – and a bathroom.

'But there's no door between the rooms', Blanche objects: '[W]ill it be decent?' (*Streetcar*, 13). The Lord Chamberlain, vetting the script for the British premiere in 1949, did not think it would be. He insisted on 'the exclusion of any references to "the four letter word" [...] and other sexual references (e.g., "ruttin'", Stanley's "kidneys")'.[21] It is interesting that this last example should have been considered a sexual reference. The exchange comes in III.1 (Scene 7 in the reading text), when Stanley wants to know how much longer he will have to wait to get into the bathroom:

BLANCHE. Not so terribly long! Possess your soul in patience!
STANLEY. It's not my soul, it's my kidneys I'm worried about!
(*Streetcar*, 72)[22]

It seems that any allusions to physical functions could be considered proximate to the erotic. The bathroom onstage makes uncomfortably vivid the terms of intimacy on which the characters are forced to live. Just behind a closed door Blanche lies in a bathtub, while Stanley hops from foot to foot waiting to urinate.[23]

Williams works up the awkwardness of these close quarters to delicate comic effect in the poker night scene. Blanche's first meeting with Mitch comes at the bathroom door as he comes out, towel in hand, while she, just home from her night out with Stella, is looking to get in. After Stella reappears from the closet and performs the introductions, Mitch tries to make his getaway:

> (*He starts forward, awkwardly, but cannot pass between the girls.*) Excuse me, please. (*Girls ad lib – 'Oh excuse me'. Mitch makes way past girls, stumbling below Stella, and above Blanche* [. . .] *The girls turn to watch him, smiling at his confusion. At door, he realizes he still is clutching towel. Overcome with embarrassment, he steps back into room and hands it to Stella.*) (*Streetcar*, 33)

It is partly Mitch's lack of physical self-confidence that attracts Blanche – Mitch, who later confesses to anxiety about his tendency to perspire that makes him wear light alpaca jackets, so unlike Stanley, who makes no difficulty about changing in Blanche's presence when 'my shirt's stickin' to me' (*Streetcar*, 18). Sure enough, we see Mitch put on his jacket and pop 'Sen-Sen into his mouth' to freshen his breath before preparing to go into the bedroom again on a second visit to the bathroom (*Streetcar*, 36).

Whether or not this visit is really necessary – Mitch offers the gauche explanation, 'We've – been drinking beer' – it is soon turned into an occasion for flirtation. 'The Little Boys' Room is busy right now', says Blanche with infantilising coyness (*Streetcar*, 36). With the curtains of the portieres firmly drawn and the paper lantern affixed to the light bulb to dim the scene, Blanche seeks to turn the bedroom into a feminine space suitable for the intimate exchanges with Mitch about his dead fiancée and the inscribed cigarette case she bequeathed to him. Mitch is to be lured away from the homosocial poker school into the twilight zone of Blanche's enchantment. It is this, as much as the radio switched on a second time against Stanley's fierce injunctions, which ultimately leads to his explosion of berserk violence. Losing at poker, he finds his masculine dominance also being sapped by Blanche's success in distracting Mitch from the game. After Stanley has run amok, thrown the radio out the window and hit his pregnant wife, Mitch is left helplessly repeating what he takes to be the moral of the story: 'Poker should not be played in a house with women' (*Streetcar*, 41).

The Kowalskis' apartment becomes a contested territory between Blanche, who comes with a substantial wardrobe trunk of costumes and accessories, monopolises the bathroom for her therapeutic baths and puts up light-shading paper lanterns, and Stanley, who wants the place cleared for his poker nights, not to mention the privacy of the bedroom to get 'them coloured lights going' with Stella (*Streetcar*, 80). The sense of the fractious abrasions of living within that confined space is all the more effective theatrically because it is not literally realised. Apart from the curtained portieres, the rest of the division between the two rooms is invisible. Mielzener's 'impressionistic X-ray' design allows us to see the interior of the apartment as an inset, visible only when lit, within the structure of the two-storey house with its outside staircase winding up to the Hubbells' above. While our attention is concentrated on the life-and-death fight for territory in the Kowalskis', the noises from Steve and Eunice supply a second-level counterpart.

In II.1 (Scene 5), there is a mini-replay between the Hubbells of the violent quarrel and reconciliation of Stanley and Stella that we have watched in full in the previous two scenes. 'A disturbance breaks out in apartment above', and snatches of the row can be heard from below:

EUNICE (*above*). I know about you and that blonde!
STEVE. That's a God-damned lie!
(*Streetcar*, 52)

When 'Eunice, above, screams as though she had been kicked', Blanche enquires of Stella with bright irony: 'Did he *kill* her?' Minutes later Eunice runs downstairs, 'rubbing her backside', screaming, 'I'm going to call the police. I'm going to call the police.' Stanley, entering, asks casually, 'What's the matter with Eun-uss?'

STELLA. She and Steve had a row. Has she got the police?
STANLEY. Naw, she's gettin' a drink.
STELLA. That's much more practical.
(*Streetcar*, 53)

Though Steve goes after Eunice in furious pursuit, calling her a 'ruttin' hunk' – one of the adjectives that had to be omitted from the London production at the Lord Chamberlain's insistence – it is no surprise to see them returning later in the scene, she 'sobbing luxuriously', he 'cooing love words' (*Streetcar*, 53, 55).[24]

The equivalence set up between the Kowalskis' marriage and that of the Hubbells normalises both. This is the way such relationships go – violent quarrels followed by loving rapprochement, the physical abuse matched by the exhilaration of the lovemaking that follows. That sense of the congruence between the two couples was accentuated in the Sydney Theatre Company's 2009 production directed by Liv Ullmann, starring Cate Blanchett as Blanche.[25] Ralph Myers's set design for that production included one room of the Hubbells' apartment, so that the audience could see figures move around in it, either clearly visible when a door was open or in silhouette when lit from behind a window. So, for instance, all through the poker night, Eunice was onstage, sitting alone upstairs. When Stella took refuge there, she could be seen in outline through the window blind as Eunice answered Stanley's increasingly desperate, repentant phone calls. The suspense was increased until we saw the shadow of Stella rise from the table, come out the door and descend the staircase to her sobbing husband. At several points in the production, the relationship between the two apartments and the two marriages was underlined. So, for instance, through the scene of the failed birthday party (III.2, Scene 8), Steve was slumped at the table in the upstairs room. When Stella went out onto the porch while Blanche was trying to phone Mitch, the shadow of Eunice was seen to come up behind Steve and embrace him. As Stanley was pleading with Stella about 'getting the coloured lights going' again, when they had regained their privacy, the couple above moved out of shot, as though to an unseen bedroom. And in the final scene, as Blanche packed to leave, Eunice was visible upstairs holding the baby, the new dimension in the Kowalskis' relationship (Figure 5.2).

How good or bad a marriage do Stanley and Stella have? Susan Koprince makes out a persuasive case for the Kowalskis as a couple 'trapped in a cycle of domestic abuse'; Stanley is 'a batterer – a man whose aggressive masculinity and desire for control are perfectly consistent with the profile of an abuser', while Stella 'matches the sociological profile of the battered woman'.[26] Elia Kazan, preparing to direct the play, emphasised in his notes the 'terrific price' Stella pays for her relationship with Stanley.[27] Picking up on a phrase in the text referring to Stella's state of 'narcotized tranquility' the morning after her impassioned lovemaking with Stanley in the wake of

Figure 5.2   Tim Richards, Jason Klarwein, Joel Edgerton, Michael Denkha,
Mandy McElhinney and Robin McLeavy in *A Streetcar Named Desire*, Sydney
Theatre Company, 2009.

their quarrel, Kazan saw Stella as existing in a 'sensual stupour', a state that
could not be prolonged indefinitely. 'Stella [. . .] cannot live narcotized
forever. There is more to her. She begins to feel, even in the sex act, *taken*,
unfulfilled – not recognized.'[28] Kazan is projecting here beyond what
the text actually shows as a means of gaining a full understanding of the
character according to the Method acting style in which he was trained.
But the comment may reflect also an uneasiness with the play's apparent
return to status quo ante in the final scene, where Stella chooses to accept
Stanley's lie about the rape and the last tableau has her once again in her
husband's arms, while he '*speaks to her voluptuously*: Now, honey. Now,
love. Now, now, love. Now, now, love. Now love. . .' (*Streetcar*, 103).[29]

     To accept that the Kowalskis' relationship can revert to the way it was
before Blanche arrived might seem implicitly to condone the rape. That is
why the ending of the 1951 Warner Brothers film of the play directed by
Kazan was changed. In this version, as Blanche is driven away in a car with
the sinister doctor and matron, Stella rejects Stanley's embrace, saying he is
never to lay a finger on her again. As she goes up to Eunice's apartment,
she whispers to her baby, 'We're not going back in there. Not this time.
We're never going back.'[30] The finality of this is underlined by the ringing

cries of 'Stella!' from Stanley, repeated from the famous ending of the poker night scene, when Stanley (Marlon Brando) and Stella (Kim Hunter) were so dramatically reunited. There will be no reunion this time. From the viewpoint of the informal Hollywood censor Joseph Breen, Stanley had to be 'condignly punished for his lust'.[31] Beyond this need for conventional moral justice to be seen to be done, what makes the ending of the play more generally disquieting is the apparent acceptance of violence as a permanent feature of ordinary married relationships. Even if Stanley's rape is regarded as indefensible, the alternation of domestic violence and passionate sex is shown to be a standard rhythm of marital life, not pathologically abusive behaviour to be stigmatised and deplored. Violent sexuality, at its worst in rape, is not something antithetical to tender, loving marriage but something endemic within it.

The inside of her head

At the time of the first production, some viewers were not disquieted by the representation of the Kowalskis' marriage, to judge at least by the captions under a set of photographs included in *Life* immediately after the premiere. Under the graphic scene of Blanche being restrained by the doctor and matron, the legend concludes: '[Blanche's] sister and husband can now resume their happiness, proving Williams's thesis that healthy life can go on only after it is rid of unwholesome influence.' This is consistent with the tone of the captions throughout. The 'fierce quarrel' between Stanley and Stella earlier in the play was 'brought about by Blanche's endless meddling'. Even Stanley's rape of Blanche is more or less her own fault: 'For weeks she has been insulting and trying to attract him. When his wife is in the hospital having a baby, Blanche hysterically attacks him with the top of a broken bottle. In a half-drunken fury, Stanley rapes her.'[32] Startlingly prejudiced as this viewpoint seems now, it is easy to see how for some audience members in 1947 Blanche – compulsive liar, alcoholic, nymphomaniac – would have appeared as the home-wrecking sister-in-law from hell breaking up a sister's 'healthy' marriage.

Williams was conscious of the problem of maintaining sympathy for Blanche. In the acting text, he wrote in a new opening stage direction for 11.1 (Scene 5):

> The scene is a point of balance between the play's two sections, Blanche's coming and the events leading up to her violent departure. The important values are the ones that characterize Blanche: the function is to give her

dimension as a character and to suggest the intense inner life which makes her a person of greater magnitude than she appears on the surface. (*Streetcar*, 52)

The technical problem of the play was to maintain an essential balance of sympathy between Blanche and Stanley – no mean feat in the original production with the electrifying performance of Marlon Brando as Stanley. In a letter to Kazan before rehearsals started, Williams insisted that 'Blanche must finally have the understanding and compassion of the audience', but 'without creating a black-dyed villain in Stanley. It is a thing (Misunderstanding) not a person (Stanley) that destroys her in the end. In the end you should feel – "If only they all had known about each other."'[33]

In the first drafts of the play, *Streetcar* had a very different scenario. It was something like a reprise of *The Glass Menagerie*, in which sister and brother-in-law were trying to help the older heroine to achieve a last-hope marriage with a gentleman caller.[34] But of equal importance in the development of the play was a separate unpublished piece called 'Interior: Panic' written in 1945–46. This 'condenses the action of *A Streetcar Named Desire* into a single act', with Blanche Shannon, her sister Grace and her husband Jack Kiefaber living in 'a shot-gun cottage in a poor section of New Orleans'.[35] The striking feature of this text is Williams's attempt to render a psychological interior, as he makes clear in a stage direction:

We are seeing it through the eyes of a person in a state of panic. The rooms are exposed, upstage and down, divided by portieres. It is somewhat the way it might have been painted by Van Gogh in his feverish interiors, with an abnormal emphasis on strident color. Distortions and irregularities of design may be added to bring out the hysteria in this view. The white plaster walls of the interior are stained with lurid projections.[36]

It is striking how much of this came across into *Streetcar*: the layout of the rooms, the 'lurid projections', even the Van Gogh colours that Williams evokes in his reading text description of 'The Poker Night' (Williams, 1, 492). But the Blanche of 'Interior: Panic' is fully delusional; the rape that is to become so horrifically real in *Streetcar* is a projection of her mind. In her paranoia, she tells her sister of what she imagines as Jack's designs: '[W]hile you're in hospital having a baby, that is the horrible plan in the back of his mind! We'll be alone here together, only these loose portieres separating our beds. And he'll come stalking through them in his pyjamas!'[37] What Williams achieved in *Streetcar* was to combine this psychological 'interior' of Blanche with the realised domestic interior of the Kowalskis' apartment.

Two years after *Streetcar* came the staging of *Death of a Salesman*, which Miller originally considered calling *The Inside of His Head*.[38] With its flashbacks and its memory slips, the theatrical strategy there too was to stage a mental landscape. But the point of rendering the mental perspective of a Willy Loman was to demand identification with him in his ordinariness. That is the point of Linda's famous speech:

> I don't say he's a great man. Willy Loman never made a lot of money. His name was never in the paper. He's not the finest character that ever lived. But he's a human being, and a terrible thing is happening to him. So attention must be paid.[39]

The theatrical techniques of interiorisation were similar in the two plays; *Death of a Salesman*, like *Streetcar*, was directed by Elia Kazan and designed by Jo Mielzener. But there is a big difference between getting inside the head of a Mr Average salesman, with his dreams of making a fortune, his aspiration for his sons and his desire to plant seeds in the backyard, and that of a neurasthenic, promiscuous, faded Southern belle. Willy's tragedy is significant because he is typical; Blanche is representative of nothing but herself. How was it possible theatrically to 'suggest the intense inner life which makes her a person of greater magnitude than she appears on the surface' while maintaining the reality of the situation in which she figures?

The music is crucial to that objective. The jazz band creates the ambient atmosphere of the city and the mood music for the individual scenes, but the Varsouviana polka is Blanche's own individual tune, heard by no one but her. In the original production, it was aurally quite distinct, played on a Novachord synthesiser offstage, while the blues music was transmitted from a live band playing in a broadcasting booth on the theatre's upper floor.[40] The polka is introduced at the end of the opening scene when Stanley casually asks Blanche, whom he has just met, 'You were married once, weren't you?' As Blanche stammers – 'The boy – the boy died' – 'Distant lilt of the "Varsouviana" is heard. Blanche, listening to music, moves choppily to L. seat.' The sound seems to produce actual nausea: 'I'm afraid I'm –going to be sick.'

> Blanche sits on L. seat. Music grows more insistent. She tries to deny the sound, looking fearfully about her, as the lights dim. When music reaches a crescendo, she suddenly leaps to her feet, pressing her hands against her ears. The lights fade out quickly and curtain down. Cut 'Varsouviana'. In darkness, the sound of the jazz band playing a blues number comes up full. They play through change. (*Streetcar*, 19)

In this theatrical elaboration of Williams's original stage direction, 'The music of the polka rises up, faint in the distance' (Williams, 1, 482), an audience watches the manifestation of Blanche's inner trauma without as yet being able fully to understand its origins. By the switch of the music, however, the convention is established that distinguishes this interior psychodrama from the theatrical world that surrounds it.

In *The Glass Menagerie* already Williams had looked for a musical theme associated specifically with Laura to come 'out most clearly when the play focuses upon her and the lovely fragility of glass which is her image' (Williams, 1, 397). The difference in *Streetcar* is that the Varsouviana is heard only by Blanche and by the audience; it is a secret they share, fully revealed in the scene where Blanche explains to Mitch the circumstances from which it arose, the dance where her revolted reaction to the discovery of her adored young husband's homosexuality provoked his suicide. Though Mitch listens sympathetically to the story in this scene, he does not hear the music. And in III.3 (Scene 9), after he has been brutally disillusioned by the stories of Blanche's past, he puts down her distracted replay of the Varsouviana sequence to drunkenness: 'Are you boxed out of your mind?' (*Streetcar*, 82). The technique, like so much in the play, is proto-cinematic, one of the reasons why it transferred so successfully to the screen, where point of view shots and distorted dialogue heard through an echo chamber could render the separateness of Blanche's state of mind. The effect is to produce a split drama in which that psychological interior of the protagonist is to some extent privileged.

This is the problem with traditional readings of the play, which have focused on the conflict between Blanche and Stanley in social terms or merely in terms of a balance of sympathy between the two.[41] Kazan's view that 'Blanche is a social type, an emblem of a dying civilization, making its last curlicued and romantic exit' has been followed by many interpreters since.[42] The issue of sympathy was raised early also when, for instance, Harold Clurman, reviewing the premiere in New York, objected to Kazan's direction: 'The play becomes the triumph of Stanley Kowalski with the collusion of the audience, which is no longer on the side of the angels.'[43] The social dimension is unquestionably there in the play, not merely in the associations of Blanche with Belle Reve and an archaic antebellum plantation culture. Her major speech at the end of I.4 (Scene 4), culminating in her appeal to Stella – '[D]on't hang back with the brutes!' – implies an onward march of civilization in which Stanley is a simian throwback (*Streetcar*, 51). By contrast, Stanley's proud declaration of his citizenship insists on the progressive model of the United States as the classless melting pot: 'I am not a Polack. People from Poland are Poles, not Polacks. But what I am is one-hundred-per-cent American, born and raised in the greatest country on earth and proud as hell of it, so don't ever call me a Polack' (*Streetcar*, 78). The play without doubt demands an oscillating balance of sympathy between the pathos of Blanche's situation and the understandable frustrations of Stanley. But *Streetcar* is not primarily a drama of residual and emergent cultures, nor yet a battle for audience empathy in which we are supposed to end up on the side of the angels. The play is skewed by the asymmetry of representing Blanche's inner life as a phenomenon distinct from the world around her.

Streetcar has often been compared to *Miss Julie*, and Strindberg was evidently a major influence on Williams from his college days on.[44] The comparison, though, brings out the significant differences between the two plays. *Miss Julie* is subtitled 'a naturalistic tragedy', and it is indeed a textbook model of the form. The two principal characters are the creatures of their background and context: Jean, the upwardly mobile servant who has lived abroad, picked up French and aspires to run a hotel in Switzerland, and Julie, the decadent aristocrat daughter of a misalliance between a count and a lower-class woman. All the circumstances conspire to bring about the tragedy. It is Midsummer Night, a seasonal time of festivity and social mixing. Julie has just broken up with her fiancé, she is in a premenstrual state before her period and both she and Jean have been drinking. To underline the point, the two have matching dreams, Julie's of being on a high pillar dreading and longing to fall, Jean's of wanting to climb to the top of a tall tree to plunder the bird's nest; they appear fused in Stanley's triumphant statement to Stella: 'I pulled you down off them columns' (*Streetcar*, 80).[45] The vertical orientation of the theatrical dynamics of *Miss Julie* is apparent in the play's kitchen setting, with the commanding voice of the Count coming down to the servants through a speaking tube from above.

Strindberg and Williams had a common belief in the essence of life as struggle. Strindberg famously mocked the 'joy of life' idealised by Oswald in Ibsen's *Ghosts* as the liberating antithesis of repression. 'I find the joy of life', he declared in the preface to *Miss Julie*, 'in life's cruel and powerful struggles.'[46] In an essay published immediately before the opening of *Streetcar*, Williams professed a comparable credo: '[T]he heart of man, his body and his brain, are forged in a white-hot furnace for the purpose of conflict' (Williams, 1, 1048). Yet the conflict dramatised in *Streetcar* is not the paradigmatic struggle of class and gender of *Miss Julie*. Class hostility colours, but does not determine, the antagonism between Blanche and

Stanley. Of course, she regards him as common; when Stella says that Stanley is Polish, Blanche replies jokingly, 'That's something like Irish, isn't it?' adding in a phrase removed from the acting text, 'Only not so – highbrow?' (*Streetcar*, 13; Williams, 1, 477). Equally obviously he resents what he sees as her pretentiousness, her airs and graces and the clothes and jewellery that he takes to be evidence of her wealth. But the real struggle of the play is over the possession of Stella, with Blanche trying to draw her back into the ambience of their childhood, in which she was the dominant older sister, and Stanley fighting to maintain the marriage, in which he is the controlling partner.

This makes for a very different sexual chemistry in *Streetcar* than in *Miss Julie*. Blanche from early in the play seeks to attract Stanley but gets very little answering response. He bluntly repels her flirtatious advances to him in 1.2 (Scene 2): 'If I didn't know you was my wife's sister I'd get ideas about you' (*Streetcar*, 27). This is very different from Jean's line to Miss Julie when she playfully admires his muscles, '*Attention! Je ne suis qu'un homme!*', where the warning is in effect a come-on.[47] The physical relationship between Stanley and Blanche is well caught at the moment of their first contact in the film. Vivien Leigh as Blanche is startled by the sound of cats screeching outside and reaches out impulsively to touch Brando's vest-clad torso. He shrugs away, saying, 'Cats', doing a derisive imitation of the noise. Blanche, here as throughout, is looking for protection from a man, any man, but Stanley the alley cat is not interested.

Jean seduces Julie because he wants to see 'the eagle's back', wants to place himself above a woman of the class he has only ever seen from below. Stanley rapes Blanche as an act of brutal destructiveness that comes about almost by accident rather than being motivated by class revenge. When Stanley enters in III.4 (Scene 10), he is full of the exhilarated euphoria of being about to become a father, the ultimate proof of his masculinity. In that mood, there can be little doubt that he makes his offer of reconciliation to Blanche in good faith, inviting her to share a beer: 'Shall we bury the hatchet and make it a loving-cup?' (*Streetcar*, 90). Up to a point, he is even prepared to go along with the evident fiction of her telegram from Shep Huntleigh and the invitation to join him on a Caribbean cruise. When Blanche exults in the prospect of her escape from the two-room apartment – 'When I think of how divine it is going to be to have such a thing as privacy once more – I could weep with joy!' – there is only a casual sneer in Stanley's rejoinder: 'The millionaire from Dallas is not going to interfere with your privacy any?' (*Streetcar*, 90–91). But that phrase, here used merely sarcastically, is to become the fulcrum point at which banter turns into physical menace.

For much of the scene, it is Blanche who appears terrified of the threat of Stanley, almost, like her predecessor in 'Interior: Panic', projecting her own paranoid fear. Though Stanley becomes increasingly physically aggressive, he is not up until the last point sexually menacing. The change comes when Blanche tries to escape by running into the bedroom and closing the curtains. Stanley follows '(*pushing drapes open*). You think I'll interfere with you? (*Softly*) Come to think of it – maybe you wouldn't be bad to – interfere with . . .' (*Streetcar*, 93–94). The first 'interfere with' here glances back to Stanley's contemptuous reference to Blanche's fictitious millionaire not interfering with her privacy. But on second utterance, the phrase changes its meaning as the idea of rape comes into his mind. 'Interfere with' (*OED* n. 4d) meaning 'to molest or assault sexually' was just entering the language: *OED*'s first citation is 1948. The fact that it was unpremeditated in no way extenuates the viciousness of the rape itself. It helps rather to illustrate what Williams meant when he said, 'It is a thing (Misunderstanding) not a person (Stanley) that destroys [Blanche] in the end.'

A recent book on Williams has argued persuasively that sexual desire rather than politics is at the centre of his work.[48] The other dimension differentiating *Streetcar* from *Miss Julie* is that it was written by a still-closeted gay playwright who needed to use the codes of an enforcedly straight mainstream theatre. Homosexuality could only be attributed to a dead man in the play's backstory, and even then it was almost literally unspeakable. This was how Blanche expressed her discovery about her young husband, Allan Gray:

> Then I found out. In the worst of all possible ways. By suddenly coming into a room that I thought was empty – which wasn't empty, but had two people in it . . . the boy I married and an older man who had been his friend for years. (*Streetcar*, 68)

Even this very discreet reference had to be curtailed in the London production and omitted altogether from the film. It was to fill the gap left by her lost love that Blanche took to 'intimacies with strangers'; she sought to give to young men the tenderness she had failed to give to the 'boy' Allan (*Streetcar*, 85). That at least the film was able to suggest with the Varsouviana playing behind the scene where Blanche has to stop herself seducing the young man collecting for the *Evening Star*.

Blanche has often been seen as a stand-in for the gay playwright. John Clum, for instance, maintains that Williams's 'protection of his homosexual subtext is achieved by hiding it within the actions of a heterosexual female character'.[49] Blanche's passion for dressing up can be played as a form of camp. There is a line that Williams attributes to Blanche in his *Memoirs*, though it does not appear at all in the play and only in abbreviated form in the film:

> Mitch has told her he'd thought that she was 'straight', and she has replied, 'What is straight? A line can be straight, or a street, but the human heart, oh, no, it's curved like a road through mountains!'[50]

Williams cites this line in relation to the emergence of his own gay sexuality, having described in some detail his first (and only) straight affair. Certainly, in this play, desire does not run on the straight tram tracks of a streetcar. As author surrogate, Blanche may well have something of the admiring gay male gaze expressed in Williams's introductory description of Stanley in the reading text: 'He is of medium height, about five feet eight or nine, and strongly, compactly built. Animal joy in his being is implicit in all his movements and attitudes' (Williams, 1, 481). But Stanley's brutally heterosexual force also exposes Blanche's vulnerable fragility. Though she flirts with him, she in no way invites the rape with which he destroys her as an act of violent male domination. The mother's boy Mitch does not have that force; Blanche has little difficulty in fending off his assault when he finally tries to take 'what I been missing all summer' (*Streetcar*, 87). And that is no doubt partly why Blanche needs him in the first place. Gender roles are not as clear and stable as the antagonism between the hypermasculinity of Stanley and the superfemininity of Blanche would suggest.

In the play's final scene, the rape has tipped Blanche over from extreme neurosis into full mental derangement. The stage is occupied by the characters of the real world, who collude in preparing a charade to humour her mad self. Her obsession with cleanliness, which has kept her in the bathroom for so much of the action, is extended to a fantasy of her deathbed, in which she will die of eating an unwashed grape. The very thought of the city is a contamination to her: 'Ah, those cathedral bells, they're the only clean thing in the Quarter' (*Streetcar*, 98). This is the study in mental alienation that Williams had sketched in 'Interior: Panic'. Blanche's inner world has finally come unmoored altogether from the actualities of the two rooms, the poker game and the life that Eunice insists must go on even if it means Stella accepting Stanley's lie about the rape. But an audience is not let off the terror of experiencing this state of delusion. The play's theatrical strategy of making an audience live within

Blanche's head means that we have to follow her out on the arm of the doctor, leaving behind a 'reality' diminished by her loss. That was the logic of the final tableau of the Sydney Theatre Company production that held Cate Blanchett alone in the same lighting in which she was isolated at her first entrance.

John Cheever saw the first production of *Streetcar* in New York in 1948 and summed up his reaction in his journal: it was '[a]s decadent, I think, as anything I've ever seen on the stage, with gin-mill or whore-house jazz in the dark between the scenes'. He went on, however, to speak admiringly of the play's effect:

> At the same time, Williams gives the theme some universality, and, having taken a daughter of joy, he makes her seem, without irony, to possess a pure heart. There is much else; the wonderful sense of captivity in a squalid apartment and of the beauty of the evening, although most of the chords struck seem to lie close to insanity. Anxiety, that is – confinement, and so forth. [...] he avoids not only the common clichés but the uncommon cliché [...] and also works in a form that has few inhibitions and has written its own laws.[51]

It's a striking perception. Blanche, the 'daughter of joy' – one assumes a euphemism for a prostitute – had indeed some sort of purity or at least intensity of feeling that survives her multiple 'intimacies with strangers'. The play's design manages to combine the claustrophobia of life in the 'squalid apartment' and its enforced physical proximities with the opening out into an atmospheric cityscape beyond. The dramatic form developed by Williams for the play, fluid, proto-cinematic, mixing realism with subjective expressionism, can fairly be said to have escaped cliché and 'written its own laws'. For some later critics, however, the play still suffers from too many inhibitions.

For interpreters from a more forthright period, *Streetcar* remains irredeemably a play of its own repressed time. Williams is accused of 'heterosexist discourse', and it is argued that in the play he 'was much more successful at dramatising the closet than at presenting a coherent, affirming view of gayness'.[52] Some modern revivals have tried to out the play more thoroughly. So, for example, a 2009 London production at the Donmar Theatre 'made Allan Gray a visible ghost, with an actor (Jack Ashton) appearing onstage several times, notably to kiss his older lover in front of Blanche and to stimulate the moment of his suicide'.[53] The radical rewrite of the play as the 'queer/camp production' *Belle Reprieve* (Split Britches/

Bloolips, 1991) subverted gender roles throughout. 'Mitch (Precious Pearl) is "a fairy disguised as a man"; Stella ([Lois] Weaver) is "a woman disguised as a woman"; Stanley (Peggy Shaw) is cast as a "butch lesbian"; and Blanche ([Bette] Bourne) is "a man in a dress", a drag queen.'[54] The aim of such a production was to show that all 'gender is unstable, performative'.[55] As with the Mabou Mines *Dollhouse*, the impulse here was, by a playful deconstruction of the canonised classic of the past, to give new militant force to its meaning. *Streetcar* can in fact be seen as a sort of halfway house, if the pun can be allowed, in the movement from more stable forms of naturalistic representation in the earlier twentieth century to the more thoroughly destabilised versions beyond. The see-through forms of the play blur the distinction between interior and exterior, allow the city to spill over into the home on the stage, render the expressive subjectivity of the individual living in a confined space. The violent love of Stanley and Stella calls in question conventional concepts of happy marriage, and the pathos accorded to the role-playing, histrionic Blanche confuses 'straight' readings of moral sympathies. Still, the play remains within the representational theatrical idiom, and the playwright himself would come to be 'despised by the alternative theatre'.[56] Nothing in *Streetcar* would prepare an audience for the all-out assault on that idiom in the work of Beckett.

CHAPTER 6

Endgame: *in the refuge*

In his first completed play, *Eleutheria*, written in French in 1947, Beckett put not one but two homes on the stage. This was a simultaneous set with a difference. Williams, with the aid of Mielzener's design, had granted audiences X-ray eyes by which they could see both inside and outside the Kowalski apartment, the streetscape behind the building and the city beyond. These, however, were contiguous spaces. Beckett juxtaposed the sordid rented room of the central character Victor in the Impasse Enfant-Jésus, far off in the Parisian 15° arrondissement, with the salon of his impeccably bon bourgeois family the Kraps. There was to be no dividing wall between the two, but rather the salon was to be an 'enclave' of Victor's flat, the flat taking up two-thirds of the stage: 'Victor's room moves imperceptibly into the Kraps' salon, as the dirty into the clean, the sordid into the respectable, emptiness into clutter.'¹ In the first two acts, there was to be a main action with dialogue in one of the two stage spaces and a silent marginal action in the other, with a progressive alteration in the scenography: 'Victor's room is seen from a different angle in each act; in the first act it is, to the audience, left of the Krap enclave, and in the second act, to their right. Hence, in both acts the main action remains on the right. This also explains why there is no marginal action in the third act, as the Krap side has fallen into the orchestra pit during the change of scene' (*Eleutheria*, 6).

Eleutheria is a polemic piece of work attacking simultaneously the conformity of conventional middle-class life, with its attachments and engagements in the world, and the representational norms of the conventionally well-made play. The cross-linguistic puns in the French names of the characters have their own contemptuous animus. At the start of the action, the sister of Mme Krap arrives unexpectedly to announce that she has married the hideous-looking Dr Piouk. The friend of the family, a highly respectable widow of a general, is Mme Meck, *meck* being French slang for 'pimp'. The fiancée of Victor, whom he has rejected, is unpromisingly called Mlle Olga Skunk. The dialogue in the Krap salon satirises and renders absurd the conventions of bourgeois life: Jacques, the too deferential footman, who has never learned that as a footman you do not knock at the door when you enter the room; Mme Krap, who refuses her sister a glass of port because it is teatime. This is all but Oscar Wilde. What disrupts this Wildean comedy of manners is the most un-Victorian explicitness with which the physical condition of the characters is discussed, whether it is the prostate condition of M Krap – 'He can't pee any more' (*Eleutheria*, 17) – the prolapsed wombs of both Mme Krap and Mme Meck, and the issue of whether or not Mme Piouk is past the menopause. The combination of excremental names and degenerative bodily disorders turns the characters, with their formal salon small talk, into grotesques.

The satiric ridicule of the bourgeoisie is matched by an equivalently aggressive subversion of theatrical conventions. There are mocking metatheatrical jokes. The instant that the nay-saying refusenik Victor in his frustration breaks a window with his shoe at the start of Act II, a glazier appears to fix it. The glazier's boy Michel, sent to fetch a diamond, reappears within seconds – 'You took your time', he is told (*Eleutheria*, 67). When Victor tries to hide from Mme Meck, his place of concealment is revealed by the Glazier: 'He is under the bed, Madame, as in Molière's day' (*Eleutheria*, 69). The Glazier, in fact, becomes the spokesman for the proper theatrical values that Victor's unmotivated refusal to act so signally flouts. 'I've come across plenty of ham actors but never one as bad as you. If you were absolutely determined to get yourself booed you couldn't have done any better' (*Eleutheria*, 87). Victor does not show any feeling for his mother or his fiancée, no grief at the news that his father has died, nor is he sacrificing all those normal emotions to a splendid cause. The Glazier who tries to fix the window that Victor has broken, who looks to put a lock on the door of his flat, wants to seal the story into a correctly framed theatrical narrative in the proper theatrical interior. In Act III, the metatheatrical attack is taken further with the intervention of the Spectator who climbs out of his box and crosses over onto the stage to protest at the play: '[W]ho wrote this rubbish [. . .] Samuel, Béké, Béké, he must be a cross between a Jew from Greenland and a peasant from the Auvergne' (*Eleutheria*, 136).

It is hardly surprising that, given the choice between *Eleutheria* and *Waiting for Godot*, Roger Blin should have chosen the latter for production; it is indeed surprising that he considered staging *Eleutheria* at all. Quite apart from its large cast and multiple sets, the play is doctrinaire avant-garde in the crudity of its satire and its elaborate and long-winded

dismantling of the conventions of naturalism. In *Godot*, Beckett was to find his true vein by abandoning the middle-class milieu and the domestic → IRISH
interior altogether. Intriguingly, Peter Snow, the designer for the English-language premiere of *Godot* in London, considered putting the road back into a box-set frame. Katharine Worth has shown how Snow tried out an idea for enclosing the road and the tree within a standard stage room complete with two doors.[2] This would have been to turn the play back towards the metatheatrical surrealism of *Eleutheria*, against the minimalist style of the play. However, Beckett did return to a version of the domestic interior in *Endgame* (1957). Though shorn of the social specificities of *Eleutheria* and without its theatrical polemics, it continues by other means the radical challenge to the representation of home on the stage and of its family-like inhabitants.

Terminal interior

In the preliminary draft for the play, which Beckett labelled 'Avant *Fin de partie*', the situation of the isolated master and servant was given a precise location in time and place. It was set in Picardy, 'and more precisely in Boulonnais... near Wissant'. F (for factotum) describes to his master (known only as X) their shared space: 'Your living quarters, erected on a cliff, are composed of a living room and a hallway transformed into a kitchen' – Beckett uses the English 'living room' in the French text. The house, it seems, was 'progressively destroyed in the autumn of 1914, the spring of 1918, and the following autumn, under mysterious circum-stances'.[3] But these geographical and historical details were taken out of later versions of the play according to the process Gontarski calls 'undo-ing', Rosemary Pountney 'vaguening'.[4] Beckett 'undoes' or 'vaguens' the text so that everything tying characters, actions and dramatic setting to an extratheatrical reality is removed. As Beckett, over the course of his career, went from the Dublin-landmarked stories of *More Pricks Than Kicks* to the nameless spaces of his later fiction and drama, so within the genetic sequence of imagining individual works early specificities were erased.

By the time of the first full two-act draft of the play, the two characters, now A and B, inhabit an unlocated 'bare interior with two high windows and an open door front left', as in the final version.[5] But this text is spectacularly non-naturalistic, a playacting combination of slapstick and surrealism. At the start of the play, the curtain rising on A (= Hamm) falls and has to rise again. At one point, 'a large, mechanical rat crosses the front of the stage'. A and B (= Clov) sing a duet on their endlessly iterated dialogue – 'Every day, ev-er-y day / All we do is repeat ourselves, / Repeat ourselves' – and are rewarded with 'frantic recorded applause'. B dons disguises to play the roles of wife/mother and little boy in A's staged plays within the play. Most bizarre of all is the coffin that is placed beside A's chair and from which a head appears at strategic points in the action.[6] In this form, the play was a ostentatious mockery of the restrained verisimilitude of representational naturalism.

Yet if one phase in the genesis of the play involved the undoing of the realising location of the action, another entailed the stripping out of this sort of gratuitous metatheatrical absurdity. At the next stage of gestation, the cast was doubled with the addition of 'mémé' and 'pépé', alias Nagg and Nell, in their dustbins, but the mechanical rat, the recorded applause and the jack-in-the-coffin head all disappeared.[7] The characters and situation in the final *Fin de Partie/Endgame* are no doubt strange and unexplained but no longer deliberately unbelievable. As Harry White puts it, for all its subversion of theatrical conventions, 'the play notably advances in naturalistic sequences which sustain the illusion of realist drama'.[8]

What is more, this process of simplifying and even, in a sense, naturalising *Endgame* went on beyond the play's premiere. When Beckett directed the play himself in German for the Schiller Theater in 1967, he took out traces of earlier stylisation from the production. So, for instance, he removed the contrast between the red faces of Hamm and Clov and the white faces of Nagg and Nell, considering them '*trop recherché*'.[9] Beckett's production assistant, Michael Haerdter, recorded in his rehearsal diary the decision to omit any metatheatrical references from the text:

> All replies which refer to the public have been removed ('a multitude in transports of joy!' etc.): the action is to be entirely concentrated on the dwellers of the lair. There is surprise when Beckett explains this by means of a principle of naturalistic theatre – 'the play is to be acted as though there were a fourth wall where the footlights are'.[10]

This does not, of course, turn *Endgame* into a naturalistic play, if only because it so determinedly refuses to yield the explanations naturalism must give its audience: who are these characters, what are their motives, where is the action happening? Beckett famously refused elucidation in an often-quoted letter to his American director Alan Schneider: 'Hamm as stated, and Clov as stated, *nec tecum nec sine te*, in such a place, and in such a world, that's all I can manage, more than I could.'[11] The challenge of the play is in fact the way in which it imprisons an audience in that place, that world, without the let-out of symbolism or allegory. For all the ingenious attempts to decode the names of the characters – Hamm as hammer; Clov, Nagg, Nell as versions of nail in French or German – they remain stubbornly opaque, unlike the sneering soubriquets, the Kraps and Piouks of *Eleutheria*.

When first imagined, what became the refuge in *Endgame* was a World War I ruin in Picardy.[12] But the play was written in the 1950s in the wake of a still more devastating war, and with the new threat of cosmic destruction, so catastrophically illustrated by the bombs on Hiroshima and Nagasaki, what had been myths or fantasies about the end of life on Earth took on a new literal reality. In 'Avant *Fin de Partie*', already F and X take themselves to be terminal survivors: 'Dommage que nous soyons les derniers du genre humain' ['Pity that we should be the last of the human race'].[13] This is implied in the final text but never stated as such, and no explanation is ever offered as to what has caused the apparent extinction of life outside the refuge. The explicitness of the postnuclear scenario in the controversial 1984 production of the play by JoAnne Akalaitis for the American Repertory Theatre may have been one of the reasons Beckett objected to it so much. The setting in a burned-out underground tunnel with derailed subway cars was designed to suggest 'an American city, probably New York, after nuclear holocaust'.[14] Beckett would have none of this. 'Any production of *Endgame* which ignores my stage direction is completely unacceptable to me. My play requires an empty room and two small windows. The American Repertory Theatre production which dismisses my directions is a complete parody of the play as conceived by me.'[15]

The imagination of *Endgame* reaches back to the archetype of the deluge – in an early draft, B/Clov reads 'the passage on Noah's flood' to A/Hamm.[16] In its own contemporary context, it must necessarily have awakened the fear of nuclear devastation. Yet Beckett does not allow his audience's attention to move off into these other fields of interpretation. To quote Yeats's line from the very different context of 'Meditations in Time of Civil War', 'the key is turned / On our uncertainty'.[17] Uncertainty there undoubtedly is in *Endgame*. The reference to Clov's 'visions', for instance, by Beckett's own account 'allows his perception of life (boy) at the end and of course the rat to be construed as hallucinations'.[18] Or again, there is Hamm's story of the mad painter and engraver 'who thought the end of the world had come'.

> I used to go and see him, in the asylum. I'd take him by the hand and drag him to the window. Look! There! All that rising corn! And there! Look! The

sails of the herring fleet! All that loveliness! (*Pause.*) He'd snatch away his hand and go back into his corner. Appalled. All he had seen was ashes. (*Pause.*) He alone had been spared.[19]

The blind Hamm, the Clov who, on his instructions, inspects the earth and sea through the two windows and can detect 'zero' there, may be as deranged as the painter and engraver. But watching the play, we can hardly comfort ourselves with that thought. The unexplained enigma of the text is far from the epistemological game-playing Beckett originally envisaged in 'Avant *Fin de partie*', where the Hamm character first declares he is not really blind and paralysed as he appears to be, and then raises the possibility that he was lying when he said so.[20]

Hamm and Clov, Nagg and Nell are apparently the last surviving people, subsisting on an ever-decreasing stock of necessary materials. One of the play's repeated motifs is the running out of supplies: there are no more bicycle wheels, sugar plums, coffins and, most cruelly for Hamm, when the often-deferred moment comes, 'there's no more painkiller' (Beckett, 127). For an audience watching the play, this state of increasing indigence matches the withholding of normal dramatic stimulation, a sort of strategic sensory deprivation. In *Eleutheria*, the emptiness of Victor's garret invaded the clutter of the Krap salon, so that by the end of the play all that was left was his single bed pushed to the edge of the footlights, with Victor himself lying on it with his back to the audience. *Endgame*, however, begins where *Eleutheria* left off, with a comprehensively cleared stage, featuring only the covered shapes of Hamm's chair and the two ashbins. A picture, the set's one decorative feature, faces the wall in a gesture comparable to Victor's turned back. An audience comes to watch and enjoy a play, to be drawn into and decode its mise-en-scène: *Endgame* wilfully frustrates such expectations.

As Hamm is taken by Clov on his tour 'right round the world' of the room, he remarks that beyond the wall is 'the . . . other hell' (Beckett, 104). Vivian Mercier maintains that Sartre's issueless hell in *Huis Clos* (1944) was Beckett's model here: '*Godot*, *Endgame*, *Play* are all offspring of *Huis Clos*.'[21] Mercier is often an acutely perceptive interpreter of Beckett, but this seems to me a mistaken judgement. The differences between *Huis Clos* and *Endgame* are significant. Sartre develops the concept of three characters who serve as one another's torturers: Garcin, the sadistic husband and self-convicted coward; Estelle, the coquette who has killed her own baby in part to spite her lover; and the lesbian Inez, who has driven her lover to suicide. The twists and turns of the relationships among the three, the permutations and combinations of their emotional dynamics, make for an ingenious form of drama. There is an impish wit in the discovery that rather than being submerged in freezing fire or boiling oil, the damned are subjected to dwell for all eternity in a room of Second Empire décor – truly hell for someone of Sartre's class and generation. But the whole play works as a philosophical parable building to its most quoted line: 'Hell is … other people.'[22] The contrast between *Huis Clos* and *Endgame* provides an exact illustration of Adorno's contrast between existentialist drama and that of Beckett. 'Absurdity in Beckett is no longer a state of existence thinned out to a mere idea and then expressed in images.'[23]

The naturalistic home on the stage points outward towards the community beyond as paradigm or epitome. But beyond the grey walls of *Endgame*, there is nothing, or at least we cannot know for certain that there is anything. Hamm may raise the possibility of a continuing pastoral elsewhere. 'Did you ever think of one thing?' he asks Clov. 'That here we're down in a hole. (*Pause.*) But beyond the hills? Eh? Perhaps it's still green. Eh? (*Pause.*) Flora! Pomona! (*Ecstatically.*) Ceres!' (Beckett, 111). The ridiculous archaism of the invocation of these goddesses in such an environment is a guarantee of its ironic inauthenticity, as unreal as Hamm's dream of escape southwards on a raft with Clov (Beckett, 109). Hamm and Clov, Nagg and Nell cannot stand in for something other than themselves because there is nothing left for which they might stand. They are equally booby-trapped against symbolic or metaphorical interpretation: 'We're not beginning to … to … mean something?' asks a disquieted Hamm. 'Mean something!', Clov replies with sardonic amusement. 'You and I, mean something! (*Brief laugh.*) Ah that's a good one!' (Beckett, 108). That necessarily turns audience intention inward to the inhabitants of the room-cum-offstage kitchen. Beckett in *Endgame* provides a drastically reduced version of home on the stage, but also in Nagg and Nell, Hamm and Clov a subversive vision of the three-generational family that might be expected to live in such a home.

The old folks at home

Eleutheria represented a particularly fierce and disgusted rejection of family life and its supposed obligations. The 'freedom' of the title that Victor seeks is the freedom from having to respond to the family's claims, the claims in particular of the women. In Act II he complains that he is 'being constantly disturbed. Yesterday it was my mother, today it's the general's widow [Mme Meck], tomorrow it will be my fiancée' (*Eleutheria*, 73).

There is in fact a distinct misogynist twist to the play's dissidence. Mme Krap is the monstrous *mère de famille* demanding that her son shape up; Mme Meck is her delegated agent. Olga, Victor's fiancée, can only imagine that if he no longer wants to sleep with her, it is because he has fallen in love with someone else. By contrast, there is a sense of affinity and affection between Victor and his father. M Krap is a writer like Victor who, like him, aspires to freedom: 'My son is in the right [. . .] I've loosed my chains' (*Eleutheria*, 28). At one point, the father pulls out a razor with the intention of killing Mme Krap, only to discover he is too weak to get out of the chair: 'Not easy to sit up, even to kill your wife' (*Eleutheria*, 54). Though Victor refuses to provide the emotional response to the news of his father's death that Mme Meck expects, the wordless marginal action of Act II, in which he 'sits down in his father's armchair under the floor lamp', remaining 'motionless for a long time' (*Eleutheria*, 7–8), is intended to show the loss he is feeling. What is more striking is that this sense of loss is also experienced by the servant Jacques, an automaton figure in Act I, who in Act II turns out to be the only person to whom Victor responds fully and openly.

No doubt coded into *Eleutheria* is something of Beckett's own feelings about his parents – his sense of grief at his father's unexpected early death, his difficult relationship with his managing mother. By contrast with such emotional complexity, in *Endgame* there is a savagely reductive paradigm of the father-son relationship expressed in the exchange between Hamm and Nagg:

HAMM. Scoundrel! Why did you engender me?
NAGG. I didn't know.
HAMM. What? What didn't you know?
NAGG. That it'd be you.
(Beckett, 116)

Parenting is here no more than the blind drive of the will to reproduce, with no necessary implication of personal bonding. Nagg, for Hamm, is the 'accursed progenitor' who is responsible for his existence, and is now merely an infantilised dependent demanding 'me pap'. 'The old folks at home!', Hamm exclaims in sardonic disgust: 'No decency left! Guzzle, guzzle, that's all they think of' (Beckett, 96). From Nagg's side there is an equally satiric travesty of paternal caring. It is, Nagg acknowledges, 'natural' that Hamm should cheat him of the promised sugar-plum: 'After all I'm your father. It's true if it hadn't been me it would have been someone else. But that's no excuse. [. . .] Whom did you call when you were a tiny boy, and were frightened, in the dark? Your mother? No. Me. We let you cry. Then we moved you out of earshot, so that we might sleep in peace' (Beckett, 119).

Nagg is 'accursed' because responsible for begetting Hamm. In *Endgame*, the whole abhorrent business of reproduction is to be stopped at all costs. Dr Piouk in *Eleutheria* had his own plans 'to resolve the situation of the human species':

> I would ban reproduction. I would perfect the condom and other devices and bring them into general use. I would establish teams of abortionists, controlled by the State. I would apply the death penalty to any woman guilty of giving birth. I would drown all newborn babies. I would militate in favour of homosexuality, and would myself set the example. (*Eleutheria*, 44–45)

However, within the context of that surreal extravaganza, Piouk is merely an absurd theoretician contrasted with the more seriously grounded life denial of Victor. The terminal situation of *Endgame* gives dramatic force to Hamm and Clov's strenuous efforts to prevent life from starting up again. The archetypal deluge myth is driven by the imperative of survival; that is why Noah must gather into the ark two of each species. In the postnuclear age, the typical scenario of end of the world narratives is to depict the hope against hope that some human beings may escape the devastation. Nevil Shute's 1957 novel *On the Beach* and its 1959 film adaptation would be representative in this. Against such narrative norms, Hamm's horror at the appearance of a flea on Clov is the more strikingly perverse: 'But humanity might start from there all over again! Catch him, for the love of God!' (Beckett, 108).

Reproduction is to be deplored; the human species should not be continued. Yet even in Piouk's prescriptions for extinction, the sexual urge is something that could only be controlled or redirected rather than eliminated. In the early drafts of *Endgame*, sex play was still necessary to the Hamm character, even if only with the help of his factotum in a female wig. The identity of the partner did not matter: 'Mother, wife, sister, daughter, harlot. It's the same to me. A woman. Two breasts and a vulva.'[24] In the final text, all that remains of this is Hamm's yearning for quiet and sleep: 'If I could sleep I might make love' (Beckett, 100). Nagg and Nell, identified by their original names, 'mémé' and 'pépé', as grandparents in the three-generation configuration of the family, are the play's only representatives of a once-reproductive couple. 'What is it, my pet?', says Nell, summoned by a knock on her bin lid by Nagg for her first and only appearance, 'Time for love?' (Beckett, 99). Sex is here treated with typical Beckettian grotesquerie, the habit of desire long outliving physical capacity. The legless pair cannot even strain their heads far enough together to kiss, much less make love.

There is something more like tenderness in the treatment of Nagg and Nell than anything else in the play, at least in the spirit of Nagg's concern and his saving of half his dog biscuit for Nell. Yet their brief dialogue represents a sceptical anatomy of the companionate marriage. Their merriest moment is in the shared memory of 'when we crashed our tandem and lost our shanks', but even then they 'laugh less heartily' as each detail of the circumstances is recalled (Beckett, 100). This perfectly illustrates Nell's proposition that '[n]othing is funnier than unhappiness', but also her comment that 'it's like the funny story we have heard too often, we still find it funny, but we don't laugh any more' (Beckett, 101). Nagg's many times repeated joke about the tailor and the trousers then follows, with even Nagg himself admitting that it had lost its original effectiveness – 'I never told it worse' (Beckett, 102). But did it make Nell laugh in the first place, when Nagg told it to her on Lake Como the day after they had got engaged? Nagg insists that it did:

NAGG. You were in such fits that we capsized. By rights we should have been drowned.
NELL. It was because I felt happy.
NAGG. (*Indignant*) It was not, it was not, it was my story and nothing else. Happy! Don't you laugh at it still? Every time I tell it. Happy!
NELL. It was deep, deep. And you could see down to the bottom. So white. So clean.
(Beckett, 102)

Again, it is characteristic of Beckett to show what is apparently a moment of joyful mutuality as illusory, here the self-regarding male performer's projection onto a solitary and inward female mood of transcendence.[25] This vestigial marriage is slowly ebbing away and is given the most antidramatic conclusion possible. Clov is instructed to look in Nell's bin: 'Go and see is she dead'. 'Looks like it', comes the reply (Beckett, 122).

The central relationship of the play, of course, is that between Hamm and Clov. But what relationship is it, master/servant or father/son? There is Hamm's story of the poor man who came whining to him for bread and asked that he and his little one – 'little boy [. . .] as if the sex mattered' – be taken into Hamm's service (Beckett, 117). Hamm imagines his solitude in the refuge with no one left: 'I'll have called my father and I'll have called my ... (*he hesitates*) ... my son' (Beckett, 126). This could be construed as his final recognition of Clov's status, just as the unfinished story could be a fictional version of Clov's arrival in the refuge. But Beckett will not allow us to be certain. One significant clue in the French *Fin de partie*, which is less evident in the English *Endgame*, is the way Clov addresses Hamm consistently with the 'tu' form. In the first sketch for the play, 'Avant de *Fin de partie*', 'F [the Clov character] insists on maintaining the social familiarities of rank [...] but X insists that F use the "tu" pronoun'.[26] Whether Clov is Hamm's adopted son or not, in the final play they have been together so long that any standard class barriers of master and servant have gone.

Clov and Hamm exist as in a bad marriage or a long-standing relationship that has gone wrong. The Latin epigram from Martial that Beckett alludes to in his letter to Alan Schneider sums up their situation: 'nec tecum nec sine te vivere possum', 'I cannot live with you or without you.'[27] Their mutual dependence involves continuous mutual provocation and frustration. It is Hamm who plays the emotional games, alternating between apparent bids for sympathy and brutal reassertions of authority. Clov's strategy is to try not to respond, to outmanoeuvre the sadistic stratagems by a deflating stoicism: 'Something is taking its course' (Beckett, 107). But of course he cannot always succeed and at times is driven to violent outbursts when he can bear Hamm's riling no more. 'Yesterday', derides Hamm, when Clov tells him that he oiled the casters of the armchair yesterday. 'What does that mean? Yesterday!'

> That means that bloody awful day, long ago, before this bloody awful day. I use the words you taught me. If they don't mean anything any more, teach me others. Or let me be silent. (Beckett, 113)

But the moment of Caliban-like revolt – 'You taught me language, and my profit on't / Is I know how to curse' – passes, and Clov returns to merely weary, dissident submission.[28]

Hamm, for all his physical helplessness, is in a position of complete power and control throughout. It is, as he points out to Clov, 'my house' (Beckett, 109). All that Clov can claim within it is the minimum separation of his own space: 'my kitchen, ten feet by ten feet by ten feet [...] Nice dimensions, nice proportions.' It is no more than an antechamber where Clov can 'lean on the table, and look at the wall, and wait for him to whistle me', but nonetheless it allows for a temporary escape from Hamm's sphere (Beckett, 93). This shades the situation back towards the master/servant relationship, with the servant in an adjacent place within reach of the living quarters that he never himself inhabits. Jacques in *Eleutheria* is such an officious attendant that Mme Krap complains sarcastically, 'Yesterday he let a good quarter of an hour go by without sticking his nose in. I thought he was dead' (*Eleutheria*, 21). The situation in *Endgame* is the opposite. The kitchen is Clov's room of his own, however little a room, however minimally his own, and his drive is always to try to get away to it: 'I'll leave you. I have things to do' (Beckett, 97). Equally persistently Hamm tries to retain him out of perversity, out of a need for company or as a pure exercise of power.

'Do you remember when you came here?' Hamm asks Clov as one of his ploys for keeping the conversation going. 'No', responds Clov. 'Too small, you told me.' Hamm persists: 'Do you remember your father?' When he receives the 'same answer', he proclaims, 'It was I was a father to you.'

CLOV. Yes. (*He looks at Hamm fixedly.*) You were that to me.
HAMM. My house a home for you.
CLOV. Yes. (*He looks about him.*) This was that for me.
(Beckett, 110)

Clov's grimly meaningful answers here bespeak the play's dark reading of home and paternity. Hamm is the ultimate tyrannical patriarch, whether as the viciously aggressive Oedipal son of Nagg, the brutally controlling master or the emotionally blackmailing pseudo-father of Clov. The family living room, which should be the nurturing space of comfort and consolation, is reduced to the barest of grey interiors, where the older generation is dying discarded in garbage bins and the survivors play out an unending loveless travesty of parental-filial bonds.

This may in part account for the sharply negative reaction to the play by critics who had admired Beckett's previous writing. Vivian Mercier was an early Beckett enthusiast, but *Endgame* so 'turned me against his work' that he wrote nothing more about Beckett for a period of twelve years. Mercier explains that there were personal reasons why the play was so distressing to him – his wife had been recently diagnosed with multiple sclerosis – but he is still forthright in his denunciation of it: 'I loathe the play and wonder whether the ability to make one's audience suffer is a valid artistic criterion.'[29] Kenneth Tynan, who had championed the cause of *Waiting for Godot* as a theatre critic, also reacted against *Endgame*. In his review of the premiere of *Fin de partie*, staged at the Royal Court in 1957, he protested against the relentlessness of the work: 'For a short while, I am prepared to listen in any theatre to any message, however antipathetic. But when it is not only disagreeable but forced down my throat, I demur.'[30]

Endgame is a deeply antihumanist work, and it is this 'philosophy of despair' to which both Mercier and Tynan objected so sharply. Clov's major concluding speech turns a cold eye on all the normal sources of human comfort, extinguishing them one by one.

> They said to me, That's friendship, yes yes, no question, you've found it. They said to me, Here's the place, stop, raise your head and look at all that beauty. That order! They said to me, Come now, you're not a brute beast, think upon these things and you'll see how all becomes clear. And simple! They said to me, What skilled attention they get, all these dying of their wounds. (Beckett, 131–32)

But the form that the play's despair takes is significant. Many of the plays in this book – almost all of them – dramatise dysfunctional families. However, the very term implies the norm of a functional family by which we judge its failure. Even in the ruins of the doll's house, Torvald Helmer can still hope for the 'miracle of miracles' that Nora has said might allow them to create a real marriage. But for Nagg and Nell, Hamm and Clov, there can be no alternative to the reduced, anguished, unillumined lives they lead. And insofar as these people in the 'refuge' stand in for all that remains of humankind, they challenge the very idea of a functioning family at home.

Irishing *Endgame*

Fin de partie is a forbidding play, incarcerating its audience in the dim living space of the four characters, a terminally attenuated home on the stage. Its impact derives, in Beckett's much quoted phrase, from 'the power of the text to claw'.[31] When the playwright translated it, he hardly lightened the English text. Indeed, he cut back on the description of the boy viewed by Clov near the end who might be read as a representation of continuing life without.[32] But he did add to the language a degree of colour in the occasional Hiberno-English phrasing that made it possible to give to the action a local habitation if not a name. I want here to look at the effect of this Irish dimension to English-language productions of the play and how it affects the perception of its stage space.

Beckett was willing, where he thought it appropriate, to write a fully developed and consistent Irish English dialogue. This is most obviously true of *All That Fall*, his first radio play, in which he meticulously re-creates the conditions of the Dublin suburb of his youth, 1920s Foxrock. It is in one sense his most representational play, even as it parodically mocks the medium of representation itself. Class structure is precisely observed in the different register of the middle-class Rooneys and the likes of the carter Christy, who tries unsuccessfully to interest Maddy in a load of 'stydung'. 'Yep wiyya to hell owwa that', is Beckett's rendering in Dublinese of Christy's effort to urge on his jennet – 'Get up with you to hell out of that' (Beckett, 173). By contrast, the genteel voices of Protestant South County Dublin are rendered in all their mincing formality.

Even more striking, because quite arbitrary, was Beckett's decision to render Robert Pinget's radio play *La manivelle* into Hiberno-English. The language used as the two old men remember and misremember their youth from before the First World War is very much the stage Irish popularised by O'Casey. At times, Beckett even borrows catchphrases from O'Casey characters: a 'darling name' from Joxer in *Juno and the Paycock*, 'going beyond the beyonds' from Fluther in *The Plough and the Stars* (Beckett, 338, 341). The unpunctuated flow of talk is there in Pinget's French, but Beckett constantly adds idiosyncratic Irish speech mannerisms that have no equivalent in the French. 'Ah maladroit que je suis' becomes 'Ah what ails me all bloody thumbs.'[33] The older, lower-class Gorman accepts correction from his superior Cream about his memory of using a rubber watering hose back in the warm summer of 1895: 'mais c'est vrai, c'est vrai pour l'arrosage vous avez raison, bien sûr qu'est-ce que je dis avec mon caoutchouc, nous n'avions pas l'eau courante à l'époque, ou est-ce qu'on l'avait' ['but true for you the watering you're right there, me and me hose how are you when we had no running water at the time or had we'].[34] This sort of pastiche stage Irish language, upping the ante of colloquialism, is maintained all the way through the text.

That was not Beckett's normal practice in relation to the translation of his own texts. He was quite prepared to let Irishisms into his English, but not as any sort of consistent medium. So, for instance, in *Waiting for Godot*, there are a handful of identifiably Irish words or expressions: 'blathering', 'what ails him?', 'cod' ('fool'), 'banjaxed' ('destroyed') (Beckett, 11, 24, 30, 72).[35] But much of the language of Vladimir and Estragon is formal English, and some of it retains a Gallicist strangeness from the literalness of the self-translation. It is a similar pattern of an occasional Irish colouring to the dialogue in *Endgame*. When Nagg cries insistently for 'Me pap', and later 'Me sugar-plum', it could perhaps be taken as second-childhood baby talk or the Irish pronunciation of 'my': compare Gorman's 'me and me hose' (Beckett, 96, 118–19). But the wit of the exchange between Hamm and Clov – 'You're a bit of all right, aren't you?' / 'A smithereen' (Beckett, 97) – depends on the way the standard

English colloquialism is literalised with the countering Irish word. Hamm's irritable enquiry as to what Nell is saying, 'Qu'est-ce qu'elle raconte?' is rendered as 'What's she blathering about?' (*Fin de partie*, 39; Beckett, 103). Clov ironically responds to a time before he was 'in the land of the living' with the nostalgic piety of Irish speech, 'God be with the days!', in French, 'La belle époque!' (Beckett, 114; *Fin de partie*, 63). But none of this makes the characters clearly Irish any more than the odd Hiberno-English turn of phrase in *Godot* turns Didi and Gogo into Irish tramps.

The Irishing of *Endgame* really began with the casting of Patrick Magee and Jack McGowran as Hamm and Clov in the 1964 Royal Court production in London – Magee and McGowran, who were by then among Beckett's favourite actors. McGowran had already played Clov in the 1958 London premiere of the English-language version of the play, in a double bill with *Krapp's Last Tape*, which Beckett had written specifically for Magee. The two had played together in *The Old Tune*, Beckett's version of Pinget's *La manivelle*, broadcast by the BBC in 1960. The Irishness of the actors in the 1964 production made the play more accessible because recognisable: 'These two players [Magee and McGowran] really seem to understand their author, and that makes it much easier for us. Master and servant, father and son, their interdependence veers constantly between love and hate in a richly Irish idiom.'[36] 'Despite its universal application, this work by an Irishman sounded, naturally enough, like the voice of Erin raised once more in complaint and lamentation.'[37]

The ethnic origins of the principal actors were again picked out for comment in the 1976 Royal Court production, where Patrick Magee was joined by Stephen Rea as Clov. It seems likely, in fact, that Rea – who had just begun to make a name for himself with his performance as Christy Mahon in the contemporaneous National Theatre *Playboy of the Western World* – might have been cast specifically because of his Irishness. Certainly this is what reviewers saw in it. Michael Billington spoke of the superb acting of Magee and Rea, 'their undoubted Irishness underlining the sense of a family relationship'.[38] John Barber echoed this with his comment that 'much of the poetry, and the ironic gaiety, is due to the Irish lilt in the voices of Patrick Magee and Stephen Rea'.[39] But it was the *Daily Mail* review that brought out most crudely the essentialist reading of the actors' nationality: 'Between [Magee and Rea] they prove what a musical advantage it is to hear Beckett played in the original Irish. Stephen Rae [sic] even *stands* in an unmistakable Irish way. His jaw hangs loose in that melancholy line that only Irish jaws can assume' (Figure 6.1).[40]

Figure 6.1   Patrick Magee (Hamm) and Stephen Rea (Clov) in *Endgame*, Royal Court
Theatre, London, 1976.

Other London productions have added a comparable Irish dimension, as in the 2009 Theatre de Complicité staging at the Duchess Theatre, where Tom Hickey as Nagg and Miriam Margolyes as Nell were played with strong Irish accents and Hickey, wakened from sleep to listen to Hamm's story, was heard to mutter to himself an Irish-language version of the Lord's Prayer.[41] But the version that most fully domesticated the play to an Irish setting was the film of the play made in 2000 for the *Beckett on Film* project.[42] It was directed by the playwright Conor McPherson, very much in his own realistic style. Michael Gambon as Hamm, sitting with yellowed teeth in a dirty old dressing gown, spoke in an educated Dublin voice that hardly needed to be raised to impose its sadistic control over Clov. The English actor David Thewlis played a scrawny Clov with an Irish accent discernibly downmarket from Hamm's. Charles Simon and Jean Anderson, both of them actually over ninety at the time of filming, were a convincingly aged Nagg and Nell.

The acting, the costuming and the setting all helped to naturalise the play. The rhythm of a day in the life was enforced by the progressive changes in Clov's clothes. He appeared first in pyjamas and cardigan; later he had got into trousers with braces and, later again, a shirt and waistcoat. His last entrance, in his overcoat dressed for departure, was thus a visually logical last stage. The room itself, with its high six-paned windows at the back and discoloured wallpapered walls with chipped plaster at the corners, gave the impression of a derelict attic. In the right-hand corner, a set of steps protected by a rickety wooden bannister led down to Clov's kitchen, from where clanks preparatory to Clov's laboured appearance could be heard when Hamm whistled. A soundscape supported the impression of an external world matching the realised interior. A high wind could be heard from outside throughout the film, and when Clov looked out the window on the sea side, there was the clang of a bell as if from a buoy. In this *Endgame*, the refuge might plausibly be imagined as the top story of some old house looking out over Dublin Bay, with Hamm and his entourage its last denizens.

Such a naturalisation of *Endgame* may stand at the opposite extreme from the style of the original production of *Fin de partie*. Roger Blin, who directed and played Hamm, emphasised the mythic dimension to the play: 'I slanted Hamm toward King Lear. From set designer Jacques Noel I asked an armchair evoking a Gothic cathedral, a bathrobe of crimson velvet with strips of fur, and a sceptre like a gaff for Hamm.'[43] By contrast with such distancing stylisation, to be able to identify the characters and the scene as Irish is to make it at least in some sort familiar. To see Hamm and Clov played by Patrick Magee and Stephen Rea was to 'hear Beckett played in the original Irish', 'their undoubted Irishness underlining the sense of a family relationship'. The placeless space of the refuge is relocated and becomes something much more like an identifiable domestic interior in the Conor McPherson film. This might be construed as a return to stock, making of Beckett's estranged theatrical image a recognisable dwelling. But it is in line with Beckett's own progressive naturalisation of the play and perhaps even with a general itch for location of actors, directors and audience faced with a room on the stage.

Endgame has the last fully represented living space in Beckett's theatre.[44] Krapp appears in his writer's den in *Krapp's Last Tape*, but all an audience can see is the area illumined by the light over the table with the tape recorder. Thereafter, as the Beckettian characters can move less and less, there is an equivalent restriction in the stage space available to them. And, minimally explained as the situation in *Endgame* is, it is more accounted for than anything later on. Nagg and Nell are legless in bins because they lost their shanks in a cycling accident in the Ardennes. No reason is given why Winnie should be buried in the mound in *Happy Days*, why M, W1 and W2 in *Play* should appear as heads in urns. As bodies in later Beckett drama are reduced to body parts or restricted to mechanically repeated actions, they are afforded no theatrically supporting environment. After *Endgame* there is no place in Beckett's theatre for characters to be, much less to go.

Beckett's drama in the middle of the twentieth century changed everything and changed nothing. He revealed all that theatre could do without: conventionally causal plot and narrative, motivated characters, representational space onstage. But no playwright could actually follow where he led, insofar as his practice pushed towards silence and a purity of image that approached the status of art installation rather than the action from which drama takes its name. Dramatists after Beckett might imitate his irrationalism, his non sequiturs of speech and movement, his surreal situations, but by his standards their plays were fleshed out in representation, with recognisable story arcs. Among the traditional attributes of theatre that returned in spite of Beckett's radical deconstruction were realised living spaces. This is clearest in Harold Pinter, Beckett's most direct heir in the English-speaking theatre, strikingly so in *The Homecoming*, the subject of the next chapter.

CHAPTER 7

The Homecoming: *men's room*

For Harold Pinter, a generation younger than Beckett, the discovery of the writer came like a revelation. Reading an extract of *Watt* and then *Murphy*, he said, 'I suddenly felt that what his writing was doing was walking through a mirror into the other side of the world which was, in fact, the real world.'[1] He went with excited anticipation to see *Waiting for Godot* in its first English-language production in London in 1955.[2] The impact of that experience is obvious in one of Pinter's own first plays, *The Dumb Waiter* (written in 1957). The whole of its single act is taken up with two men waiting in a basement in a state of uncertainty. Ben, like Beckett's Vladimir, seems more sure of himself; Gus, the Estragon of the partnership, needs repeatedly to be reminded of where they are and what they are there for. There is an unseen person called Wilson who may or may not appear – and in fact, he does not show up. However, a plausible explanation for Ben and Gus's situation emerges soon enough. They are hired killers who lurk in the basement to murder their target, who will be lured there by Wilson, their boss. Gus is drilled by Ben through the accustomed routine for the killing. And the play's climactic ending comes when Gus himself turns out to be the target. *The Dumb Waiter* is Beckett crossed with film noir.

The basement in which Ben and Gus hang out waiting to do their job is carefully and realistically set up, with its door off left leading to a kitchen and a lavatory with an annoyingly delayed flush, a door right from which the murder victim is to enter. The conversation is convincingly banal, Ben engrossed in his newspaper, Gus trying to distract him with talk of cricket or football, fidgeting around with the biscuits he has brought with him, preparing to make tea. Inexplicable abnormality enters the play only when an envelope containing matches is slid under the door at the right, and subsequently bizarre orders for food start to descend through the dumb-waiter, a ghostly revival of the days when the building used to be a restaurant, the basement its kitchen. The apparently stable, sordid environment in which two hit men await their assignment acquires a life of its own, animating the stage space as though with an alien invading force.

This was to be the strategy for several of Pinter's early plays. In *The Room* (1957), the talkative Rose ministers to her entirely silent husband Bert; their room, like the cooked breakfast she serves him, provides comfort and warmth and security. As Rose says repeatedly, '[T]his room's all right for me. I mean, you know where you are.'[3] In this it is contrasted with the basement with its running walls: 'Those walls would have finished you off. I don't know who lives down there now. Whoever it is, they're taking a big chance. Maybe they're foreigners' (Pinter, 1, 87). Below the safety of the contained living space of the room, there is estrangement and danger. But Rose's confidence in the security of the room is disturbed by visits from the landlord Mr Kidd, who does not seem to know how many floors there are in his own house, and Mr and Mrs Sands, the couple in search of accommodation who have been told by a man in the basement that Rose and Bert's room is vacant. Finally, up from the basement comes the 'blind Negro' Riley, who has insisted on seeing Rose alone, greets her as Sal and brings a message from her father asking her to come home. The play ends with Bert returning transformed into a masterful and aggressive personality and beating Riley up. The identities that have seemed fixed within the ordinariness of the room are undermined with an accompanying destabilisation of the spaces around it.

In *The Birthday Party* (1958), as in *The Room*, the familiar living accommodation is presided over by the overmothering woman. The all but infantilised husband Petey accepts the nurturing care of Meg, the seaside boarding-house landlady, while the lone lodger Stanley resists it, but all three appear to live within a settled routine. The arrival of the unexplained Goldberg and McCann turns the action into a catch-as-catch can struggle between the men, culminating in the Walpurgisnacht games of the birthday party. Hunted by his predatory captors, Stanley can deflect the violence launched at him only by assaulting the women, trying to rape Lulu and strangle Meg. By Act III, the balances of male power have shifted: Stanley has been lobotomised into conformism and will be shipped in a van to be 'cared for' by the mysterious unseen Monty; the previously dominant Goldberg needs to have his confidence reflated by his erstwhile sidekick McCann; and it is only the quiescent Petey who registers a feeble and ultimately vain protest at what is taking place. Pinter excluded women altogether from *The Caretaker* (1960); his three-handed cat-and-mouse game between Davies, Aston and Mick is an all-masculine battle for territory from the start. In that play, the room, with its surreal collection of objects, is no longer a normative marital space but somewhere between a refuge and a treasure trove, with the men fighting over who has ownership or rights of occupancy there.

Throughout this early work, Pinter established his characteristic configuration of setting and theme: the confined space of the room with its unstable surroundings, the infiltration of the banal by the bizarre, territorial gender dynamics. Writing in the late 1950s, he was soon seen as one of the Anglophone followers of the postwar European avant-garde, included by Martin Esslin in his expanded edition of *The Theatre of the Absurd* as one of the 'proselytes' of Beckett, Eugène Ionesco and Jean Genet.[4] Yet the differences between Pinter and Beckett are obvious and readily understandable. Beckett emerged from the heady experimentalism of 1930s European modernism and came late to the drama. His first two completed plays, *Eleutheria* and *Waiting for Godot*, were written largely as an escape from the concentrated creative effort of composing his great, dense trilogy of novels. Pinter, by contrast, was a professional actor who had played in countless major and minor repertory roles in Ireland and in Britain. Though he had written Dylan Thomasish poems and an autobiographical novel, his theatrical background made drama his most obvious medium, and a drama at least initially approximating to the play situations he knew so well from the commercial theatre. All of his plays, like none of Beckett's, begin with what looks like a familiar setting, what appears to be a conventional action, and move on from there. In *The Homecoming* (1965), he approached still closer to a stock subject with the return of a long-absent son and brother to the family home. The aim of this chapter is to consider what becomes of the image of the home and family poised, as it is in Pinter, between traditional naturalism and the more radical defamiliarisation of Beckett.

A house in north London

The earliest extant draft of *The Homecoming* is a brief manuscript dialogue between A and B, prototypes of Teddy and Ruth, consisting of edgy exchanges over who will go to bed first.[5] In an extended typescript version of this, they are joined by C, already very obviously Lenny, who propositions B in A's absence in a conversation that includes the substance of the two stories of his violence against women, his beating up the diseased whore and his abandoned attempt to help the old lady with the immovable mangle (though in this version of the latter he does not actually hit her).[6] The unlocated dialogue appears to take place in A's house, where C is hiding out, having been taken in as 'a man at the end of his tether', sounding in C's account like Stanley escaped from *The Birthday Party*: 'I was picked up last week and brought here in a closed car. As I was on the run at the time I thought I had come to the end of the line. But it wasnt the case.'[7] A and B are lovers; according to B in conversation with C, they have just come back from their honeymoon in Venice, but A suggests that B is actually married to someone else and has been in Venice with her husband. From A's strong assertion that 'there's nothing homosexual' in his relationship with C, it is to be suspected that there is.[8] The dance of sexual relations that Pinter planned is suggested by a manuscript schema at the end of the typescript:

Jealousy
A of B & C
C of B & A
B of A & C[9]

This was the sort of drama Pinter had already created in *The Collection*, his 1961 television play in which the four characters, three men and a woman, offer their alternative, evidently unreliable, versions of their sexual relationships. It was to be perfected in the triangulated Jamesian manoeuvres of *Betrayal* (1980).

Between these early fragments and the first complete draft, the initially planned play of sexual desire came to be housed in a family and a local habitation. Michael Billington in his critical biography of Pinter established the facts out of which the dramatic situation was imagined. Morris Wernick, one of the very close group of friends Pinter had known from school days at Hackney Downs Grammar School, explained in a letter to Billington:

> I married in 1956 and left immediately to start life in Canada. I never told my father that I was married and for the next ten years continued to keep up this 'pretence' even on my infrequent visits to England. [. . .] [I]n 1964 I brought my whole family to England where my father met his daughter-in-law and grandchildren. I do not need to tell you that it was one of the memorable moments in my life.

Wernick concealed his marriage because his wife was Gentile and, because of the matrilinear principles of Judaism, this was an especially feared form of marrying 'out', as Pinter elucidated. 'For a Jewish man to bring back a *shiksa* was in those days a dread thing to do. I heard later that one or two people I knew at school had done so. Their families considered them to be dead.'[10] Other details were apparently taken from Wernick's family situation as well: he was one of three brothers, he had an uncle who was a cab driver and another of Pinter's friends claimed that Max in the play was a 'dead ringer' for Wernick's father.[11]

In the first full draft of the play, Pinter included some details to indicate that the family were Jewish. The father's close friend at that stage was not MacGregor but Berkowitz; Lenny, on a night out with his friends, eats the distinctively Jewish dish of chopped liver, and tells Susan (the Ruth figure) that he would have drink in the house for 'a celebration, you know, a barmitzvah or something like that'.[12] All of these specifying details Pinter was to remove from the final text, and he himself maintained that 'it wasn't a play about Jewish society. The fact that it makes sense in all sorts of languages and communities not remotely Jewish bears that out.'[13] And it is certainly striking that, even in the first draft, the goyishness of the daughter-in-law is never even mentioned. When Teddy and Susan appear downstairs in the morning, Max (still only an unnamed 'Father') attacks her as a 'lousy tart' and 'a filthy scrubber off the street', disregarding Teddy's insistence that they are married; Teddy never gets as far as confessing that she is Gentile.[14]

The removal of the specifying particulars in Pinter's play can be compared with the 'undoing' or 'vaguening' undergone by Beckett's texts in the process of composition, the situation of *Endgame* changing from a ruined house in the Ardennes after World War I to its final unlocated 'refuge'. But the results, in terms of the stage situations in the completed plays, are in fact quite different. The grey emptiness of *Endgame*, with its two high windows looking out on nothing, gives no clue as to where it is or what it signifies. The 'house in North London', by contrast, is exactly what it says it is. Outside Beckett's refuge, life is apparently extinct. The characters who come and go from the house in Pinter, by contrast, move through a network of city landmarks. Sam, the chauffeur, tells anyone who will listen about his day driving a customer around.

> Picked him up at the Savoy at half past twelve, took him to the Caprice for his lunch. After lunch I picked him up again, took him down to a house in Eaton Square – he had to pay a visit to a friend there – and then round about tea-time I took him right the way out to the Airport. (Pinter, III, 20)

Due to Sam's collapse at the end of Act II, Teddy will not have the benefit of his uncle driving him to London airport – 'right up the M4' (Pinter, III, 19). When Teddy says, 'I'll just go up the road to the Underground', Max is on hand with the standard Londoner's offer of alternative routes: 'Listen, if you just go the other way, first left, first right, you remember, you might find a cab passing there. [. . .] Or you can take the tube to Piccadilly Circus, won't take you ten minutes, and pick up a cab from there out to the Airport' (Pinter, iii, 87).[15]

Pinter's stage spaces were from the first realistically conceived. But in *The Room* and *The Dumb Waiter*, their solid familiarity was disturbed by the apparent instability of the surroundings. The environments of *The Birthday Party* and *The Caretaker* are less disorienting, and in *The Homecoming* the setting is thoroughly naturalised. In terms of the representation of home on the stage, in fact, it could be seen as something of a return to the older conventions of naturalism. Williams and Miller in plays such as *Streetcar* and *Death of a Salesman* had developed a flexible dramaturgy in which the stage space could represent simultaneously family accommodation, states of mind and urban living conditions. Pinter, however, disliked 'composite sets' with 'cut-away wall, staircases, screens, and front doors'. According to John Bury, the designer of the first production of *The Homecoming*, the knocked-through wall was a device to naturalise what was in fact a composite set, where you could see 'the hall, the front door, and the staircase', by turning it into a 'single living area'. The design therefore featured the brick pillars and supported rigid steel girder that such a conversion would have demanded, on Pinter's instructions deliberately softened so as to make it less obvious, though 'you could see the steelwork and the difference of texture between the two piers as being whitewashed brick as opposed to wallpaper in the rest of the house'.[16]

Harold Bloom called Pinter 'the legitimate son of Samuel Beckett', but the differences between the two are at least as important as the perceived creative filiation.[17] The underpinning of Beckett's drama is existential and philosophical, however little he countenanced its interpretation in these terms. Pinter's dramatic focus, following the empiricist bent within the Anglophone theatrical tradition, is essentially social and psychological. His characters in *The Homecoming* may not be specifically Jewish or Gentile, but they are otherwise immediately recognisable: Max, the retired butcher; Sam, the former cabbie turned private chauffeur; Joey, the trainee boxer with his day job in demolition; Lenny (rather implausibly a milkman in the first draft) driving an Alfa Romeo on the earnings of the prostitutes he runs in Soho. Martin Esslin was prepared to argue for 'the validity of the play as a realistic and perfectly explicable series of events as they could, in fact, happen to a family living in the circumstances outlined and clearly indicated by the author'. Max and MacGregor could have been 'members of the London half-world of pimps and gangsters'; the dead wife Jessie a whore; Ruth, as a former nude photographic model, 'a prostitute or near-prostitute when she first met Teddy'.[18] Such a hypothesis involves a good deal of speculative reconstruction of the backstories of the characters that Pinter deliberately leaves out. But the very fact that it can be offered, whether convincingly or not, suggests how different these figures are from the Beckettian grotesques, Hamm and Clov, Nagg and Nell. There is nothing inherently strange about Pinter's characters in *The Homecoming* but their unexplained and unmotivated behaviour.

Stripping down the family

The relentlessly dark image of humanity in *Endgame* repelled even some of Beckett's champions, and it took quite a time for it to make its way theatrically in spite of the fame of *Waiting for Godot*. There was some outrage at *The Homecoming*, especially in its try-out performances, where audiences walked out or booed. But, when the Royal Shakespeare Company production opened in London, on the whole the reaction was one of bewildered puzzlement at the unaccountable actions of the characters. 'The thing is perfectly turned', remarked Philip Hope-Wallace, 'but to what end?' He went on to contrast the normal principles of dramatic irony, by which the audience knows more than the characters onstage. 'In Pinter it is the other way up. It is *we* who are in total ignorance: the actors who are exchanging wreathed smiles and knowing nods of complicity.'[19] The arbitrariness of Ruth's behaviour in Act II was attributed to the peculiarity of the family by the *Times* reviewer. 'The play sets out to present a close family unit but no such unit takes shape. And as a result there is no motive for the wife's action. She is not succumbing to the gravitational pull of the household but merely choosing, for no reason, to stay there.'[20] Harold Hobson, lone champion of the execrated first production of *The Birthday Party*, found *The Homecoming* disturbing: 'I am troubled by the complete absence from the play of any moral comment whatsoever. [...] [W]e have no idea what Mr Pinter thinks about Ruth or Teddy, or what value their existence has.'[21] The emotional vacuum of the play, the amoral detachment from the action and the strangeness of the family's behaviour have remained the talking points in most subsequent interpretations of *The Homecoming*.

There can be no doubt that the apparent lack of motivation and reaction in the characters was a deliberately chosen effect in the play. So, for example, there is a long speech by Teddy in Act II in which he tells his family how incomprehensible they would find his philosophical writings:

'You wouldn't understand my works. You wouldn't have the faintest idea of what they were about' (Pinter, III, 69–70). In the typescript first draft, there were interspersed directions indicating tone and mood: 'breathless', 'hoarse', 'feverishly'.[22] In the final text, there is none of this, but instead the breaks of ellipsis dots are used to register the breakdown in Teddy's struggle to maintain some sort of illusion of superiority: 'Might do you good … have a look at them … see how certain people can view … things … how certain people can maintain … intellectual equilibrium' (Pinter, III, 70). Similarly, in the first draft, when Wally (Max) and Lenny have first broached the idea of keeping Susan (Ruth) and putting her on the game, Teddy's response to Wally's taunt is significant:

> Wal – [. . .] What do you think, Teddy,? That'll solve all our problems.
> Ted – Yes. (clenching eyes) Yes, it would.[23]

In the final text, there is no such explicit indication of the pain that Teddy may be enduring in hearing his wife's future treated in this way.

Paul Rogers, who played Max in the first production, considered that the apparent impassiveness was part of the game the family play with one another: 'The rules of this game are that nobody ever shows a blow actually register.'[24] Lack of demonstrativeness is certainly part of the cool attitude that the family members adopt with one another. This is the first encounter of Lenny and Teddy, meeting unexpectedly late at night after six years:

TEDDY. Hullo, Lenny.
LENNY. Hullo, Teddy.
Pause.
TEDDY. I didn't hear you come down the stairs.
LENNY. I didn't.
(Pinter, III, 33).

Pinter's famously pregnant 'pauses', calibrated against the longer 'silences' and the slightly shorter ellipses, must imply the weight of what the characters may be feeling, while the surface of speech remains flat and toneless.

The lack of emotional colouring in so much of the characters' dialogue was echoed in the stage setting and costuming in the original production. The bareness and emptiness of the set was remarked on by many of the reviewers. 'The family inhabits a vault of a living-room, all blacks and bleached greys with a vast beam dividing the back wall and a high, thin, flight of stairs beyond.'[25] The world of the play, according to J.C. Trewin, was 'a vast, chilly, grey room [. . .] the sort of place, sparsely furnished, a chair islanded here, another there, that is clearly a Pinter creation [. . .] Just out of sight is a front door. Before us a stair leads upward. But the entire world is confined to this room.'²⁶ For Paul Rogers, the set was expressive of the all-male household in the wake of Jessie's death. '[T]hey'd thrown out all her rubbishy bits of furniture':

> [T]hey made it so that no woman would live there. They knocked down that wall to make one big room. It looks like a waiting room. That's the way they like it, clear and masculine, like a butcher's shop.²⁷

The domestic space is cleared of all merely incidental appurtenances, to provide an arena of combat for the main action of the play.

The 1973 film version very closely follows the original stage production, and its austere monochrome set is reflected also in the costuming.²⁸ All the men in the opening scene wear shades of grey and black. Max in his grey cardigan and (never removed) cap, with dirty plimsolls, sits in an uncovered upholstered armchair with grey patterning. Lenny is seen in a dark suit, relieved only by a maroon tie, on a black leather sofa. These are his signature colours: when preparing to go out, he puts on a three-quarter-length black leather jacket, and in the late-night scene with Teddy and then Ruth, he appears in a patterned maroon dressing gown. Sam, as befitted his chauffeur's role, wears a neutral suit, while Joey shuffles about in a grey jersey with holes in the back. The status of Teddy and Ruth as visitors from elsewhere, when they first enter, is marked by their light white overcoats, the overcoat in which Teddy will finally exit back to America. When Ruth comes downstairs in the morning, she is wearing a black dressing gown with flowers picked out on the back. Whether or not this was an indication that she had gone over to Lenny's dark side, the use of a very restricted range of colour throughout was no doubt intended to accentuate the starkness of the action.

In the stripped-down domestic space of the all-male household, the power dynamics are all the more perceptible. The stage directions specify that the play should open with the dark-suited Lenny sitting on the sofa studying the racing form in the newspaper. 'Max comes in, from the direction of the kitchen. [. . .] He wears an old cardigan and a cap, and carries a stick.' Even the form of his first question is accusatory: 'What have you done with the scissors?' Lenny's studied silence in the face of his father's demands for a response, like his wilful misunderstanding –

MAX. [. . .] I want to cut something out of the paper.
LENNY. I'm reading the paper.
MAX. Not that paper. I haven't even read that paper. I'm talking about last Sunday's paper.

– is a declaration of unmoved ascendancy. He does not even have to raise his voice when he contemptuously turns on Max: 'Why don't you shut up, you daft prat?', and the impotence of Max's gesture of lifting his stick and threatening his son is emphasised when it is followed by him sitting down in the armchair and asking Lenny for a cigarette (Pinter, III, 15–16). The retired father, with his cap, cardigan and stick, has to yield to the son who is still out working, up to date with the current news, not relegated to catching up with last Sunday's paper in the back kitchen.

Max comes in from the direction of that kitchen, looking for the scissors to cut out an advertisement for 'flannel vests' (Pinter, III, 16). In the all-masculine household, some of the men have to take on traditionally female roles and occupy spaces such as the kitchen, while Lenny, the alpha male, dominates the living room at the front of the house. Max's position as cook is another occasion for needling abuse by his son.

LENNY. Dad, do you mind if I change the subject?
Pause.
I want to ask you something. The dinner we had before, what was the name of it? What do you call it?
Pause.
Why don't you buy a dog? You're a dog cook. Honest. You think you're cooking
        for a lot of dogs.
(Pinter, III, 18–19)

Not only is Max feminised by having to take on the woman's function as cook, but he is a rotten, inept cook, inadequate thus both as father and mother.

In his initial idea for the play, Pinter seems to have had in mind the geometry of the sexual triangle, the permutations of jealousy and desire between his three characters, A, B and C. In *The Homecoming*, this is transferred to the changing configurations of power between the men. The vectors of force in the scene between Lenny and Max are altered by the entrance of Sam. Sam, as the weak brother, is a target on whom Max can lay off the aggression he has been unable to resist from his son. Sam is twitted with his inability to get a wife: 'It's funny you never got married, isn't it? A man with all your gifts' (Pinter, III, 22). He is mocked by an imagination of his finally getting a partner at the age of sixty-three, with the suggestion that he would not be able to satisfy her without help from the other men of the house:

> When you find the right girl, Sam, let your family know, don't forget, we'll give you a number one send-off, I promise you. You can bring her to live

here, she keep us all happy. We's take it in turns to give her a walk around the park. (Pinter, iii, 23)

Sam can get back at Max only by sly counterinsinuations. When accused of 'having a good bang on the back seat' of his car, he hints, 'I leave that to others', a hit that evidently finds its mark from Max's angry reaction: 'What others? You paralysed prat!' (Pinter, iii, 23). Meanwhile, Lenny draws his uncle out, asking him details of his day's work, with a tone somewhere between ironic mockery and a studied courtesy, in marked contrast to his brutal curtness with his father. In the men's manoeuvring for position, Sam, the generally despised gamma male, can still be useful as a shield for Lenny in his war with Max.

In the war games of the family, Joey, the all but brain dead wannabe boxer, is too insignificant a figure to offer any real threat. He is seldom attacked by the others, though Max can keep his hand in, so to speak, by the occasional malicious putdown:

> I'll tell you what you've got to do. What you've got to do is you've got to learn how to defend yourself, and you've got to learn how to attack. That's your only trouble as a boxer. You don't know how to defend yourself, and you don't know how to attack. (Pinter, iii, 25)

A much more significant character in the configuration of conflict is the dead MacGregor. He features as Max's supersibling, the brother Sam never was. 'We took you into the butcher's shop', Max reminds Sam, 'you couldn't even sweep the dust off the floor. We took MacGregor into the shop, he could run the place by the end of a week' (Pinter, iii, 47). In Max's tough guy reminiscences of his time with his friend MacGregor, it is he himself who features as the sidekick:

> We were two of the worst hated men in the West End of London. I tell you, I still got the scars. We'd walk into a place, the whole room'd stand up, they'd make way to let us pass. You never heard such silence. Mind you, he was a big man, he was over six foot tall. (Pinter, iii, 16)

The silence and awe, we may take it, were due to MacGregor the six-footer; if Max had been so feared, how come he, rather than his opponents, has the scars? And yet, long before Sam makes his final dramatic revelation – 'MacGregor had Jessie in the back of my cab as I drove them along' (Pinter, iii, 86) – MacGregor's betrayal of Max has been heavily trailed. Sam hints as much when reminding Max how he, Sam, looked after Jessie when Max was busy: 'You wouldn't have trusted any of your other brothers. You wouldn't have trusted Mac, would you? But you trusted me. I want to remind you' (Pinter, III, 26). But the posthumous reputation of Mac, alter ego of Max, is proof even against Sam's denunciation of his infidelity, which is dismissed as a product of Sam's 'diseased imagination' (Pinter, III, 86). It may be that MacGregor's cuckolding of Max (though denied here) makes him all the more a man in Max's eyes.

Violent aggression in Pinter's language appears as a turbid eddy in a surface of casual, all but meaningless dialogue. One example comes, significantly, immediately after Sam's reflection on how Max trusted him with Jessie, where he would not have trusted Mac:

> Old Mac died a few years, ago, didn't he? Isn't he dead?
> *Pause*
> He was a lousy stinking rotten loudmouth. A bastard uncouth sodding runt. Mind you, he was a good friend of yours. (Pinter, III, 26)

The obscene insults come sandwiched between the mock casual enquiry, as of a passing acquaintance, 'Isn't he dead?', and the conciliatory gesture, '[H]e was a good friend of yours.' This exactly matches Max's own comments about Jessie in his opening scene with Lenny.

> He was very fond of your mother, Mac was. Very fond. He always had a good word for her.
> *Pause*.
> Mind you, she wasn't such a bad woman. Even though it made me sick just to look at her rotten stinking face, she wasn't such a bad bitch. (Pinter, III, 17)

The volcanic eruptions of the language are all the more disconcerting because of the blandly colloquial speech patterns they disrupt. The casual repetitions of 'Very fond', the oral buttonholing 'Mind you' and the tone of sentimental recollection in 'she wasn't such a bad woman' make the equally casual expression of hatred even more unexpected.

By the time of *The Homecoming*, this sort of stylistic switchback was an established Pinter manner, like his other characteristic technique of the long, apparently unmotivated speech that occasionally disrupted the pattern of terse, pause-laden exchanges of banalities. This could take the form of a show of strength, as in Lenny's anecdote about his meeting with the diseased woman in the dock area and his deliberations as to whether he should murder her or not, ending with the pseduocasual conclusion:

> [I]n the end I thought ... Aaah, why go to all the bother ... you know, getting rid of the corpse and all that, getting yourself into a state of tension. So I gave her another belt in the nose and a couple of turns of the boot and sort of left it at that. (Pinter, III, 39)

The playful fantasy element in this extended story is marked near the start by the nonsense nautical language in Lenny's scene setting of the docks: 'I was standing alone under an arch, watching all the men jibbing the boom, out in the harbour, and playing about with a yardarm' (Pinter, III, 38). This is a peacock display for Ruth, not an account of a real incident. Equally, Teddy's long diatribe against his family's inability to understand his philosophical writings already mentioned – 'You wouldn't understand my works' (Pinter, III, 69–70) – in its blustering unreality is an abject revelation of weakness, a claim to some sort of superior vision of things to compensate for his routed defeat.

Banal dialogue that twists towards the absurd, apparently unmotivated monologues, unheralded outbursts of violence, like Max's assault on Joey and Sam – all of these were already part of the Pinter house style by 1965. *The Homecoming*, however, was his first play to feature a full family scene, leaving audiences and critics to wonder what sort of family this was or what was the significance of the men's behaviour. There were those, from the start, who doubted if it had any. '*The Homecoming* undoubtedly works', said Milton Shulman, reviewing the premiere, 'but the nagging doubt remains that this is not drama but a confidence trick.'[29] Bert States, in a 1968 essay, expressed a more thoughtful scepticism. After a bare summary of the play's plot, he commented:

> It would be hard to conceive an action, in modern 'family' terms, which violates so many of our moral scruples with so little effort and so little interest in making itself credible. You may read causes *into* it, but the causes pale beside the facts, like the page of repentance at the end of a dirty book. The whole thing has about it a blatant improbability and artifice which depends not upon our sympathizing, or understanding its origins, but upon our seeing how far it has taken its own possibilities.[30]

Simon Trussler, in his book on the playwright, was much less circumspect in his polemic denunciation of the whole play:

> *The Homecoming* is [...] a modishly intellectualised melodrama, its violence modulated by its vagueness, its emotional stereotyping disguised by carefully planted oddities of juxtaposition and expression. To suspend disbelief in this play is to call a temporary halt to one's humanity.[31]

What all the doubters have suggested, more or less forcefully, is that the stripping down of the family to this group of irrationally warring men amounts to mere theatrical mystification.

Certainly, explanation and interpretation seem called for by the strangeness of the action, and they have not been wanting. Some critics have followed Martin Esslin's lead in looking between the lines for the omitted underplots that might make for plausible motivation. Given MacGregor's affair with Jessie, there is the possibility that one of the sons might have been Mac's rather than Max's. This has led to a sort of 'spot the bastard' game with various votes as to which is the odd son out.[32] There is a suggestive passage in which Max remembers his father: 'He used to come over to me and look down at me. My old man did. He'd bend right over me, then he'd pick me up. I was only that big' (Pinter, III, 27). This could be put together with the invitation to Teddy, '[W]hy don't we have a nice cuddle and kiss, eh? Like the old days?' (Pinter, III, 51) to suggest a pattern of child abuse replicated from generation to generation. Ruth's statement that she came from the neighbourhood – 'I was born quite near here' (Pinter, III, 61) – together with her hesitant remark that 'I was . . . different . . . when I met Teddy . . . first' (Pinter, III, 58) and her memories of being a 'photographic model for the body' (Pinter, III, 65) have lent credence to the widespread view that the play is Ruth's homecoming, a return to the seedy North London milieu from which she came.

Filling in the gaps, however, can only go so far in explaining the unaccountable behaviour of the family in *The Homecoming*. It has been commoner to look for interpretations of the deep structure of the play to make sense of it. So, Martin Esslin, while justifying the plausibility of the story, argues that 'its real, its realistic, action is a metaphor of human desires and aspirations, a myth, a dream image, a projection of archetypal dreams and wishes'. He then offers a psychoanalytic reading in which 'from the sons' point of view [. . .], *The Homecoming* is a dream image of the fulfilment of all Oedipal wishes, the sexual conquest of the mother, the utter humiliation of the father. From the father's point of view the play is the terrifying nightmare of the sons' revenge.'[33] Vera M. Jiji relates this Freudian pattern to a ritualistic interpretation: 'Pinter dramatises the ancient archaic rite of the sacrifice of the ritual king and the mating of the fertility goddess with the new conqueror.'[34] Irving Wardle sees the play in terms of a territorial struggle, drawing upon the study of ethology made popular in the 1960s by Robert Ardrey, Desmond Morris and Konrad Lorenz. 'Ruth's relations with the family consist of extended bargaining: she has sex to offer, they have territory, and in the end they strike a deal.' The play, as a result, becomes a 'ritualised tournament in which the two instincts of sexual desire and territorial aspiration fight it out under the scrutiny of an emasculated observer on the sidelines'.[35]

Pinter in *The Homecoming* created a family stripped of affect, unrestrained by moral scruple, and cleared back the domestic living space into an arena for combat. There were those who reacted sceptically, or indeed indignantly, to this spectacle of value-free family relations. But for those who admired the play, it was the cool denial of traditional beliefs that made it satisfying. The father and three sons, competing for the prize of the one woman, were portrayed as nothing else but the war of all against all. This could be understood as the deep truth of the family in its merciless exposure of the dynamics of power, its uncovering of the shaping form of the Freudian family romance or the approximation of human behaviour in the home to the territorial imperatives of other animals. Structuralist thought, still so fashionable at the time of the play's production, will have lent persuasiveness to this sort of perception. Within such interpretations, however, what produced most moral queasiness and required most justification was the role of Ruth in the play's conclusion. Nora Helmer's declaration that her highest duty was to herself and not to her husband and children, so shocking in 1879, might have been taken as read by the 1960s. Still, Ruth's decision not just to abandon her marital and maternal responsibilities but to stay on with her in-laws, servicing all the men while earning her keep as a sex worker, remained an occasion for bemused disbelief.

The battle over Ruth

In the masculinist ethos of the North London house, feminine occupations and feminine characteristics provide the currency of insult among the men. So Lenny sneers at Max for having to take on the woman's job of family cook, and incompetently at that – 'you're a dog cook' (Pinter, III, 19). Max resents the men's demands for food: 'Who do you think I am, your mother?' (Pinter, III, 24). At the same time, he regards the kitchen as his preserve and is driven mad by Sam's ostentatious clearing up after breakfast: '[H]e's always washing up in there, scraping the plates, driving me out of the kitchen' (Pinter, III, 45). Max's preferred term of abuse is the female 'bitch', even when addressed to men. The unmarried brother Sam is lampooned as passive homosexual rent-boy: 'You'd bend over for half a dollar on Black-friars Bridge' (Pinter, III, 56). At the opposite end of this male/female spectrum is the allegedly promiscuous Joey, who has 'had more dolly than you've had cream cakes' (Pinter, III, 74). In the anecdote that Lenny urges Joey to tell to illustrate his potency, when the two of them, cruising round North Paddington, picked up two girls and 'had them' on a bomb site, Joey has to be reminded of 'the best bit', when he insisted on taking his woman without 'contraceptive protection' (Pinter, III, 75). The rawer the act of sexual penetration, the greater is the male mastery on display.

In this context, emotions stirred by the dead wife and mother Jessie are especially volatile from that first reference to her by Max already quoted: '[S]he wasn't such a bad woman. Even though it made me sick just to look at her rotten, stinking face, she wasn't such a bad bitch' (Pinter, III, 17). In the relaxed postprandial mood of the beginning of Act II, he is in sentimentally reminiscential mode. 'Mind you', he tells Ruth, 'she taught those boys everything they know. She taught them all the morality they know. I'm telling you. Every single bit of the moral code they live by – was taught to them by their mother' (Pinter, III, 53–54). (In the light of the sons' moral code as represented in the play, there has to be some degree of irony here.) This is followed up by an elaborately roseate recollection of a happy evening at home in anticipation of a profitable business deal, bathing his young sons, pampering his wife with the promise of gorgeous clothes. Within minutes, however, the mood has changed and she is 'a slutbitch of a wife' again. Indeed, Max rants that it was he who had to carry all the burden of parenthood down to a grotesque parthenogenetic labour: '[D]on't talk to me about the pain of childbirth – I suffered the pain, I've still got the pangs' (Pinter, III, 55). By contrast with this, Sam speaks of Jessie with protective tenderness and admiration. If he married, he tells Max, he would 'never get a bride like you had, anyway. Nothing like your bride . . . going about these days. Like Jessie. [. . .] She was a charming woman' (Pinter, III, 24). Even if there is an element of needling Max in this, it is characteristic of the less assertive Sam to speak in this chivalrous fashion.

The unstable afterimage of the absent Jessie conditions the reception of Ruth in the play. When she appears downstairs with Teddy in the morning after their unseen arrival the night before, she is met with a stream of vituperative invective by Max. She is a 'dirty tart', a 'smelly scrubber', a 'stinking pox-ridden slut' (Pinter, III, 49). All of his partly repressed hatred and distrust of his dead wife is voiced in Max's denunciation of Ruth. The association of the two is set up in the apparently unintended implications of his attitude of indignant outrage at Teddy: 'I've never had a whore under this roof before. Ever since your mother died' (Pinter, III, 50). But if at breakfast Ruth is greeted as a whore, the first one to be given houseroom since the death of Jessie, by lunchtime she has replaced Jessie as beneficent mother figure, handing round the coffee cups, presiding over the family reunion. Under her warming influence, Max, Teddy, Lenny and Sam light up their cigars in what became an iconic image for both the theatrical production, in which the group appeared 'opening up like a flower', and the symmetrically

Figure 7.1 Michael Jayston (Teddy), Ian Holm (Lenny), Cyril Cusack (Sam) and
Paul Rogers (Max) in *The Homecoming*, film directed by Peter Hall,
American Film Theatre, 1973.

composed shot in the film (Figure 7.1).[36] It is so evocative, not only for
the phallic suggestiveness of the cigars, but for the inturned, intertwined
concentration of the men, not one of whom is facing another. Ruth is
first whore, then mother, before her final transformation into the two
together. When Joey and Max return from the gym to find Lenny
dancing with Ruth, Joey identifies her with a gasp of astonishment:
'Christ, she's wide open. *Pause.* She's a tart' (Pinter, III, 66). While Joey,
having moved in to take Ruth over from Lenny, writhes on the sofa with
her and Lenny caresses her hair, Max compliments Teddy on his choice:
'Mind you, she's a lovely girl. A beautiful woman. And a mother too'
(Pinter, III, 67–68). And it is as full-time *mère de famille* and part-time
professional whore that Ruth is finally invited to stay and serve the family
of men.

And what of Ruth herself in this bewildering sequence of events? From
the start, she is seen to be resistant to the suggestions and projections of the
men, the unmoved mover in the play's swirl of fantasy and desire. When

she comes in first with Teddy, she meets all his conversational openings with blank indifference or a blocking chop-logic:

TEDDY. [...] Shall I go up and see if my room's still there?
RUTH. It can't have moved.
(Pinter, III, 28)

Though she claims to be tired when they first come in, she refuses to go to bed and insists instead on going out for 'a breath of air', taking the key of the house with her. In her unexpected encounter with Lenny on return, she uses stonewalling tactics with equally successful results. His bizarre tale of the lady 'falling apart with the pox' who propositioned him on the docks and whom he considered murdering, evidently intended to shock and impress, elicits only the puncturing query, '[H]ow did you know she was diseased?' (Pinter, III, 39). The manoeuvres over the glass of water represent a chess game of sexual strategy in which Lenny comes off worst:

LENNY. [...] Just give me the glass.
RUTH. No.
Pause.
LENNY. I'll take it, then.
RUTH. If you take the glass ... I'll take you.
(Pinter, III, 42)

The normally unflappable Lenny is seriously ruffled, not to say unmanned, by Ruth's suggestion that he lie down on the floor and let her pour water down his throat. As she exits smiling upstairs, he is left shouting after her: 'What was that supposed to be? Some kind of proposal?' (Pinter, III, 43).

This is Ruth's keynote throughout: imperturbable, contrary, taking charge of situations in which she is supposed to be the passive pawn. She stands unflinching in her dressing gown under the barrage of insults thrown at her by Max at their first meeting. Her polite smiles and social compliments as the men puff on their cigars in the relaxed atmosphere after lunch are practically as noncommittal. She will not assent to Teddy's upbeat vision of their life in America – 'a very stimulating environment', as he calls it (Pinter, III, 58). Her version is anything but stimulating: 'It's all rock. And sand. It stretches ... so far ... everywhere you look' (Pinter, III, 61). She ends her roll around on the floor with Joey abruptly and takes a new imperious tone in her demands of Lenny, as though already very much in charge of the household:

RUTH. I'd like something to eat. (*To Lenny.*) I'd like a drink. Did you get any drink?

LENNY. We've got drink.
RUTH. I'd like one, please.
LENNY. What drink?
RUTH. Whisky.
LENNY. I've got it.
Pause.
RUTH. Well, get it.
(Pinter, III, 68)

Joey, who insisted on unprotected sex with his casual pickup, spends two hours in the bedroom with Ruth, without being able to 'get all the way' (Pinter, III, 74). And, of course, she manages completely to turn the tables on the men when they make their supposedly veiled proposition to her that she should go on the game, by her hard bargaining over terms and conditions: the number of rooms she would require in her flat, a personal maid, the initial outlay of capital to be counted as the men's investment, not a loan to be repaid out of income.

A measure of the unease caused by Ruth's behaviour in *The Homecoming* is the uncharacteristic willingness of Pinter to speak out about her, against his usual policy of refusing to disclose anything about his characters not stated in the play. 'The woman in *The Homecoming*', he told one interviewer, 'is not a nymphomaniac and if she is playing some kind of game she doing it for a very practical reason.'[37] He gave an even fuller defence of Ruth's decision to stay in London on another occasion:

> If this had been a happy marriage it wouldn't have happened. But she didn't want to go back to America with her husband, so what the hell's she going to do? She's misinterpreted deliberately and used by this family. But eventually she comes back at them with a whip. She says, 'If you want to play this game I can play it as well as you'. She does not become a harlot. At the end of the play she's in possession of a certain kind of freedom. She can do what she wants, and it is not at all certain she will go off to Greek Street. But even if she did, she would not be a harlot in her own mind.[38]

This has been taken to be in line with the mood of the first production, 'which was overtly biased in favour of Ruth from playwright to actors and director'.[39] Certainly Peter Hall took pains to blacken Teddy as 'the biggest bastard of the lot [. . .]. I don't think he goes out a defeated man, or a saddened man, or a martyred man. He goes back, in a way, confirmed in the family's hatred of women.'[40]

Following on from Pinter's lead, it has become a commonplace in the interpretation of *The Homecoming* to see the play's ending as a victory for Ruth. Michael Billington, calling it 'an implicitly feminist play', declares:

'[T]he inference to be drawn from the dramatic action and from the concluding image is that by the end Ruth has acquired a new freedom and that women – through strength of will and sexual authority – can achieve their own form of empowerment.' He goes on to cite approvingly Penelope Gilliatt's comment in a review of the play: 'Ruth looks on her body rather as a landlord would look on a corner-site. As soon as she has apparently been exploited sexually she really has the advantage because she owns the property.'[41] The argument here and elsewhere is that Ruth, by taking control of the situation, disproves the men's stereotyping imagination of her and other women. So Elizabeth Sakellaridou maintains that 'by the end of the play she has formed for herself a compact personality, synthesising all the aspects of the female principle, the mother, the wife and the whore'.[42] Drew Milne, however, remains sceptical about this argument that 'Ruth's rational self-determination makes her acquiescence to misogynist structures into a positive image'. 'It is difficult', he remarks, 'to perform Ruth as a positive image of female self-determination, since her power depends on her recognition and confirmation of the misogynist fantasy within which she is forced to perform.'[43] Milne's essay is a challenge to the critical orthodoxy that attributes to Pinter an acceptable sexual politics.

The debate is a significant one from the point of view of the images of home on the stage this book has been exploring. The tradition began with the defiance of the cherished ideology of bourgeois marriage and the family home in Nora's dramatic slam of the door. Through much of the first half of the twentieth century, playwrights in this tradition were concerned with the family and its various forms of dysfunction. Pinter's reduction of the family to a warring tangle of hatreds, needs and desires in *The Homecoming* could be seen as a culminating example of that sceptical anatomy, the heir of Ibsen and Strindberg. Yet as the women's movement and feminist theory continued to develop, male dramatisations of the domestic space necessarily came under suspicion. Thus, with *The Homecoming* it became essential to maintain that the play's grotesque misogyny was the characters' and not the playwright's. The house in North London might well be represented as an arena in which the men fought it out for territorial advantage, with the woman as the feared/hated/desired sexual prize. But the woman who seems simply to accept her role within that system had to be shown to have some degree of agency, to be something other than the object within the patriarchal imaginary she appears to be. Hence Pinter's anxious apologetics with its weirdly archaic terminology: even if she does get set up in Soho, 'she would not be a harlot in her own mind'. Hence the struggle to construe an acceptable feminist message from a woman's decision to give up her position as wife and mother of three children to act instead as professional prostitute and shared sexual possession. There can be no doubt that the final tableau, where she is seated in Max's armchair, with Joey's head in her lap, Lenny standing in attendance behind her, and Max himself on hands and knees pleading for a kiss, is a victory for Ruth; the interpretation of that victory was a matter of ideological politics.

When it transferred to Broadway in 1967, the RSC production of *The Homecoming* had poor reviews. Walter Kerr in the *New York Times*, whose word normally decided whether a show lived or died, was scathing: 'Harold Pinter's "The Homecoming" consists of a single situation that the author refuses to dramatize until he has dragged us all, aching, through a half-drugged dream.'[44] Yet, against the odds, the play went on to a long run and four Tony Awards, making Pinter 'commercial' enough to risk putting on *The Birthday Party*. In the cynical terms of William Goldman, it was the 'Snob Hit' of the season, fulfilling the requirements of being British and 'at least a little unintelligible'.[45] A part of the play's success may well have been its riddling inscrutability: the apparently motiveless actions of its characters, the shock of Ruth's enigmatic role. There were also the sheer theatrical skills of Pinter – 'one of the most naturally gifted dramatists to have come out of Britain since the war', as even Kerr conceded – realised by the extraordinarily gifted RSC team, director Peter Hall and designer John Bury at the height of their powers and the fine cast of actors so used to playing as an ensemble. But it represented also a return of the recognisable family home, though in a piquantly estranged form. This was the family finally stripped bare of all its pretensions to Mum and Dad and happy ever after.

From the 1970s on, that deconstruction of the family was to take other forms. Women playwrights in particular chose for the most part not to use the iconic home on the stage for their reimagination of gender. The work started by *A Doll's House* had to be advanced by other means; the naturalistic middle-class four-walls set itself, perhaps, felt too like the trap from which women playwrights needed to escape. Much drama of the 1970s and 1980s, in fact, whether the left-wing British work of Caryl Churchill, David Hare and Howard Brenton or the hard-hitting American plays of Sam Shepard and David Mamet, employed a more fluid dramaturgy of episodic narrative and shifting scenes outside the home. When Tom Stoppard, one of the most formally adventurous dramatists of this period, came finally in 1993 to put a domestic interior onstage in *Arcadia*, it was not exactly domestic, was certainly not middle-class and was fixed in space but not in time.

CHAPTER 8

Arcadia: *seeing double*

Harold Pinter and Tom Stoppard were friends; they had their Jewishness, their passion for cricket and their lack of a university education in common. But there the resemblances end. Pinter began life as an actor, and his plays had their origin in the forms of conventional theatre, however estranged. Stoppard worked as a journalist, and his word-based drama was shaped by his eclectic reading and appetite for research. Though Pinter's early plays were often considered apolitical – in 1977 Kenneth Tynan could still group Pinter with Stoppard among the 'cool, apolitical stylists' of British theatre[1] – he was to develop outspoken left-wing views, famously using his Nobel Prize address, 'Art, Truth & Politics', for a violent attack on US foreign policy.[2] Stoppard, an early admirer of Margaret Thatcher, who at one point styled himself as a 'conservative with a small c. [. . .] conservative in politics, literature, education and theatre', directed his political activism against the Communism of the Eastern bloc.[3] Pinter's mise-en-scène is typically concentrated in a single set, a single situation, while Stoppard delights in a fluid dramaturgy of scene-shifting theatricality. The contrast can be pointed by the way the two playwrights absorbed the impact of *Waiting for Godot*. In *The Dumb Waiter*, Pinter realised the waiting pair as Hemingwayesque killers in the basement of an English provincial city. Stoppard, in *Rosencrantz and Guildenstern Are Dead*, reimagined them as the attendant lords of *Hamlet*, spinning out time in an offstage no-man's-land before they arrive at their happenstance destiny.

A Stoppard play characteristically starts with a picture puzzle. So, for example, *After Magritte* (1970) shows a bizarre interior with a fruit basket hanging from the ceiling, one figure in a bath towel lying on an ironing board with a bowler hat on her stomach, a second in a ball gown on her hands and knees on the floor, and a third bare-chested in evening dress trousers and long waders, all of them observed by a police constable looking through a window. This may have been inspired by René

Magritte's painting *The Assassin Threatened*, but the play is not in fact surrealist: by the end of the one-act *After Magritte*, an explanation has been given for each detail in the whole strange scene.[4] This is Stoppard's strategy in many of his plays. *Jumpers* (1973) begins with a collage of disconnected stage images: a singing star breaking down in her performance; the striptease act of a woman swinging back and forth into the light, shedding clothes as she goes; a hole blown in a living pyramid of yellow-clad gymnasts as one of them is shot from behind. The rest of the play will be devoted to uncovering the sources and significance of this strange sequence. In other plays, the mystifying medley is aural rather than visual. *Artist Descending a Staircase* (1972), originally a radio play, turns on the playing of a series of sounds on tape that will eventually explain the death of the artist of the title. The barrage of language at the opening of *Travesties* (1974) is deliberately unintelligible, with Joyce dictating the polyglot first words of the 'Oxen of the Sun' episode of *Ulysses*, Tristan Tzara improvising a cut-and-paste Dadaist poem and Nadya excitedly telling her husband Lenin in Russian that there has been a revolution in Moscow. As the action goes on, the compositional techniques of Joyce and Tzara are elucidated, and at the beginning of Act II there is even a reprise of the first scene with the Russian translated for the audience's benefit.

In such plays, the play of images is intended to support the play of ideas. As we come to construe the scenes before us, we are led into the intellectual themes that they reflect: the conflicting languages of art, politics and history in *Travesties*; the position of an unconvinced and unconvincing theism in the aggressively secularist world of *Jumpers*, where philosophy has become no more than mental gymnastics. Almost all of the early work of Stoppard was produced in the state-subsidised theatres of Britain, which could both afford his technically elaborate staging and expect their well-educated audiences to enjoy the range and reach of his thought. *Night and Day* (1978), written for the West End, used a more conventionally naturalistic dramaturgy, and a more straightforwardly action-based plot. In *The Real Thing* (1982), also produced in the commercial theatre, is was as though Stoppard, so often stereotyped as an intellectual exhibitionist, set out to prove that he could write a moving domestic drama of love and marriage.

Henry, the upmarket playwright protagonist of *The Real Thing*, author of a Sartre play, 'Jean-Paul is up the Wall', is without doubt some sort of stand-in for Stoppard himself.[5] Henry is defensively aware of the weakness of his women's parts, a charge often levelled at Stoppard, and confesses, 'I don't know how to write love. I try to write it properly, and it just comes out embarrassing.'[6] The play is in some sense an attempt to overcome that difficulty, to write 'properly' about love. But the very title makes problematic the issue of what is 'the real thing'. The play opens with what appears to be an edgy scene between husband and wife, the husband confronting the wife with what he takes to be evidence of her adultery. But Scene 2 reveals that what we have been watching is the start of Henry's play *House of Cards*, performed by Charlotte, Henry's actress wife, and Max, the real-life husband of Henry's lover Annie. The metaphor of the house of cards is literalised in the play within the play as we see Max's cardhouse collapse as Charlotte comes in, slamming the door – itself a witty inversion of the ending of *A Doll's House*. Running through the play's representation of love relationships – Henry and Annie disentangling themselves from their marriages, but then having their love threatened by Annie's affair with a younger actor – is the suggestion that any such relationship may be no more than such a vulnerable house of cards. The living rooms in which most of the love scenes take place are all but interchangeable. In Scene 3, where Max discovers Annie's actual adultery, we are told that 'the disposition of furniture and doors makes the scene immediately reminiscent of the beginning of Scene 1' – that is, the *House of Cards* opening.[7] The play works by advertising its own theatricality, implying the performativity of love itself. The cover image of the Faber first edition nicely highlights this theme, with a mise-en-abyme image of a dress-suited showman within a curtained proscenium arch gesturing towards a miniature version of a showman within a curtained proscenium arch. Love, sex, marriage – it's all theatre; it can never be the real thing.

That was not the way the play was received, at least by some critics. Frank Rich, the *New York Times* critic, called it 'not only Stoppard's most moving play, but also the most bracing play that anyone has written about love and marriage in years'.[8] And Henry in the play is given a defiantly romantic assertion of the existential truth of love: 'Carnal knowledge. It's what lovers trust each other with, knowledge of each other, not of the flesh but through the flesh, knowledge of self, the real him, the real her, *in extremis*, the mask slipped from the face.'[9] *Arcadia* (1993), in a deflating self-referencing gesture, opens with the young Thomasina's innocent question to her tutor, 'Septimus, what is carnal embrace?', and its deadpan answer, 'Carnal embrace is the practice of throwing one's arms around a side of beef.'[10] When forced to admit that it in fact means 'sexual congress', Thomasina wants to know, 'Is it the same as love?' 'Oh no', says Septimus, 'it is much nicer than that' (*Arcadia*, 4). *Arcadia* takes a distinctly cool attitude towards sex and its relationship to love. It moves away from *The*

Real Thing, also, and Stoppard's earlier work generally, in the solidity of its single setting. The audience of *Arcadia*, as in no other play of Stoppard, looks in at just one room from start to finish of the action. But of course that one room is represented in two time periods, 190 years apart. And that makes this a distinctly different version of home on the stage.

Space and time

The *Doll's House* model of theatrical domestic space involved a coding of the home represented onstage as it bespoke the family living there, a potential metonym for the society at large. The Helmers' living room, Ranevskaya's old nursery, the summer house of the Tyrones or the Kowalskis' apartment had the condition of the lives of the characters written into the walls, the windows, the furniture. Contemporaneity and familiarity were also key features of this paradigm, at least in origin. The middle-class audiences in the theatre would immediately recognise versions of themselves and their own living conditions in the homes on the stage. Even where the scene was placed back in time, as in *Long Day's Journey*, or moved down into a working-class milieu, as in *Streetcar*, the specificities of the characters' situation made them credible and immediately recognisable.

For the purposes of his double period staging in *Arcadia*, Stoppard elides as much of such environmental detail as he can. The stage direction for the opening 1809 scene stresses the empty neutrality of the room:

> The room looks bare despite the large table which occupies the centre of it. The table, the straight-backed chairs and, the only other item of furniture, the architect's stand or reading stand, would all be collectable pieces now but here, on an uncarpeted wood floor, they have no more pretension than a schoolroom, which is indeed the main use of this room at this time. What elegance there is, is architectural, and nothing is impressive but the scale. (*Arcadia*, 1)

Stoppard most definitely does not want the self-conscious Regency period piece so standard in TV adaptations of Jane Austen, with every item of furniture contributing to the costume drama historicity. The schoolroom represented in the 1809–12 scenes is a purely functional space rather than one of the showpiece reception rooms of the house. And for the modern scenes, it is even more indeterminate, having been stripped of all surplus belongings to turn it into a passageway for outside visitors on their way to the ladies' toilet at the coming dance.

The distinctiveness of Stoppard's use of the stage space here is the more obvious when compared with *The Cherry Orchard*. The nursery setting of Chekhov's Act I and IV action is comparable to the schoolroom in *Arcadia*, a presumably less than central space in the large Gayev country house. But everything about it is made significant. The nursery where Ranevskaya and Gayev, then Anya and Varya (and presumably the dead son Petya) lived and played as children, is a repository of memory, a concretisation of the continuity of the family's life in the house. The iconic bookcase, which not even the most postmodern production can omit, is embraced by Ranevskaya, apostrophised by Gayev as mute witness to their shared past. The cherry orchard itself, so evocative of the estate and all it represents in the past and present, is designed to be visible through the windows. What we see onstage in *The Cherry Orchard* makes the present a moment in a registered history of the family and of the country.

Stoppard's scene is thus not historical but transhistorical. The house of the Crooms, still in the possession of the same family nearly two hundred years on, might well have represented the stable tradition of the English upper classes. This, however, is not Stoppard's concern, for all his small *c* conservatism. The scenes in the different time zones are juxtaposed situations, equally present in the theatre, rather than contrasted as a historical before and after. What holds the two together is our awareness of their coexistence on the stage, with the characters in the latter period trying painstakingly to reconstruct what we have watched spontaneously enacted before us. The props that figure between the time zones have a special status beyond their realising function. Part of the playful fun of the drama is seeing the casually handled objects of 1809 become the intensely scrutinised, and generally misleading, archaeological clues of 1993. So, for instance, we see Thomasina in Scene 1 draw in a figure on the landscape architect Noakes's plans for remodelling the garden: 'I will put in a hermit, for what is a hermitage without a hermit?' (*Arcadia*, 13). In Scene 2, the garden historian Hannah reverently shows to Bernard, the Byron scholar with his own research mission at Sidley Park, Thomasina's John the Baptist–like doodle: 'The only known likeness of the Sidley hermit. [...] Drawn in by a later hand' (*Arcadia*, 25). Though objects are carried over from the scenes of one time period to another, the stage direction indicates that 'books, etc., used in both periods should exist in both old and new versions' (*Arcadia*, 15). The Noakes sketchbook, therefore, with its drawing of the hermit, is not a surviving witness of the past, like Gayev's bookcase, but a theatrical replica of such.

By emptying the stage set of *Arcadia*, Stoppard reverses his previous picture-puzzle strategy. Where previously he started his plays with a wildly unstable and unreadable collage of visual images to be gradually comprehended as the action went on, here he presents one unvarying and relatively bare room and directs most of the audience attention to an unseen and also unchanging offstage, as the stage direction makes clear:

> The upstage wall is mainly tall, shapely, uncurtained windows, one or more of which work as doors. Nothing much need be said or seen of the exterior beyond. We come to learn that the house stands in the typical English park of the time. Perhaps we see an indication of this, perhaps only light and air and sky. (*Arcadia*, 1)

The original National Theatre production went for the latter option, with little beyond one overhanging tree visible through the windows (Figure 8.1).

Yet the look of the garden is a key issue throughout the play. In 1809–12, it is in the process of being transformed, much to Lady Croom's disgust, from Capability Brown–style naturalness to the Gothic picturesque of Richard Noakes, standing in for the real-life landscape gardener Humphrey Repton. Lady Croom gestures indignantly to Noakes's before-and-after sketchbook, which replicates Repton's Red Books:

> Here is the Park as it appears to us now, and here as it might be when Mr Noakes has done with it. Where there is the familiar pastoral refinement of an Englishman's garden, here is an eruption of gloomy forest and towering crag, of ruins where there was never a house, of water dashing against rocks where there was neither spring nor stone I could not throw the length of a cricket pitch. (*Arcadia*, 12)

But in 1993, Hannah is assisting the latter-day Lady Croom in excavating a still earlier layout of the grounds, a formal Italian garden from the first half of the eighteenth century. She provides a relativising perspective on the idea of the Capability Brown natural style as 'the real England': it was as much a construction as the Gothic that replaced it.

> English landscape was invented by gardeners imitating foreign painters who were evoking classical authors. The whole thing was brought home in the luggage from the grand tour. Here, look [at Noakes's sketchbook again] – Capability Brown doing Claude, who was doing Virgil. Arcadia! And here, superimposed by Richard Noakes, untamed nature in the style of Salvator Rosa. It's the Gothic novel expressed in landscape. (*Arcadia*, 25)

But Hannah's lament for the lost formal garden shows that the nostalgia for an Arcadian original receding back into time is universal: 'There's an engraving of Sidley Park in 1730 that makes you want to weep. Paradise in

Figure 8.1   Bill Nighy (Bernard) and Felicity Kendall (Hannah) in *Arcadia*,
National Theatre, London, 1993.

the age of reason. By 1760 everything had gone – the topiary, pools and terraces, fountains, an avenue of limes – the whole sublime geometry was ploughed under by Capability Brown' (*Arcadia*, 27). The Regency room in *Arcadia*, with its outlook on the park, is not there to represent the particular historical transition from the classical to the Romantic age, but to afford the audience a perspective in which such transitions are recurrent and generic.

Tristan Tzara in *Travesties* wonders 'what possible book could be derived from reference to Homer's *Odyssey* and the Dublin Street Directory for 1904'.[11] A reader who did not know *Arcadia* might equally puzzle over what work could draw upon the history of landscape gardening, James Gleick's *Chaos: Making a New Science* and A.S. Byatt's Booker Prize–winning novel *Possession*. Gleick's popular science book was used in the play for two of the fields in which chaos theory was developed, the animal populations of Valentine's studies of grouse and fractal geometry – the 'New Geometry of Irregular Forms discovered by Thomasina Coverly' (*Arcadia*, 43).[12] *Possession* had an alternating time scheme with narratives both for a Victorian poet and his love affair and the investigations of two literary scholars in the present. According to Ira Nadel, who gives a detailed analysis of the similarities between the two works, 'Stoppard told Byatt he had pinched the plot of *Arcadia* from her novel.'[13]

The use of a double time setting was of course not a novelty; two other contemporary precedents for this feature of *Arcadia* have been suggested.[14] What is so striking in Stoppard's play is the use of the same unaltered stage space with objects from both periods appearing together. This was in fact his starting point, as he explained in a 1995 interview: 'the idea of having a room that doesn't change, and you see what happens in the room in the past, and you see what happens in the room 180 years later'.[15] The formal convention for this is established in the stage direction introducing Scene 2, the first set in the present. 'During the course of the play the table collects this and that, and where an object from one scene would be an anachronism in another (say a coffee mug) it is simply deemed to have become invisible' (*Arcadia*, 15). However, Stoppard no sooner sets up this principle than he deliberately breaks it by having objects from one time zone reappear visibly in the other. So, for example, the apple offered by the mute Gus as a token of love to Hannah in Scene 2 is sliced open by Septimus minutes later in Scene 3. By Scene 7, when the characters from the different periods come to share the stage, there is a miscellaneous litter of things on the table: 'the geometrical solids, the computer, decanter, glasses, tea mug, Hannah's research books, Septimus's books, the two portfolios, Thomasina's candlestick, the oil lamp, the dahlia, the Sunday papers' (*Arcadia*, 96). Such a pile-up of stage properties underscores the point that Stoppard is not representing an actual room of any given time but a fictive theatrical space that is its own place.

The alternating periods of the play are not merely a theatrical device; they work to highlight the theme of time as it is articulated in the play, most formally in the debate between Thomasina and Septimus in Scene 3. Thomasina is horrified by the destructiveness of time, all the great works of the past lost by the frivolous actions of such as Cleopatra, the 'noodle', as Thomasina calls her:

> Oh, Septimus! – can you bear it? All the lost plays of the Athenians! Two hundred at least by Aeschylus, Sophocles, Euripides – thousands of poems – Aristotle's own library brought to Egypt by the noodle's ancestors! How can we sleep for grief?

Septimus's stoical reply counters with a perspective in which nothing is ever lost forever:

> We shed as we pick up, like travellers who must carry everything in their arms, and what we let fall will be picked up by those behind. The procession is very long and life is very short. We die on the march. But there is nothing outside the march so nothing can be lost to it. The missing plays of Sophocles will turn up piece by piece, or be written again in another language. Ancient cures for diseases will reveal themselves once more. Mathematical discoveries glimpsed and lost to view will have their time again. (*Arcadia*, 38)

In this exchange, Septimus the urbane tutor seems to have the greater theatrical authority over the outburst of his passionate but naive pupil.[16] What is more, the action of the play validates his last comment. Thomasina's 'glimpse' of a mathematical way of measuring irregular forms has its proper time in the late twentieth century, with the discovery of chaos theory. The excitement of that latter moment is expressed by Valentine: 'It's the best possible time to be alive, when almost everything you thought you knew is wrong' (*Arcadia*, 48).

Countering that buoyant sense of exhilaration in the experience of new knowledge, even if it was preknown at some previous period, is the principle of entropy, imagined as Thomasina's other intuitive discovery. In this case, Septimus confirms her observation about the dispersal of the jam in the rice pudding: '[Y]ou cannot stir things apart.'

> No more you can, time must needs run backward, and since it will not, we must stir our way onwards mixing as we go, disorder out of disorder until

pink is complete, unchanging and unchangeable, and we are done with it for ever. (*Arcadia*, 5)

This inevitable movement towards disorder, with the heat loss that becomes the second law of thermodynamics, produces a very different sense of time from Septimus's reassuring cycle, in which everything in human history is sooner or later rediscovered. It is the imagination of the heat death of the universe envisioned in the opening lines of Byron's poem 'Darkness' that Hannah quotes in Scene 7:

> I had a dream that was not all a dream.
> The bright sun was extinguished, and the stars
> Did wander darkling in the external space,
> Rayless, and pathless, and the icy earth
> Swung blind and blackening in the moonless air . . .
> (*Arcadia*, 79)

Against the optimistic vision in which loss is always recoverable overhangs this sense of slow degeneration to an inevitable end.

In a more immediate way, the play makes us conscious of irrecoverable loss in the fact of death and the waste of human talents. One possible model for Thomasina was Ada Lovelace, Byron's daughter. Ada, in spite of protracted periods of illness as a child and again as an adult, marriage at the age of twenty and three children, did take an active interest in mathematics and is widely credited with a part in the invention of what became the modern computer. She died at thirty-six of uterine cancer, unlike Thomasina in the play, who is killed in a fire at the age of sixteen. But Stoppard makes clear the unlikelihood of someone of Thomasina's gifts in her time and situation being allowed to realise her potential, even had she lived. When Lady Croom is reminded of Thomasina's age – 'Sixteen years and eleven months, mama, and three weeks' – her response is, 'We must have you married before you are educated beyond eligibility' (*Arcadia*, 84). Accomplishments are all very well for an aristocratic young woman; learning, scholarship and serious science are regarded as disabilities. The feminist undercurrent of the play, which dramatises the tragic frustration of women's creative capacity throughout so much of human history, is placed within a view of love, sex and marriage radically changed from that in earlier plays.

Sex and literature

'Sex and literature. Literature and sex. Your conversation, left to itself, doesn't have many places to go. Like two marbles rolling around a pudding basin. One of them is always sex' (*Arcadia*, 63). Hannah, speaking to the sexually self-preening Bernard here, is the anti-romantic voice of the play. It is she who extols the formal gardens of the early eighteenth century as 'Paradise in the age of reason' (*Arcadia*, 27), she who denounces the 'nervous breakdown of the Romantic Imagination' (*Arcadia*, 25). She brushes off Valentine's proposal – 'Can't we have a trial marriage and I'll call it off in the morning' – 'I don't know when I've received a more unusual proposal' (*Arcadia*, 75). She is much more blunt with Bernard's equivalently more direct suggestion that she come with him to London for sex, insisting that it is overvalued: 'Chaps sometimes wanted to marry me, and I don't know a worse bargain. Available sex for not being allowed to fart in bed' (*Arcadia*, 63). Hannah is the most authoritative figure in the modern section of the play; Stoppard's sympathies, as a fellow professional writer, tipped towards her against the arrogant and exhibitionist academic Bernard. Stoppard may be taken to speak through Hannah also in rejecting the obsessive interest in sexual motivation in human action: 'Einstein – relativity and sex? Chippendale – sex and furniture. Galileo – "Did the earth move?"' (*Arcadia*, 63).

In *The Real Thing*, Stoppard sought to meet the criticism that he could not write convincingly about love with a play where its very elusiveness is the subject. Still, he was prepared to allow Henry his affirmation of an ideal of love consummated: 'Carnal knowledge. It's what lovers trust each other with, knowledge of each other.' In *Arcadia*, he tried another tack, sidelining sex, disconnecting it from love. There is as much sex in the play as in a Feydeau farce, but it is all extramarital, not marital or even premarital. The Regency Lady Croom is attracted to/has an affair with Byron, who sleeps with Mrs Chater, who has had sex with Septimus as well as being the mistress of Captain Bryce. Humiliated by Byron's liaison with Mrs Chater, Lady Croom takes Septimus as her lover, only to replace him some years later with Count Zelinsky. The modern Lady Croom sublimates her attraction to Bernard by lending him her bicycle – 'Lending one's bicycle is a form of safe sex, possibly the safest there is' (*Arcadia*, 51). Bernard will finally be banished from Sidley Park when caught *in flagrante* with the all too willing Chloë, who has seen his potential from the start – 'a lot of sexual energy there' (*Arcadia*, 33) – but first self-denyingly offered him to Hannah. The play as a whole seems to correspond to Chloë's personal chaos theory: 'The universe is deterministic all right, just like Newton said, I mean it's trying to be, but the only thing going wrong is people fancying people who aren't supposed to be in that part of the plan' (*Arcadia*, 73).

Sexual desire is an irrational and disruptive force in *Arcadia* unconnected with marriage or the family. In the nineteenth-century action, Lord Croom is an absent figure, obsessively addicted to shooting, having ordered the fashionable remaking of the garden but otherwise leaving his wife to indulge in whatever or whomever she currently fancies. We see nothing of the modern Lord Croom either, but he is sketched in as a stereotypically eccentric aristocrat, allergic to homosexuals, typewritten letters and Japanese cars. The young people in both periods – Thomasina and Lord Augustus, Valentine, Chloë and Gus – might as well be parentless for all that is shown of their familial relationships. That is part of what makes the representation of the living space in *Arcadia* so distinctively unlike most of the homes on the stage considered earlier in this book. It is not the home of a given family by virtue of operating between two time zones; it is not really focused on the family at all.

From *A Doll's House* on, with its critical scrutiny of the patriarchal marriage, the concern of modern playwrights exploring this model of the domestic space has been to interrogate the workings of the family, its functions and dysfunctions. In *The Cherry Orchard* it is the extended family of the Russian big house, its semi-feudal molecular structure assisting in its drifting dissolution. The Tyrones in *Long Day's Journey* are locked in Oedipal stasis, bound to one another in need, hatred and love. *Streetcar* dramatises the incapacity of heteronormative married love in modern urban society to tolerate the otherness of other forms of desire. The attack on the family in later plays has been much more ferocious. *The Homecoming* exposes it as a system of power in which sexual relations are nothing else but a struggle for possession and dominance. The very rationale for the family as the means to self-perpetuation of the human species is called in question by Beckett's grotesque parody of intergenerational dynamics in *Endgame*. The ultimate nightmare for Hamm and Clov in their almost-terminal state is the prospect that life might start up again.

Stoppard's *Arcadia* is by no means as comfortless as this. Sex – 'much nicer than love', as Septimus judges it to be – is an undeniable pleasure, though one unconnected with love or procreation. There is none of the appalled revulsion that typically characterises Beckett's treatment of the physical act of making love. But Stoppard tends to imply that it is 'trivial' in the sense that Valentine uses the word (*Arcadia*, 60), a superficial distraction from more serious matters. 'Does carnal embrace addle the brain?', asks Thomasina, as she hands him a billet-doux from the torrid Mrs Chater. 'Invariably', replies the cool Septimus (*Arcadia*, 14).

Thomasina has no time for the great love stories of the past: 'I hate Cleopatra', she declares.

> Everything is turned to love with her. New love, absent love, lost love – I never knew a heroine that makes such noodles of our sex. It only needs a Roman general to drop anchor outside the window and away goes the empire like a christening mug into a pawn shop. If Queen Elizabeth had been a Ptolemy history would have been quite different – we would be admiring the pyramids of Rome and the great Sphinx of Verona. (*Arcadia*, 38)

Admittedly, this is the prepubescent Thomasina of not quite fourteen, but Stoppard uses the outburst to cast a cold eye at the glamorisation of the Antony and Cleopatra story, *All for Love*, or *The World Well Lost*, as the Dryden version had it.

Shaw anticipated Stoppard in this. In the preface to his *Three Plays for Puritans*, he explains why he felt the need to write his *Caesar and Cleopatra* as a Puritan's corrective to Shakespeare:

> Shakespear's Antony and Cleopatra must needs be as intolerable to the true Puritan as it is vaguely distressing to the ordinary healthy citizen, because, after giving a faithful picture of the soldier broken down by debauchery, and the typical wanton in whose arms such men perish, Shakespear finally strains all his huge command of rhetoric and stage pathos to give a theatrical sublimity to the wretched end of the business, and to persuade foolish spectators that the world was well lost by the twain. (Shaw, II, 37)

Stoppard has fairly often been compared with Shaw, though Stoppard himself has been uncomfortable with such comparisons.[17] They were both accused of not being able to write satisfactory women's parts and being incapable of dealing with love. *Man and Superman* was Shaw's response to the challenge by A.B. Walkley, the theatre critic of the *Times*, to write a Don Juan play; the result was a play in which John Tanner, Shaw's Don Juan figure, is not the philandering predator but the reluctant prey of his Donna Anna. Shaw's experience as a drama reviewer through the 1890s left him allergic to the well-made plays of his time, with their dominant love interest. Stoppard is almost equally sceptical. In *The Invention of Love*, he has Oscar Wilde declare: 'We would never love anybody if we could see past our own invention. [. . .] In the mirror of invention, love discovered itself.'[18]

Arcadia, Elisabeth Angel-Perez says, reads as if 'inspired by Shaw (particularly by *Heartbreak House*)'.[19] Certainly, Stoppard's play as a big house comedy of ideas is more like Shaw's than any other text considered in this book. The disorientating bewilderment of Bernard on his first introduction to Sidley Hall, with the unexplained comings and goings of Valentine, who passes through muttering, 'Sod, sod, sod, sod, sod, sod . . .' (*Arcadia*, 17), and Gus, who withdraws saying nothing, is quite like Ellie Dunn's exposure to the bizarre inhabitants of Heartbreak House. More significantly, though, for both Shaw and Stoppard the amorous adventures that make up such a large part of the action in both houses are diversions from more serious matters. Shaw, like Shotover, is impatient with the love affairs of his 'demon daughters'. Stoppard, like Hannah, dismisses the reductive point of view of men like Bernard who see everything in terms of 'sex and literature', the 'two marbles rolling around a pudding basin'. There is, however, a crucial difference. In *Heartbreak House*, the distaste for the distractions of love is a male-centred longing for an all-male world. 'When you have found the land where there is happiness and no women', Shotover says to Mangan, 'send me its latitude and longitude; and I will join you there' (Shaw, v, 131). The objections to romance in *Arcadia* come from a feminist point of view. Heroising Cleopatra, Thomasina complains, 'makes such noodles of our sex', denies them a brain. Hannah refuses to accept the brash and arrogant Bernard's stereotyping view that she is uptight and repressed – 'You should let yourself go a bit' (*Arcadia*, 63) – nor yet Valentine's claim that her 'classical reserve is only a mannerism; and neurotic' (*Arcadia*, 75). Hannah remains her own woman for all the male projections upon her.

Arcadia and *Heartbreak House* are comedies of ideas, specifically not traditional romantic comedies designed to end with marriage and happy ever after. After all the on/off negotiations over whether Ellie will or will not marry Mangan, and her passionate infatuation with Hector Hushabye, she gives herself in a 'mystic marriage' to Shotover, a purely symbolic, spiritual union. Dance is the figure that represents the closure of marital matching in any number of comedies, but in *Arcadia* there is no future for either dancing couple. Hannah waltzes awkwardly with the mute genius Gus, 'Thomasina's gifted artistic avatar', as he has been called.[20] And the Thomasina whom we see in the arms of Septimus we know already will die that very night. In neither Shaw's nor Stoppard's play is there any of the promise of continuity afforded by the marriages of comedy. Instead, in *Heartbreak House*, after the explosion offstage that has killed the 'two burglars', we are left with the uncertain prospect of potential apocalypse tomorrow. The dance in *Arcadia* takes place in an impossible timeless zone threatened by ultimate entropy, shadowed by death.

Death and the dance

Stoppard sets up the alternation between the two time periods as the governing principle of his play and then proceeds to play games with it. So, for instance, Scene 4, set in 1993, ends with a change of lighting in the empty room: 'From a long way off, there is a pistol shot. A moment later there is the cry of dozens of crows disturbed from the unseen trees' (*Arcadia*, 52). That is the end of Act 1. An audience comes back after the interval primed for a scene in the Regency period in which the occasion of that offstage shot, the threatened duel between Septimus and Chater, will be revealed. Instead, they are given a continuation of the modern-day story with Bernard rehearsing his sensational lecture in which he will 'prove' that it was Byron who fought the duel with Chater and killed him. We have to wait until the start of Scene 6 and a 'reprise: early morning – a distant pistol shot – the sound of the crows' (*Arcadia*, 67) before we get the *éclaircissement* we expected: there was no duel, the Chaters have left and the shot was only Septimus killing a rabbit, which will be misidentified as a hare and mis-attributed to Byron's gun in the Sidley Park game book. The theatrical fun, of course, comes from the deferral of the true explanation, which shows how egregiously wrong is the modern researcher's reconstruction.

So much so straightforward; the dramatic device of withholding know-ledge for a time from the audience only helps to reinforce the irony of our understanding so much more than the characters. Yet we are hardly prepared for what happens in the long final Scene 7 – it occupied a full forty-five minutes in the original production[21] – where the two time streams flow together and characters from both periods occupy the stage simultaneously. In one sense, the effect is to provide the audience with a clarifying omniscience, being able to see both past and present, a bit like the idea of the afterlife that Hannah so deplores, 'the great celestial get-together for an exchange of views', with its answers 'in the back of the book' (*Arcadia*, 75). The juxtaposition of the nineteenth- with the twentieth-century characters does indeed provide us with the answers to the puzzles the original situation set up. So, for instance, in one of the Regency sequences of dialogue (*Arcadia*, 79–82), a number of the missing pieces of the jigsaw come into place. The dwarf dahlias, the key piece of evidence showing that Chater died in the West Indies and was not shot in a duel by Byron, are referred to by the earlier Lady Croom, just as 'Hannah sits back in her chair, caught by what she is reading' (*Arcadia*, 83), evidently the entry in the 1810 garden book that documents the dahlias. From the sour references by Lady Croom to Byron's appearance at

Devonshire House in the company of his then-mistress Lady Caroline Lamb, it is clear that Hannah was right in identifying the two of them in a drawing by Fuseli used on the cover of her book; Bernard in his patronising way had claimed this was a mistake. And Septimus casually mentions that his brother was the editor of the London journal the *Piccadilly Recreation*, a missing link explaining why it was he and not Byron who published the two reviews of Chater's book there. It all comes together like the roundup by the detective at the end of the thriller.

Yet the experience of this scene does not correspond to that simply satisfying sense of having all the t's crossed and the i's dotted. That is in part because of the shock we receive when we learn of Thomasina's death and the way in which we receive it. Hannah and Valentine are arguing about the significance of Thomasina's calculations, which Valentine has been developing on the computer. Valentine refuses to accept that Thomasina was a genius ahead of her time; if she had been 'she'd be famous'.

HANNAH. No, she wouldn't. She was dead before she had time to be famous . . .
VALENTINE. She died?
HANNAH . . . burned to death.
VALENTINE (*realizing*). Oh . . . the girl who died in the fire!
HANNAH. The night before her seventeenth birthday.
(*Arcadia*, 76)

For Valentine, Thomasina's death is ancient history, an incident of the distant past of his family, 'the girl who died in the fire'. For us, who are witnessing the extremely attractive sixteen-year-old Thomasina still very much alive in the stage present, there is a horror in knowing that she is just about to die.

Stoppard took the title for his play from a series of seventeenth-century paintings, the most famous of which is that by Poussin in the Louvre; in fact, the playwright originally wanted to call the play *Et in Arcadia ego*, before 'brevity and box-office sense prevailed'.[22] The Poussin image, showing four shepherd figures grouped around a tomb, has two of them pointing to the inscription, 'Et in Arcadia ego'.[23] Stoppard's text highlights the motto when it is cited by Lady Croom as the peroration of her paean on her garden in its Capability Brown style: '[I]t is nature as God intended, and I can say with the painter, '*Et in Arcadia ego!*' 'Here I am in Arcadia.' She is disconcerted by Thomasina's response to this: 'Yes, mama, if you would have it so.' 'Is she correcting my taste or my translation?' 'Neither are beyond correction, mama', replies the cheeky daughter (*Arcadia*, 12). It is in fact Septimus who supplies the correct translation: '"Even in Arcadia, there am I!"', to which Thomasina with all the insouciance of her thirteen years responds, 'Oh, phooey to Death!' (*Arcadia*, 13). In Stoppard's Arcadia of the garden, which is of course a palimpsest of all the different ways a garden Arcadia has been conceived over a seventy-year period, death is the dark presence.

Both Thomasina's anachronistic 'discoveries' – the second law of thermodynamics and the fractal geometry of natural forms – feature prominently in Scene 7. With her intuition about the jam in the rice pudding confirmed by 'a prize essay of the Scientific Academy in Paris' (*Arcadia*, 81), she sketches a diagram of heat exchange, showing why the latest technical invention, the Newcomen steam engine of which Noakes is so proud, will never yield the full power it takes to drive it.[24] It is this, with the essay that Septimus sets her to explain the diagram, that is to drive Septimus himself mad in the years of sequestration in the hermitage that are to follow her death. We are told early in the play by Hannah, giving the one account of the hermit that survives into the modern period, that after his death his refuge was discovered 'stacked solid with paper. Hundreds of pages. Thousands. [...] He'd covered every sheet with cabalistic proofs that the world was coming to an end' (*Arcadia*, 27). In Scene 7, we come to realise that these were not cabalistic proofs but attempts to follow through on Thomasina's theory of entropy. Her terrible end is matched by the grotesque imagination of Septimus's demented efforts to verify her idea. The tragic dimension to the play turns on the loss and waste of human life and talent as much as on the heat loss that is dooming the world to eventual extinction.

As against that, there is Thomasina's 'rabbit equation', which becomes the iterated algorithm in which the outcome of one calculation becomes the input for the next – hence the explanation of its resemblance to a rabbit: 'it eats its own progeny' (*Arcadia*, 77). When Valentine feeds this rabbit equation into his laptop, it produces what he calls the 'Coverly set'; '[H]ow beautiful!', exclaims Hannah, looking at the images on the computer screen. Stoppard is here borrowing the 'Mandelbrot set', the graphic illustrations by Benoit Mandelbrot in which 'each picture is a detail of the previous one, blown up'. The colour images of the Mandelbrot set reproduced in James Gleick's book are indeed beautiful.[25] This is what evokes Valentine's expression of wonder in the play: 'In an ocean of ashes, islands of order' (*Arcadia*, 76). The imagery here is significant. The 'ocean of ashes' is the latter-day extinct world to which entropy dooms us. But at the same time, the new science of chaos theory allows an entrancing vision of order in what appears to be the randomness of nature.

More than one critic has pointed to the ways in which the form of Stoppard's play gives body to the science with which it is concerned.[26] Scene 7 perfectly illustrates this. On the face of it, the merging of the two time periods in the one space is a wilful breach of the play's own conventions, producing a bewildering collocation of characters and images. Emblematic of this is the disorderly debris on the table, 'a considerable mess of papers, books and objects' from both time zones, through which Valentine has to root to find Thomasina's diagram of heat exchange (*Arcadia*, 92–93). Yet the interweaving juxtaposition of the different situations yields its own symmetries, its own choreography. The scientist Valentine matches Septimus; the daughter of the house Chloë is the equivalent of Thomasina; and a previously unseen Lord Augustus provides a counterpart for the modern Gus – the action is arranged so they can be doubled by the same actor. Having the 1990s figures put on Regency clothes out of a dressing-up box for the occasion of the Saturday night dance brings the two sets of characters closer together while emphasising the theatrically costumed status of both. Sequences of action from one period alternate with those of the other, and these are punctuated by snatches of conversation intercut between the two, with dialogue echoing and answering across the time gap. This rhythm of repetition with variation culminates in the double dance that ends the play.

Septimus is finally persuaded to teach the impatient, now sixteen-year-old Thomasina to do the waltz, the latest fashionable dance, scandalous at the time because of the way the partners held one another throughout in close physical proximity. It expresses the discovery of love between the two, a love that Septimus insists should not be consummated, in spite of Thomasina's urgent wishes. The determinedly nondancing Hannah dances with her autistic admirer Gus, the awkwardness of their dance contrasting with the fluency of the other couple. Neither of these relationships is going anywhere; their harmonious union exists only for the moment of the dance. Scene 7 as a whole dramatises the complexity of human behaviour; the anarchic disruptiveness of desire that, as in Chloë's personal chaos theory, drives Newton's determinist universe off course; the finitude of lives bounded by death. Against that sense of randomness, the only order is the theatrical aesthetic form temporarily picked out of flux and process. Septimus looks forward in dismay to the prospect of an unillumined universe: 'When we have found all the mysteries and lost all the meaning, we will be alone, on an empty shore.' 'Then we will dance', replies Thomasina, suiting the action to the word (*Arcadia*, 94).

Arcadia has turned out to be a one-off for Stoppard. His subsequent plays have never again used the format of the single set. For the memory play *The Invention of Love* (1997), scenes from various stages of the life of the dead poet and scholar A.E. Housman weave in and out of the action. The epic sweep of the trilogy *The Coast of Utopia* (2002) tracks its nineteenth-century Russian intellectuals across many European countries and thirty-five years of history. *Rock 'n' Roll* (2006) uses 'smash-cuts', instant scene changes to shuttle back and forth between Cambridge and Prague through times between 1968 and 1990. *Arcadia* is significant for this study because of its distinctive rendering of the home on the stage. Earlier plays made one dramatic space and one family group living within it stand in for a broader-based community. In Beckett and Pinter this becomes a figure for the nature of the family, or indeed a basic paradigm for human relationships. However the equation, space plus character equals meaning, $s + c = m$, remains the same. Stoppard adds a different dimension to the equation by retaining the stable space but doubling the sets of characters and time periods, $s + c_1 + c_2 = m$. This both relativises and makes more abstract the patterns of meaning, as they run between past and present. But it also highlights the theatrical space in and for itself as the scene of significance in which the different representations fold in upon one another.

Stoppard's play was hugely successful on its first production in London, and has gone on to many other stagings, including the Comédie-Française in 1998 and revivals in London (2009) and New York (2011). Many critics regard it as Stoppard's finest work to date. One of the sources of its popular success, no doubt, is the sense of glamour associated with its historical setting. The audience are teleported at will across the centuries into an aristocratic Regency country house, with Byron himself tantalisingly just off stage. Where the original naturalistic model of the Ibsenian home on the stage depended on an identification of middle-class audiences with middle-class characters and setting, spectators at *Arcadia* enjoy the pleasure and privilege of being taken out of themselves in time and space. The 1809–12 schoolroom of Sidley Park is like the home of no one watching the play in the twentieth or twenty-first centuries. For my last case study in this book, I want to move to a play as far as possible from the gracious elegance of *Arcadia*, though it too takes an audience away from a familiarly recognisable setting. Suzan-Lori Parks's *Topdog Underdog* (2001) is not set in a middle-class home either but in a 'seedily furnished rooming house room' in New York.[27] With its cast of two African American brothers jockeying for position in this sordid rented space, it moves any likely audience of the play outside their comfort zone and calls in question their basic assumptions about what constitutes the norms of home and family.

CHAPTER 9

Topdog/Underdog: *welcome to the family*

When *Topdog/Underdog* was first produced in 2001, the admirers of
Suzan-Lori Parks were taken aback by the form of the play. As Una
Chaudhuri put it in her review, 'at first glance *Topdog/Underdog* strikes
one as a retreat for Parks, a move backwards both in terms of dramatic
history as well as in terms of the poetic imagination that illuminates her
earlier plays'.[1] Robert Brustein, similarly, thought it 'far from Parks's most
ambitious writing'; he explained why he had gone along with the verdict of
his fellow committee members in awarding the play the Pulitzer Prize for
Drama in 2002: 'Prizes often go to the lesser achievements of good playwrights whose better stuff has been previously ignored.'[2] For some theatre
reviewers, on the other hand, the change in style was a welcome one. Ben
Brantley called the play 'its author's most consumer friendly and outright
entertaining work to date, [which] should establish an expanded audience
for Ms Parks, who has often been regarded as overly opaque'.[3] Artemis
Furie, reviewing the production when it transferred to Broadway, was even
more forthright: 'Parks is an avant-gardist; typically her work is an exercise
in ardently cerebral and resolutely obtuse game-playing [. . .] *Topdog* breaks
through the boundaries of this endearing, yet outmoded, aesthetic.'[4]

Whether regarded as a retrograde departure from her own best practice
or an admirable breakthrough into a more accessible mode, *Topdog* was
certainly something different for Parks. In her essay 'Elements of Style', she
explained her position in relation to naturalistic form:

> We should understand that realism, like other movements in other art-
> forms, is a specific response to a certain historical climate. I don't explode
> the form because I find traditional plays 'boring' – I don't really. It's just
> that those structures never could accommodate the figures which take up
> residence inside me.[5]

Those figures that occupied Parks's imagination in her first plays were
certainly quite strange ones. The play that brought her to prominence,

winning her an Obie Award in 1989, *Imperceptible Mutabilities in the Third Kingdom*, has three distinct narrative centres and a chorus of characters called Kin-Seer, Us-Seer, Shark-Seer, Soul-Seer and Over-Seer. In a mode that one critic called 'allegorical absurdism', Parks began to work with what was to become her characteristic theme: the recovery of the lost voices of African Americans.[6] She declared this as her mission in an early essay called 'Possession': '[B]ecause so much of African-American history has been unrecorded, dismembered, washed out, one of my tasks as playwright is to [. . .] locate the ancestral burial ground, dig for bones, find bones, hear the bones sing, write it down' (*The America Play*, 4). These dead voices, vatically ventriloquised, necessarily found utterance in fragmentary snatches, not in coherent, continuous narratives. So, for example, her 1992 play *The Death of the Last Black Man in the Whole Entire World*, a powerful dramatisation of African American suffering, works through an expressionist collage of stereotypes, characters called Black Man with Watermelon and Black Woman with Fried Drumstick, speaking a defiantly nonstandard Black English.

Combined with her polemic politics of race in many of Parks's plays of the 1990s was a strong feminism. Her play *Venus* (1996) combined the two, centring on Saartjie Baartman, the historical Khoikhoi woman from South Africa, who because of her unusual physique was exhibited as a freak in London and Paris in the early nineteenth century. Again, the dramatic technique is one of deliberate alienation, its multiply metatheatrical effect being to identify the theatre audience with the scopophilic gawkers at the freak show. *In the Blood* (1999) and *Fucking A* (2000) were both rewritten versions of Hawthorne's *The Scarlet Letter*, bringing out the more desperately entrapped situation of the African American equivalents of Hester Prynne: Hester La Negrita, the exploited, illiterate lone mother on welfare of *In the Blood*, and the branded abortionist Hester in the dystopic world of *Fucking A*. Although *In the Blood* is marginally more naturalistic than her other plays, it too uses Parks's characteristic episodic structure, choric interludes and nonindividualised characters. Nothing in her experimental theatre, with its lack of located setting, its extravagant use of multiple personae and its discontinuous narratives, could have prepared audiences for *Topdog*, a well-made play for two male actors, fighting for dominance in a single room.

Parks with *Topdog* can be placed with other avant-garde playwrights returning, reluctantly or otherwise, to the scene of the realised family home. Commenting on this phenomenon in the introduction to this book, I quoted Sam Shepard's wry remark about *Buried Child*: 'It's sort of a typical Pulitzer Prize–winning play. It wasn't written for that purpose; it was kind of a test. I wanted to write a play about a family.' And of course Parks, like Shepard, did indeed win the Pulitzer Prize for this more recognisable sort of play. She ends her little preface to the published text of *Topdog* with a sardonic comment: 'This is a play about family wounds and healing. Welcome to the family' (*Topdog*, n.p.). In the light of the range of domestic spaces explored in this book, the sordid rooming-house room where Lincoln and Booth are holed up is a drastically reduced form of the family home. This chapter considers what the focus on this minimal version of the home on the stage, the concentration on the family in a male two-hander, signifies in the work of Parks as an African American woman playwright.

History

Topdog/Underdog was an outgrowth of Parks's earlier *The America Play* (1994). As she herself put it, '[I]t was underneath that play for years. *The America Play* was working on, writing *Topdog/Underdog*.'[7] *The America Play* is a surreal extravaganza centred on the 'Foundling Father', 'a man who was told that he bore a strong resemblance to Abraham Lincoln. He was tall and thinly built just like the Great Man. His legs were the longer part just like the Great Mans legs. His hands and feet were large as the Great Mans were large' (*America Play*, 159). However, this Lincoln look-alike is black. The Foundling Father is therefore an ironic pun for the fatherless 'Lesser Known', who is not part of the official genealogy of American history, the founding 'fathers' of Lincoln's Gettysburg address. The play uses a variety of simulacra to guy the received versions of the past. It is set in 'a great hole. In the middle of nowhere. The hole is an exact replica of the Great Hole of History' (*America Play*, 159). The Great Hole of History is a theme park visited by the Foundling Father and his wife Lucy on their honeymoon in which visitors can gaze down on the legendary figures of the past. The play's replica setting has been created by the Foundling Father out west as a mimic version of the original, which is of course itself a synthetic mausoleum.

The ironic satire of *The America Play* has multiple targets. The Great Hole of History not only mocks the emptiness of so many received narratives but also suggests the absence of the African Americans who make no part of those narratives. Parks provides an apparatus of footnotes to the published text, citing facts and sources in deadpan mockery of scholarly scruple. Within the play, Lucy tells her son Brazil all she knows of his father's end: 'Heresay says he's past. Your Daddy. Digged this hole then he died. So says hearsay' (*America Play*, 181). The punning reference to 'heresay/hearsay' glances at the historian's distrust of oral testimony, the only testimony available to people whose lives are never registered in print. The fetishisation of great figures of the past is linked to the equally satirised cult of the dead. The Foundling Father was a gravedigger by trade who aspired to become an undertaker, with his son trained up as a professional mourner and Lucy as a 'Confidence', the person deputed to hear the dying person's last words. The America of *The America Play* is death-obsessed, backward-looking, a manufactured and gapped construction of its own imagined past.

One of Parks's key theatrical techniques is what she calls 'Rep and Rev', repetition and revision, derived from 'the Jazz esthetic in which the composer or performer will write or play a musical phrase once and again and again [. . .] – with each revisit the phrase is slightly revised' (*America Play*, 8–9). In *The America Play*, it is the assassination of Lincoln that is so repeated in revised versions. The Foundling Father finds himself a job sitting in Lincoln getup, as it were in the theatre, while people pay in turn to stand behind and 'shoot' him in the guise of John Wilkes Booth. This scene is played out repeatedly through the action, the several assassins using the variant words attributed to Booth at the moment of the shooting: 'The South is avenged', 'Thus to the tyrants' (*America Play*, 165, 171). The metatheatrical awareness generated by this replaying of the assassination scene is heightened by extracts from *Our American Cousin*, the play Lincoln was actually watching when he was shot; his loud laughter, 'Haw Haw Haw Haw' (*America Play*, 164), is the cue each time for the person playing Booth to make his murderous entrance. This bizarre charade sends up the absurdity not only of people's desire to touch fame, to get inside history, but also of the implied grudge of all these volunteer Booths against the American president identified with the emancipation of African Americans from slavery. Whether shooting the Foundling Father as the black man he is or as the imago of the liberationist Lincoln, they represent the wish-fulfilment backlash of white ascendancy.

The creation of *Topdog/Underdog* was an extraordinary imaginative literalisation of the central trope of *The America Play*. The two brothers are really called Lincoln and Booth, a tasteless joke on the part of their father, it appears. Lincoln has an actual job in an arcade in which he whites up as his namesake, donning the iconic beard, frock coat and stovepipe hat, employed to be shot by those who pay to be Booth for their amusement. There is an equivalent grounding of the setting. The hole in

Figure 9.1   Eric Berryman (Booth left) and KenYatta Rogers (Lincoln right) in
Topdog/Underdog, Everyman Theatre (Baltimore, MD, USA), 2013.

the middle of nowhere that reproduced the Great Hole of History was a
virtual conception at several removes from any real locality. By contrast,
Booth's room in the rooming-house – its place 'here', its time 'now'
(*Topdog*, [2]) – is given a sordidly detailed theatrical materialisation. The
set, according to one review of the original production, had 'the bruised,
brown-toned look of a faded old photograph';[8] when that production was
staged in London, 'Booth's grungy tenement room' was described as 'all
peeling walls, scrounged furnishings, bare bulbs and haunted-house
shadows'.[9] Parks's play demands such a setting. Even though a recent
Baltimore revival in 2013 flanked the action with projected images as though
from the arcade where Lincoln worked, a photo showing Lincoln's first
entrance in the play reveals in what meticulous detail the stage directions
were realised, down to the girlie magazines under Booth's bed (Figure 9.1).[10]

Parks herself, when writing the play, felt the constricted confinement of
the space as against the expansiveness of her early work. 'In this play, there
is no escape for the two men, there is no escape from this one room that
they share. In other plays, I can fan out and become other people and have
multiple perspectives, but here I have to deal with what these guys are
going through first hand.'[11] Where *The America Play* was set in a hole in

the middle of nowhere, a timeless, placeless place of pure phantasmagoria, the action of *Topdog* moves relentlessly through a week in the life of the two brothers in their comfortless quarters. No home onstage explored in this book is so isolated from any offstage surroundings. Even in *Endgame*, Clov has his kitchen to which he can retreat, the dead 'corpsed' world beyond the windows he scans through the telescope. The rooming house of *Topdog* must have other rooms, other tenants, but we never hear of them; Booth's room has a bathroom 'down the hall' (*Topdog*, 15), but Lincoln prefers to pee into a plastic cup where he is. The two men come and go into a city with buses and saloons and shops for shoplifting, but we never know what city it is. The characters are locked into their one-room situation, and the audience is locked in with them.

And yet, subtended beneath the immediacy of the here and now action of *Topdog* is the African American history that Parks dramatised with such imaginative ambition in *The Death of the Last Black Man* or *The America Play*. It is there most obviously in Lincoln's grotesque whiteface makeup, so strikingly displayed in his first entrance, illustrated in the Baltimore production. The absurd unreality of this mask and the ridiculousness of the actor in his Lincoln gear are designed to talk back to the racist traditions of the blacked-up white minstrel singers. Booth is startled by the silent appearance of his brother in costume: '[T]ake off that damn coat, man, you make me nervous standing there like a spook, and that damn face paint, take it off' (*Topdog*, 11). Lincoln's whited-up face does indeed make him look ghostly, but there is a hint of a pun here; a 'spook' is of course not only a ghost but a derogatory word for an African American, the unintended double meaning that gets Coleman Silk, the protagonist of Philip Roth's *The Human Stain*, into so much trouble. For Booth, his brother's job is a degrading pretence, 'dressing up like some crackerass white man, some dead president and letting people shoot at you'. But for Lincoln, 'Its honest work' (*Topdog*, 22).[12] Though Booth forces him to acknowledge that he gets less pay than a white man playing the part would, Lincoln claims that he can maintain his own identity underneath the disguise:

> [I]t dont make me. Worn suit coat, not even worn by the fool that Im supposed to be playing, but making fools out of all those folks who come crowding in for they chance to play at something great. Fake beard. Top hat. Dont make me into no Lincoln. I was Lincoln on my own before any of that. (*Topdog*, 30)

As much as in the theme park 'Great Hole of History' of *The America Play*, in *Topdog* Parks mocks the taste for a simplified, white-dominated version of history. In one of the most-quoted passages from the play, Lincoln reflects on the desire for a familiar sanitised story of the past:

> People are funny about they Lincoln shit. Its historical. People like they historical shit in a certain way. They like it to unfold the way they folded it up. Neatly like a book. (*Topdog*, 52)[13]

The ironic distance of the remark, however, does not free the character of Lincoln in the play, or his brother, from the consequences of that history. In theatrical terms, they are overdetermined by their very names to act out the parts they do. From the moment Booth pulls his gun, in shocked surprise at the unobserved entrance of his brother, an audience will guess that the play ends with the younger brother carrying out the role of his namesake. In the original production, this sense of the overhang of the fated parts they have been assigned was rendered by the lighting, which cast giant shadows of the figures at key points on the wall behind them.[14]

Lincoln is a retired hustler, a star of the three-card monte scam who has renounced his former profession in favour of what he thinks of as 'honest work'. Against Booth's scepticism, he insists that the charade in which he is employed is not a hustle: 'People know the real deal. When people know the real deal it aint a hustle' (*Topdog*, 22). Playing the about-to-be-assassinated president as an African American in whiteface and phony clothes does not fool anyone, nor yet compromise his individual identity as Lincoln in his own right. But just as we know that the character called Booth will end up shooting his brother Lincoln, we know that Lincoln will be forced to return to his role as hustler. It is the story arc of the Western, where the famous gunslinger who has vowed to go straight, settle down and raise a family will inevitably be called out of retirement for one last showdown. For Lincoln, however, whose marriage has broken down, and who is forced to share his brother's single-room apartment, the 'honest' life consists of a dead-end job pretending to be shot at discriminatory low wages – and even from that he is fired, made redundant by a wax dummy. The 'heroic' past to which he then returns is as the street hustler.

The behaviour of Lincoln and Booth has been linked to the attitude known as 'cool pose', of which the hustle is one type.[15] Richard Major and Janet Mancini Bilson define African American cool pose as 'a ritualized form of masculinity that entails behaviours, scripts, physical posturing, impression management, and carefully crafted performances that deliver a single, critical message: pride, strength, and control'. Hustling, they main-tain, 'compensates for lack of income, goods and services, and status. It gives the cool cat a kit bag of identity tools for creating a sense of power, prestige, pride and manhood.'[16] It is his skill as a card hustler that has made Lincoln top dog for his younger brother; it is the skill to which Booth longingly aspires, even though he has his own special virtuoso role as shoplifter. Sure enough, when Lincoln returns to street hustling, he reenters the room apostrophising himself in triumph: 'Link, you got it back, you got it back you got yr shit back in thuh saddle, man, you got back in business' (*Topdog*, 83). That return to form means money, the admiration of the whole bar where he could buy the drinks, the adoration of any number of available women who 'knew I'd been throwing the cards'.

> Theyd heard word and they seed uh sad face on some poor sucker or a tear in thuh eye of some stupid fucking tourist and they figured it was me whod just took thuh suckers last dime, it was me who had all thuh suckers loot. They knew. They knew. (*Topdog*, 84)

The rewards of hustling are indeed 'a sense of power, prestige, pride and manhood', but above all the exhilaration of having conned the suckers out of their last dime.

There is a whole history of previous American theatre behind *Topdog*, not only *True West* (1980), Sam Shepard's battle of brothers, which is often cited as its antecedent, but the life-lies of the skid-row characters in O'Neill's *The Iceman Cometh* (1946) and the competitive scams of David Mamet's *Glengarry Glen Ross* (1984). O'Neill's down-and-outs, however, have at least the community of illusion represented by Harry Hope's saloon. Mamet's realtors, jockeying for position in their con talk salesmanship, stand in for mainstream capitalism. The African American Lincoln and Booth are at the bottom of that heap with no one but one another as audience for their performances of fantasised success, no space but the one confined room they share. '*Topdog*', Parks said in an interview, 'is about personal history, and family history, and about the overriding history that they can't escape.'[17] The overriding history is not only the heroised backstory of the assassination of Lincoln at his moment of victory but the continuing lives of the descendants of those black slaves he freed. The personal and family drama of Lincoln and Booth in *Topdog* represent that larger history writ small.

Brothers

On the page, *Topdog* can read as a pretty grim play: the sordid struggle for supremacy of the two brothers living hand-to-mouth in their squalid tenement. In performance it feels quite unlike that, if only because it is so very much a performance. In the first production at the Joseph Papp Public Theatre, the back wall reproduced in all its dingy particulars the atmosphere of the rooming-house room: the battered door, the grubby wallpaper lime green/yellow below, brown above. But with the audience on three sides of the thrust stage, there could be no more of the room represented, nor any fourth-wall illusionism. Booth's opening three-card patter was played out to the audience, winning laughs if only for its ineptitude, like the traditional clown in the circus who absurdly mimics the graceful skills of the tightrope walker or acrobat who will follow him. This style and setting were retained even in the Broadway transfer to the Ambassador Theatre with its proscenium arch stage. Indeed, with the replacement of the more subtle actor Don Cheadle by the rapper Mos Def in the role of Booth, the clowning was increased on Broadway. The comedy was much broader, with new music-hall routines for Jeffrey Wright also, who continued in the part of Lincoln.

The play was written, according to Robert Brustein, 'in the style of black vaudeville, the homeboy equivalent of *Waiting for Godot*'.[18] In that style, the brothers, for all their competitiveness, play the routines together as a double act. Right through the action, the two of them have scenes where they are playing in sync, their joint performance registered by high fives. They are bros, acting out their roles, lulling an audience into the false security of simply enjoying the show. In this, the three-card monte act itself has a special place. As a recurrent routine, it is a good example of Parks's 'Rep and Rev' technique. We see it first as very badly played by Booth. We are tantalised, as Booth is, by the hope of seeing the maestro Lincoln throwing the cards. There is a trailer for this in Scene 4 when 'he sees a packet of cards. He studies them like an alcoholic would study a drink. Then he reaches for them, delicately picking them up and choosing 3 cards' (*Topdog*, 56). In his patter, so infinitely slicker than Booth's, significantly it is the black card rather than the red that is the winner. The play will climax in Lincoln's monte lesson for Booth in Scene 5 and in Scene 6, where the game is finally performed in earnest, with money on the line.

For much of the action, it may appear that even when at their most competitive Lincoln and Booth are still game-playing brothers. But of course they are brothers in more senses than one. Booth asks Lincoln about his 'Best Customer', the regular who comes in every day to shoot him:

BOOTH. [...] He's a brother, right?
LINCOLN. I think so.
BOOTH. He know yr a brother?

LINCOLN. I dunno.
BOOTH. Hes a *deep* black brother.
(*Topdog*, 34–35)

Lincoln cannot be sure if the customer is an African American because the routine requires the Booth stand-in to approach from behind, and he cannot tell if the assassin knows if he is black in his whiteface getup. The customer is a 'deep black brother' if he acts out this white-on-white killing aware of their shared race. It is he who whispers in Lincoln's ear the philosophical question of identity: 'Does thuh show stop when no ones watching or does thuh show go on?' (*Topdog*, 34).

This meaning of 'brother' is listed in the *OED* (though still in 2003 only at 'draft entry' status) as follows: 'Chiefly in African-American use: a (fellow) black man. Also in extended use: a fellow non-white man (used esp. as an expression of solidarity).' One illustration is taken from a 1965 *Los Angeles Times*: 'Light-skinned Negroes such as myself were targets of rocks and bottles until someone standing nearby would shout, "He's a brother—lay off."' The inbuilt sense of solidarity is significant. It is assumed that in a white-dominated culture, all African Americans, indeed all nonwhites, should stand together in mutual support. It would thus be analogous to the long-standing usage by which fellow members of a religious community are brothers and sisters in Christ. The sibling rivalry of *Topdog*, paralleled in other plays of fraternal conflict such as *True West* or Athol Fugard's *Blood Knot* (1961), has an extra dimension because these warring brothers are black brothers. So far from making them allies against a racially biased society that bars them from advancement, they are driven inward to a home struggle with one another for the position of top dog, the only sort of supremacy they can know.

It has been argued that Lincoln remains top dog throughout, only pretending to play underdog to his brother. The basis of this claim by Patrick Maley is that the dealer in three-card monte can always win when he needs to do so by palming the necessary cards, and that insofar as Lincoln never shows this crucial skill to Booth, he is effectively conning him throughout.[19] This is to some extent plausible, as Booth appears always to believe that the skill of the dealer consists only in the speed of his handling of the cards and his mesmerising patter, whereas in fact the sucker is never allowed to win except as a means of drawing him into the game. However, Lincoln's determination to give up the hustle seems real enough; he is alone when we see him tempted to go back to the cards: 'He sees a packet of cards. He studies them like an alcoholic would study a drink' (*Topdog*, 56). The play would lose much of its point, or be turned into a very different sort of play, if the dramatic switchback in power positions between the brothers were only an illusion.

Lincoln has always been top dog as older brother. But in the play, Booth is on his home turf, Lincoln a guest on sufferance. 'Its my place', Booth reminds his brother. 'You dont got a place. Cookie, she threw you out. And you cant seem to get another woman. Yr lucky I let you stay' (*Topdog*, 15). In this initial face-off between the two, Lincoln the wage earner who has bought the Chinese take-away is forced to set up the food, made to exchange the meat that Booth ordered for the 'skrimps' he had bought for himself. Booth claims precedence by virtue of his position as householder, however limited the facilities of the 'house', but also in terms of his sexual potency. Lincoln has been thrown out by his wife and has found no replacement, while Booth claims, at least, to be regaining the love of the unseen and maybe imaginary girlfriend Grace. His terms of abuse of Lincoln for refusing to team up with him in the three-card hustle illustrate the interconnections of race and sex in the hierarchy of power: 'you shiteating motherfucking pathetic limpdick uncle tom' (*Topdog*, 21). A black man who is willing to white up as Lincoln is an impotent and submissive Uncle Tom. Booth's ultimate insult combining all of these charges is the claim to have cuckolded his brother: 'You a limp dick jealous whiteface motherfucker whose wife dumped him cause he couldnt get it up and she told me so. Came crawling to me cause she needed a man' (*Topdog*, 45). So much is fantasy in this play that it is impossible to be sure if Booth's claim to have slept with Cookie is true, but Lincoln does not try to dispute it here or in Booth's more detailed, almost apologetic account much later in the play (*Topdog*, 93).

Lincoln clings stubbornly to the satisfaction he gains from his 'job', humiliating as Booth considers it to be.

> I like the job. This is sit down, you know, easy work. I just gotta sit there all day. Folks come in kill phony Honest Abe with the phony pistol. I can sit there and let my mind travel. (*Topdog*, 33)

But his employment is at risk; the arcade is threatening to replace him with a wax dummy, and Lincoln is desperate not to lose his position: 'It's a sit down job. With benefits. I dont wanna get fired. They wont give me a good reference if I get fired' (*Topdog*, 53). He pleads with Booth to help him practice his Lincoln act so he can impress his employers: 'My paychecks on the line, man.' Booth, however, refuses, rubbing in his superiority as a man with a woman waiting for him: 'I got a date. Practice

on yr own' (*Topdog*, 36). He even manages to persuade Lincoln to part
with another five dollars to make his date go better.

Lincoln wants Booth's help because the younger brother is the master of
costume and performance, as we see at the beginning of Scene 2, where
Booth has his virtuoso disrobing act, producing from under his coat two
complete shoplifted outfits – suits, shirts, ties, belts, shoes and socks: 'I
stole and I stole generously' (*Topdog*, 28). 'They say the clothes make the
man', says Lincoln, contrasting these gaudy new clothes with the 'getup'
he has to put on every day (*Topdog*, 29). Against Lincoln's declaration that
he can maintain his own identity in spite of playing the president in reach-
me-down gear, Booth insists that in his stolen suit, 'You look like the real
you.'

> Most of the time you walking around all bedraggled and shit. You look
> good. Like you used to look back in thuh day when you had Cookie in love
> with you and all the women in the world was eating out of yr hand.
> (*Topdog*, 30)

This is cool pose again, male strutting with limitless sex the reward, and
Booth here is the man who can kit out his shabby brother for a return to
his former role as alpha male. In this, at least, Booth would seem to have
achieved top dog status.

And yet he is also still the needy younger brother, eager to emulate
Lincoln as three-card monte artist, even to the extent of changing his name
to '3-Card' (*Topdog*, 19). That desperate neediness is shown from the very
beginning in his pathetically amateurish efforts to practice the patter for
throwing the cards. On this, Lincoln can speak with the authority of the
past master: 'You wanna hustle 3-card monte, you gotta do it right, you
gotta break it down. Practice it in smaller bits. Yr trying to do the whole
thing at once thats why you keep fucking it up' (*Topdog*, 18). Lincoln's
refusal to return to hustling, his reluctance to teach Booth the moves, of
course only increases his brother's desire and enhances his own mystique.
In this sense, Maley is right; Lincoln lures Booth into the final contest by
the same strategy that the hustler draws in the 'mark', the sucker on the
street:

> Thats thuh Dealers attitude. He *acts* like he dont wanna play. He holds
> back and thuh crowd, with their eagerness to see his skill and their
> willingness to take a chance, and their greediness to win his cast, the larceny
> in their hearts, all goad him on and push him to throw his cards, although
> of course the Dealer has been wanting to throw his cards all along. Only he
> dont never show it. (*Topdog*, 74).

Booth is similarly driven by Lincoln's apparent unwillingness to play and his own conviction that he can win, and is similarly mistaken in that belief.

There can of course be no winners in this conflict between the brothers. Lincoln can manoeuvre Booth into betting at three-card monte and defeat him as soon as Booth's long-hoarded 'inheritance' is at stake: 'It may look like you got a chance but the only time you pick right is when thuh man lets you' (*Topdog*, 106). Even though Lincoln apparently tries to tone down his triumphalism – 'Im not laughing at you, bro, Im just laughing' (*Topdog*, 107) – this is more than Booth can take: 'Only so long I can stand that little brother shit' (*Topdog*, 108). With the fantasy of his rapprochement with Grace exposed and his confession that he shot her, there is only one way Booth can deal with his intolerable consciousness of being underdog. Lincoln is killed with the gun that an audience will have known is to be fired from the moment Booth pulls it at the very beginning of the play. The full horror of that fratricidal violence is brought out in the final sequence, where Booth's vicious denunciation of his dead brother is followed by his sobbing scream as he nurses the body. Penned into the one room with nothing for them outside but fantastic illusions of identity, they have no way but this to resolve the irresolvable conflict of top dog and underdog.

Family

Parks considers her detailed rendering of African American English a key part of her dramatic language and provides a glossary of nonstandard spellings in her essay 'Elements of Style': 'thuh' for 'the', 'k' for 'okay' and so on (*America Play*, 17). Yet within that idiom there is also room for parody, as in the sequence Booth plays out with Lincoln when he brings home the pay packet on Friday night:

BOOTH. Lordamighty, Pa. I smells money!
LINCOLN. Sho nuff, Ma. Poppas brung home the bacon.
BOOTH. Bringitherebringitherebringithere. [. . .]
BOOTH. Oh lordamighty Ima faint, Pa! Get me muh med-sin!
(*Lincoln quickly pours two large glasses of whiskey.*)
LINCOLN. Dont die on me, Ma!
BOOTH. Im fading fast, Pa!
LINCOLN. Thinka thuh children, Ma! Thinka thuh farm!
(*Topdog*, 26)

Ben Brantley particularly admired this in his review of the first production as 'the delightful, barbed spectacle of the brothers' cornpone celebration of

Lincoln's weekly paycheck, sending up the homey, rustic family they never had'.[20] Yet the parts that the two characters play here, with Booth as Ma and Lincoln as Pa, are significant for the family background they did have.

Lincoln is regularly associated with his father, Booth with his mother throughout the play. When the parents left separately, it was Booth who was given a parting inheritance of five hundred dollars by his mother and enjoined to tell no one about it, while the father gave an exactly similar parting present to Lincoln two years later. The Oedipal schema is apparent in the relationship of both sons to the parents. Lincoln burned all his father's suits after he left, banishing the spectre of the paternal presence. His father would take Lincoln with him when he visited his 'ladies', on occasions allowing him to watch the lovemaking, but 'one of his ladies liked me, so I would do her after he'd done her' (*Topdog*, 90). If Lincoln triumphed in the Oedipal struggle by replacing his father sexually, Booth is given a long bitter monologue in which he remembers acting as a voyeur on his mother's infidelity, a nightmare psychological displacement for the son. Coming upon her unexpectedly with her 'Thursday man', he recalls, 'they didnt see me come in, they didnt see me watching them, they didnt see me going out' (*Topdog*, 100).

A 'raggedy photo album' serves as prompt for childhood memories, focused for Lincoln in the house they lived in: 'We thought it was the best fucking house in the world' (*Topdog*, 64). 'We had some great times in that house, bro. Selling lemonade on thuh corner, thuh treehouse out back, summers spent lying in thuh grass and looking at thuh stars.' Booth is unconvinced by this storybook idyll': 'We never did none of that shit.' What he remembers is a 'cement backyard and a frontyard full of trash' (*Topdog*, 65). Lincoln tries to account for the parents' desertion of their sons: 'I think there was something out there that they liked more than they liked us and for years they was struggling against that more liked something.' It was this that made life in the house so significant.

> We moved out of that nasty apartment into a house. A whole house. It werent perfect but it was a house and theyd bought it and they brought us there and everything we owned, figuring we could be a family in that house and them things, them two separate things each of them was struggling against would just leave them be. Them things would see thuh house and be impressed and just leave them be. (*Topdog*, 67)

The vision here of the father shining his shoes every night, the mother putting food on the table, reading to her children, 'the clean clothes, the buttons sewed on all right' is the mirage of 'regular people living in a house' never in fact to be achieved (*Topdog*, 68).

Parks is here writing back to Lorraine Hansbury's *A Raisin in the Sun*. In Hansbury, the decision of the mother to buy a house in a previously all-white neighbourhood is not only a courageous claim for African American rights but a necessary liberation for the three-generation family fractiously living in the one small apartment. Although at the end of the play their future is uncertain, ownership of the house will give them the necessary space for dignity. *Topdog* shows how that icon of middle-class stability, the house as home to the nuclear family, is unobtainable for the likes of Lincoln and Booth. Hansbury asserts that it is only the pressures from outside that prevent the African American family from being the truly loving, mutually supportive family they really are. Parks exposes the way the low collective status of African Americans eats at the very basis of a potential family, making trust and love impossible.

The situation of the abandoned, unhoused sons is the more remarkable coming from Parks for its concentration on the deformations of the male ego. In plays such as *Venus*, *In the Blood* and *Fucking A*, she had written as a feminist African American playwright dramatising the lives of black women doubly exploited as objects of the white male gaze. Lincoln and Booth, without any sort of model of reciprocal love in their parents, without accredited social roles, must make their own self-worth out of a hustling masculinity in which women can be only prey or prize. For Booth, as for Joey and Lenny in *The Homecoming*, the ultimate sign of manhood is to have unprotected sex, to 'do it without a rubber' (*Topdog*, 39). Though he can fantasise about marriage to Grace, at the same time he resents her 'trying to make myself into a one woman man [...] One woman rubber-wearing motherfucker' (*Topdog*, 68). Monogamy amounts to emasculation. The reward for Lincoln of a return to fame as a hustler is having women 'purrrring all up on me and letting me touch them and promise them shit' (*Topdog*, 84). Only in this way can he forget about being dumped by his wife Cookie. Their illusions of cool pose sexual dominance are constantly challenged, adding animus to their struggle for macho ascendancy over one another.

Booth's single room in the rooming house could not well be further removed from the ideal of the family home. In the opening scene face-off, Lincoln challenges Booth's claimed dominance as the proprietor of the room by pointing out its lack of amenities:

LINCOLN. You dont got no running water in here, man.
BOOTH. So?
LINCOLN. You dont got no toilet you dont got no sink.

BOOTH. Bathrooms down the hall.
LINCOLN. Yuh living in thuh Third World, fool!
(*Topdog*, 15)

This shanty shelter in which the two of them live stands as an antonym to the detached suburban house with its multiple bathrooms and two-car garage that is the standard symbol of American family prosperity and achievement. One of the more unlikely of Booth's shoplifting acquisitions in Scene 2 is a folding screen 'which he sets up between the bed and the recliner creating 2 separate spaces' (*Topdog*, 25). From then on, he has 'his' bedroom to which he can retire to masturbate. The absurd division of the space is a grotesque mimicry of the claim to privacy of those who can afford rooms of their own.

At the beginning of Scene 5, immediately after the intermission, the audience returns to a changed scene.

> The monte table is nowhere in sight. In its place is a table with two nice chairs. The table is covered with a lovely tablecloth and there are nice plates, silverware, champagne glasses and candles. All the makings of a very romantic dinner for two. The whole apartment in fact takes its cue from the table. Its been cleaned up considerably. New curtains on the windows, a doily-like object on the recliner. (*Topdog*, 59)

The genteel language of the stage directions – 'nice', 'lovely', 'romantic' – provides an ironic distance from this vision of opulent transformation. There is an equivalent theatrical change of scene in Act II of Sean O'Casey's *Juno and the Paycock*, when the impoverished Boyle family believe they have come into money, and their dingy tenement flat is spectacularly refurnished. But O'Casey naturalises the scene; the 'glaringly upholstered armchair and lounge', the 'cheap pictures and photos' have all been bought on hire purchase on the basis of money borrowed from fellow tenants who have pawned their possessions to provide the cash.[21] This is a plausible rendering of a working-class economy, as is the third act stripping bare of the home, when the money turns out to have been illusory.

Parks does not work with that sort of truth-seeming naturalism. It is highly implausible that Booth, however skilful a shoplifter, could have 'boosted' such an array of goods, nor yet have chosen them so well. What Parks wants is the mirage of the sort of 'nice' romantic dinner scene her audience would least expect in this appallingly squalid room. In the original production, there was a dazzling white tablecloth covering a table with matching chairs, a candle in the centre, champagne in an ice bucket.

But later on, when Booth finally gave up on the prospect of his dinner date Grace appearing and Lincoln offered to throw the cards, the whole table setting was unceremoniously bundled up in the tablecloth and dumped. The milk crates and piece of cardboard on which Booth practiced his three-card monte in the opening scene were placed on top of the table. The whole dinner scene was palpable, disposable illusion.

Topdog does not invite us to believe in the literal reality of what is represented onstage, nor yet of the backstory of the brothers. How likely is it in fact that their two parents should have deserted them separately, two years apart, each one giving one of the sons the same exact sum of five hundred dollars in cash? How credible is it that Booth would have kept his 'inheritance' tightly knotted in the stocking in which it was given him, or indeed that Lincoln should return from his first day back on the streets hustling with the matching five hundred dollars to stake against his brother? These symmetries are there to figure a social psychological situation beyond the individual case study. Lincoln and Booth are opposed paradigms for different types of parental deprivation, anger against the rival father, hurt jealousy and resentment of the loved mother; their uses of their inheritance, Lincoln's splurging and Booth's hoarding, are contrasted ways of dealing with the emotional capital of memory. The family home, icon of stability, respectability and prosperity in the white-dominated society outside, appears only as a phantom or travesty in the claustrophobic space that is all the brothers can ever have. 'Welcome to the family.'

Conclusion: home base

In September 2012, the Royal Court Theatre in London staged *Love and Information*, a new play by veteran playwright Caryl Churchill.[1] It was not in fact a play as such but a series of fifty-seven discrete playlets, featuring a hundred different characters – only they were not characters. All that Churchill supplied by way of text were snatches of dialogue, some of them no more than a few lines, by unnamed people in undefined locations – as it were, voices caught out of the ether. What they had in common was information: withholding it, imparting it, sharing it. One person urged a resistant other to tell a secret, someone sought to explain irrational numbers to an unmathematical friend, a pair of former lovers struggled to remember the details of their long-ago affair. Some sketches were dramatic (a young woman telling her supposedly younger sibling that she is actually the mother, not the sister), some strongly political (a torture scene, a glimpse of animal experimentation in the lab), but most were funny, banal, absurd. The show was directed by James Macdonald in a plain white box, with minimal props introduced for each vignette, a split-second blackout dividing one from another with the sound of a camera click. It was a play for the twenty-first century in its unlocated, decentred collage of fragmentary stories, with people in danger of reduction to so many minibytes of information. As such, it was very successful and at the time of writing is about to open off-Broadway in the New York Theatre Workshop.[2]

Just a few months earlier, however, the Young Vic in London mounted a revival of *A Doll's House* that was even more successful, winning a best actress award for Hattie Morahan in the lead role and transferring in 2013 to two runs in the West End. It was a new version by the experienced English dramatist Simon Stephens that was lightly modernised – Nora surreptitiously ate chocolates, not macaroons – but otherwise stayed quite faithful to the original.[3] And Carrie Cracknell's production had none of the wild reimagining of the Mabou Mines version, nor the violent

Figure C.1   Set design by Ian McNeil for *A Doll's House*, Young Vic, London, 2012.

innovations of Thomas Ostermeier's production. The whole nineteenth-century storyline was there: the initial apparently happy, loving marriage of the Helmers; the threat of the intruding moneylender Krogstad; Nora's growing terror at the prospect of exposure; the final showdown between her and Torvald. Cracknell, in fact, sought to flesh out the reality of the family situation. We were shown tableaux of the Christmas Eve dinner with everyone wearing holiday hats; the older children knelt to pray before going to bed. The only new feature of the production, unsignalled in the published text, was the scene design by Ian McNeil (Figure C.1).

The set was in white painted wood, a literal doll's house with the walls cut away. A revolving stage allowed the audience to see not just inside the living room of the Helmers' apartment but Torvald's study, the dining room, Nora's single bedroom – Stephens's text specified that she and Torvald had separate rooms, dealing with the issue of the marital bedroom missing from Ibsen's text – and the corridor off which these other rooms opened. At the play's opening, the revolve turned and we saw the maid scurrying to bring Helmer a drink in his study, the bustle of the household in motion as Nora arrived in with the Christmas tree and the presents.[4] When Nora went to confide the long-kept secret of her loan to Kristine Linde, it was whispered to her in the bedroom. Krogstad's Act II confrontation with Nora in which he sneers at her plans to kill herself took place in the narrow corridor that ran the length of the apartment, with the hallway and its letter box at the end. The final blazing row between Nora and Torvald was not conducted with the two of them seated at the living room table, as stipulated in Ibsen's text, but back in the awkward confines of the bedroom. This doll's house was a place of secrets and lies, of enforced concealment within tasteful but claustrophobically cramped living conditions.

Una Chaudhuri takes *Miss Julie* as an example of how the naturalistic playwright's promise of 'an ambitious new contract of total visibility' could not be fully realised within the naturalistic dramaturgy of the time.[5] All but ubiquitous closed-circuit television and onlookers at any event with hand-held mobile phones have made this sort of panopticon a technological reality in the twenty-first century. The Young Vic *Doll's House* with McNeil's design feeds the expectation that we should be able to view not just a chosen room but the whole of a house with its multiple spaces and scenes. Tracy Letts's *August: Osage County* (2007) satisfies a similar need, representing the warring Weston family throughout their 'rambling country house outside Pawhuska, Oklahoma', from ground floor to attic space.[6] This, however, is not a new design phenomenon but a theatrical strategy that goes back to the mid-twentieth century with the designs of Jo Mielzener for *Streetcar* and *Death of a Salesman*. It is an illusionism that declares its own theatricality and does not ask us to accept the fourth-wall convention. McNeil's doll's house, though beautifully realised in detail down to the tasteful Christmas decorations, was palpably a stage set, cutaway rooms appearing on an obvious revolve. This was a home on the stage seen to be just that.

An article in the *Guardian* sought to explain the popularity of the 2012 *Doll's House* revival, which happened to coincide with others near the same time in Britain, in terms of the continued relevance of the gender issues that the play raises.[7] No doubt there is still unfinished business for the women's movement even in societies that affirm the fullest equal opportunity policies. But regular revivals of Ibsen or Chekhov or Strindberg are now standard occurrences in almost any theatre city in the world. They form a third phase of a classic European theatre repertoire comparable to Greek tragedy and the early modern drama dominated by Shakespeare. These hardy perennials are available for all comers to revive, adapt or reconceive. The Greek tragic drama provided the seminal myths of our culture: Oedipus, Medea, the Oresteia. Shakespeare has yielded narrative forms, resonant images that continue to circulate: Romeo and Juliet's love across the barricades, the meditations of Hamlet, Lear on the heath. From the nineteenth-century naturalists we get the intense focus on the human family in the secular, material context of the home.

This stage image remains a normative form, just as the nuclear family living in a specific domestic space remains a standard social icon, however much it is reconfigured in a time of global mobility and changing familial patterns. The most ambitious playwrights of the modern period, from O'Neill to Parks, have revolted against the limitations of box-set realist interiors as inadequate to their purposes in representing the deeper history and political significance of their subjects. And yet they are recurrently drawn back to this older form as though unable altogether to escape from home and family as the informing conditions of their characters' lives. The nineteenth-century home on the stage, old-fashioned and clunky as it now seems, banal as it has become in its small- and large-screen derivatives, keeps reappearing to haunt modern dramaturgy. The best that playwrights can do is to adapt it, deconstruct it or play games with it. But the history of the form testifies to its flexibility and the richness of its dramatic possibilities as reconceived both by later playwrights and by directors of revivals.

Two distinct theatrical strategies for dealing with home and family can be discerned in the plays considered in this book, one looking inward, the other outward. *A Doll's House* established a politics of the interior as a critical anatomy of the institution of marriage. The Helmers are a Norwegian middle-class couple of 1879, but that is not what is significant about them. Their relationship stands in for the social contract of marriage itself, with its skewed gender dynamics manifested in the doll's house metaphor of the home. Much later plays in totally different modes can also be seen as comparably paradigmatic. *Endgame*, as an enclosed space with the outside world obliterated, represents a sardonic *reductio ad absurdum* of the vestigial three-generation family living within it. The superficial representationalism of *The Homecoming* barely masks the territorial struggles for power and ascendancy within the house. One of the concerns of *Arcadia* is with the changing shape of the garden of Sidley Park as it reflects changing tastes over time. But of course we never get to see that garden, and instead our attention is given to the two temporally estranged groups of characters living in the simultaneous present of the theatrical space before us.

The Cherry Orchard, by contrast, is not confined within a single set, and the significance of its action resonates out beyond itself like the sound of the snapping string. 'All Russia is our orchard', declares the grandiloquent Trofimov, and the drama of the lost cherry orchard is indeed a moment in

Russian social and political history, even as it is also much more than merely that. By the time Shaw came to write *Heartbreak House*, his attempt at a *Cherry Orchard*-like 'fantasia in the Russia manner', it was in the context of the Great War. Though he deliberately occluded the presence of the war in the text, the play's house, shaped like a ship, took on urgent allegorical application. *Long Day's Journey into Night*, with its day in the life of what is so evidently the playwright's own family in his family's own re-created home, could not be more inward-looking. And yet, the Irish American family fixed in their 1912 moment bespeak the history not just of themselves but of their community. *A Streetcar Named Desire* uses its New Orleans cityscape to give specificity to the conflict between Blanche, the last fragile standard-bearer of the values of the antebellum South, and the emergent working-class Stanley. We never know in what city *Topdog/Underdog* is set, but the onstage duel of the brothers Lincoln and Booth in the one rooming-house room is a tragedy of African American men in a white-dominated history.

To divide the plays in this way into texts turned in toward the home and family as against those historicising works that highlight the informing conditions of the characters is to overstate the differences between them. Even *Endgame*, deliberately 'vaguened' by Beckett into a placelessness outside of time, may have postnuclear scenarios playing around it in the minds of audiences, and can be nudged back toward Irishness in production. A strictly sociological reading of *Streetcar* could not move us with the pity and fear we feel at the destruction of Blanche. It was a basic premise of naturalist drama that the representation of surfaces could reveal essences, that a given domestic interior dramatised in all its specificity might express fundamental truths of the human condition. As naturalism has come to seem outmoded, theatre directors have sought to find other, more symbolic, metatheatrically self-aware styles in their revivals of the major works of the late nineteenth century, just as playwrights have found it necessary to reimagine domestic spaces in their own idiom. But the objective is still the same: to find the right images to release the range of meanings immanent within the still fraught, still compelling idea of home on the stage.

Notes

INTRODUCTION: IBSEN AND AFTER

1 Eric Bentley (ed.), *The Theory of the Modern Stage* (Harmondsworth: Penguin, 1968), p. 365.

2 Émile Zola, *Le naturalisme au théâtre: les théories et les exemples* (Paris: Charpentier, 1881). The second volume, published in the same year, was *Nos auteurs dramatiques*.

3 Bentley, *Theory of the Modern Stage*, p. 351.

4 On the box set, see Dennis Kennedy (ed.), *Oxford Encyclopedia of Theatre and Performance* (Oxford: Oxford University Press, 2003), 1, pp. 178–79; for the fourth-wall convention, see Denis Diderot, *Writings on the Theatre*, ed. F.C. Green (Cambridge: Cambridge University Press, 1936), p. 157. I am grateful to Alexandra Poulain for directing me to the Diderot reference.

5 See Bert O. States, *Great Reckonings in Little Rooms* (Berkeley: University of California Press, 1985), p. 41.

6 Bentley, *Theory of the Modern Stage*, p. 363.

7 Raymond Williams, 'Social Environment and Theatrical Environment: The Case of English Naturalism', in Raymond Williams and Marie Axton (eds.), *English Drama: Forms and Development* (Cambridge: Cambridge University Press, 1977), p. 217.

8 Dates for plays are always those of first production, unless otherwise stated.

9 August Strindberg, *Miss Julie and Other Plays*, trans. Michael Robinson (Oxford: Oxford University Press, 1998), p. 66.

10 Ibid., p. 60.

11 Michelle Perrot (ed.), *A History of Private Life, 4: From the Fires of the Revolution to the Great War*, trans. Arthur Goldhammer (Cambridge, MA: Belknap Press, Harvard University Press, 1990), pp. 2–3.

12 Catherine Hall, 'The Sweet Delights of Home', in Perrot (ed.), *A History of Private Life*, pp. 47–93. By contrast, Wytold Rybczynski argues that the sense of domesticity and the dominant role of the woman within the home emerges in seventeenth-century Holland: see *Home: A Short History of an Idea* (London: Heinemann, 1988), pp. 51–75.

13 Perrot, p. 74.

14 Quoted by John Archer, 'The Place We Love to Hate: The Critics Confront Suburbia, 1920–1960', in Klaus Stierstorfer, *Constructions of Home:*

Interdisciplinary Studies in Architecture, Law and Literature (New York: AMS Press, 2010), p. 48.

15 Walter Benjamin, *Selected Writings,* vol. 3: *1935–1938,* ed. Howard Eiland and Michael W. Jennings, trans. Edmund Jephcott, Howard Eiland et al. (Cambridge, MA: Belknap Press of Harvard University Press, 2002), p. 38.

16 Charles Rice, *The Emergence of the Interior* (London: Routledge, 2007), p. 10.

17 Programme note for Provincetown Players production of *The Ghost Sonata,* quoted in Marc Robinson, *The American Play 1787–2000* (New Haven, CT: Yale University Press, 2009), pp. 167–68.

18 Thornton Wilder, *Our Town and Other Plays* (London: Penguin, 2000 [1938]), p. 22.

19 See Anne Ubersfeld, *Lire le théâtre* (Paris: Editions sociales, 1977), translated as *Reading Theatre,* trans. Frank Collins (Toronto: University of Toronto Press, 1999), and *L'ecole du spectateur* (Paris: Editions sociales, 1982).

20 Gay McAuley, *Space in Performance* (Ann Arbor: University of Michigan Press, 1999).

21 David Wiles, *A Short History of Western Performance Space* (Cambridge: Cambridge University Press, 2003).

22 Una Chaudhuri, *Staging Place* (Ann Arbor: University of Michigan Press, 1997), p. 5.

23 Ibid., p. 27.

24 States, *Great Reckonings in Little Rooms,* p. 65.

25 Ibid., p. 71.

26 I have dealt with this issue in detail in *The Politics of Irish Drama* (Cambridge: Cambridge University Press, 1999), pp. 72–76.

27 Henri Lefèbvre, *The Production of Space,* trans. Donald Nicholson-Smith (Oxford: Blackwell, 1991), p. 87.

28 Arthur Miller, introduction, *Collected Plays* (London: Cresset, 1958), 23.

29 Ibid., p. 31.

30 The term is that of Robert Brustein, *The Theatre of Revolt* (London: Methuen, 1965), though he does not deal with these playwrights.

31 Michael Billington, *State of the Nation* (London: Faber, 2007), p. 101. This traditional view of Osborne's play and its relation to the theatre that came before it has been challenged by Dan Rebellato, *1956 and All That: The Making of Modern British Theatre* (London: Routledge, 1999).

32 Glenda Leeming, commentary, in Shelagh Delaney, *A Taste of Honey* (London: Methuen, 1982 [1959]), p. xx. (The quotation is from Delaney herself.)

33 Ibid., p. 7.

34 Quoted in Fintan O'Toole, *The Politics of Magic* (Dublin: Raven Arts, 1987), p. 20.

35 Tom Murphy, *Plays: Two* (London: Methuen Drama, 1993), p. 91.

36 Marc Robinson (ed.), *The Theater of Maria Irene Fornes* (Baltimore: Johns Hopkins University Press, 1999), p. ix.

37 John Dugdale (comp.) *File on Shepard* (London: Methuen Drama, 1989), p. 39.

38 Susan Glaspell, *The Complete Plays*, ed. Linda Ben-Zvi and J. Ellen Gainor (Jefferson, NC: McFarland, 2010), p. 28.

39 There are, of course, exceptions to this generalisation. My colleague Steve Wilmer pointed me to the achievements of Minna Canth (1844–97) and a tradition of prominent women dramatists following on from her in the Finnish theatre, working with the form of domestic drama.

1 *A DOLL'S HOUSE*: THE DRAMA OF THE INTERIOR

1 Quoted from unsigned notice headlined 'Henrik Ibsen in English', *Daily News*, 8 June 1889, included in Michael Egan (ed.), *Henrik Ibsen: The Critical Heritage* (London: Routledge, 1972), p. 104.

2 Ibid.

3 James Walter McFarlane and Graham Orton (eds. and trans.), *The Oxford Ibsen* (London: Oxford University Press, 1963), IV, p. 2. All quotations from Ibsen, unless where otherwise stated, are taken from this eight-volume edition under the general editorship of James Walter McFarlane (1960–77) and are cited parenthetically in the text.

4 Einar Haugen, *Ibsen's Drama: Author to Audience* (Minneapolis: University of Minnesota Press, 1979), p. 103.

5 Michael Meyer, *Ibsen* (Stroud: Sutton Publishing, 2004), p. 321.

6 Egil Törnqvist, *Ibsen: A Doll's House* (Cambridge: Cambridge University Press, 1995), p. 18.

7 The diagram is reproduced by kind permission of Dr Törnqvist, who points out that there is a mistake in it: the back stairs indicated on the right-hand side should be drawn in a broken line to indicate they are not visible onstage.

8 See Frederick J. Marker and Lise-Lone Marker, *Ibsen's Lively Art: A Performance Study of the Major Plays* (Cambridge: Cambridge University Press, 1989), p. 53.

9 States, *Great Reckonings in Little Rooms*, p. 66.

10 Richard Hornby, *Patterns in Ibsen's Middle Plays* (Lewisburg: Bucknell University Press, 1981), p. 92.

11 Marker and Marker, *Ibsen's Lively Art*, p. 53.

12 Ubersfeld, *Reading Theatre*, p. 102.

13 Törnqvist, *Ibsen: A Doll's House*, p. 143.

14 Christmas Eve rather than Christmas Day is the main focus for celebration in Norway as in several other European countries.

15 This motif was much more obvious in the earlier draft, where Nora is portrayed as constantly in and out of the house (Ibsen, V, 313–14).

16 Austin Quigley, *The Modern Stage and Other Worlds* (New York: Methuen, 1985), p. 93.

17 Richard Hornby, for instance, dismisses the 'trip south to save Helmer's life' as 'ridiculously unscientific': Hornby, *Patterns in Ibsen's Middle Plays*, p. 91.

18 In what follows I am summarising the facts from the account in Meyer, *Ibsen*, pp. 318–20, combined with details given in Robert Ferguson, *Henrik Ibsen* (London: Richard Cohen, 1996), pp. 235–38.

19 This suggests an interestingly pseudo-marital relationship between Ibsen and Kieler. The nicknames Torvald gives Nora, which have often seemed so embarrassingly patronizing to later readers and audiences, would have been unselfconscious signs of affection at the time. Anne Martin-Fugier notes that in the nineteenth century, for the first time, '[b]ourgeois husbands and wives used the familiar *tu* and called each other by silly but touching pet names' (Perrot, *A History of Private Life*, p. 322).

20 Tracy Davis has pointed out that pink-coloured tights in the nineteenth century were 'the article most heavily invested with indexical signification of skin, eroticism, and sexual stimulation'. Quoted in Alisa Solomon, *Re-Dressing the Canon: Essays on Theater and Gender* (London: Routledge, 1997), p. 60.

21 Quoted in John Northam, *Ibsen's Dramatic Method* (London: Faber, 1953), p. 23

22 Solomon, *Re-Dressing the Canon*, p. 55.

23 Toril Moi, *Henrik Ibsen and the Birth of Modernism* (Oxford: Oxford University Press, 2006), p. 239.

24 Errol Durbach, *A Doll's House*: Ibsen's Myth of Transformation (Boston: Twayne, 1991), p. 52.

25 See Margot Norris, *Suspicious Readings of Joyce's* Dubliners (Philadelphia: University of Pennsylvania Press, 2003), pp. 217–18, for an interpretation of the relationship between the two texts. I am grateful to Anne Fogarty for this reference.

26 Kirsten Shepherd-Barr, *Ibsen and Early Modernist Theatre 1890–1900* (Westport, CT: Greenwood Press, 1997), p. 45.

27 Durbach, A Doll's House, p. 49.

28 Marker and Marker, *Ibsen's Lively Art*, p. 83.

29 Törnqvist, *Ibsen*: A Doll's House, p. 132.

30 Marker and Marker, *Ibsen's Lively Art*, p. 63, quoting from *Teatr i iskusstvo* (*Theatre and Art*, 1906/52).

31 Marker and Marker, *Ibsen's Lively Art*, pp. 63–64.

32 Ibid., pp. 65–66.

33 Ibid., p. 76.

34 Ingmar Bergman, *A Project for the Theatre*, ed. Frederick J. Marker and Lise-Lone Marker (New York: Frederick Ungar, 1983), p. 8. The quotations here are from an interview with Bergman by the editors that introduces their translated texts of the three plays in the *Project*. For the description of Bergman's production that follows, I have relied heavily on this work.

35 Ibid., p. 20.

36 Ibid.

37 Marker and Marker, *Ibsen's Lively Art*, p. 82.

38 Törnqvist, *Ibsen*: A Doll's House, p. 95; Bergman, *A Project for the Theatre*, p. 21.

39 Bergman, *A Project for the Theatre*, p. 23.
40 Ibid., p. 30.
41 States, *Great Reckonings in Little Rooms*, p. 65.
42 Bentley, *Theory of the Modern Stage*, p. 364.
43 See Marker and Marker, *Ibsen's Lively Art*, p. 67.
44 Ibid., p. 69, quoting Fredrik Schyberg.
45 Marker and Marker, *Ibsen's Lively Art*, p. 78.
46 Jonathan Kalb, 'Nora the Killer Doll', *New York Times*, 7 November 2004.
47 Ian Shuttleworth, 'Bleeding Nora', *FT Magazine*, 31 January 2004.
48 Kalb, 'Nora the Killer Doll'.
49 Lee Breuer in 'Looking for a Miracle: Reflecting on Ibsen's *A Doll's House*', documentary accompanying film of Mabou Mines *DollHouse* on DVD, 2008. The original stage production opened in New York in 2003 and was still being revived and toured in 2011. The analysis here is largely based on this film version.
50 Lynn Gardner, 'Mabou Mines *DollHouse*', *Guardian*, 27 August 2007, www. theguardian.com/culture/edinburghfestival2007, accessed 28 December 2012.
51 Martin Puchner, 'Toying with Ibsen', www.hotreview.org, accessed 28 December 2012.

2 *THE CHERRY ORCHARD*: ALL RUSSIA

1 Anton Chekhov, *Plays*, trans. Michael Frayn (London: Methuen, 1988), p. 283. All quotations from *The Cherry Orchard* are taken from this edition, cited parenthetically in the text. I have also consulted Ronald Hingley's translation of *The Cherry Orchard* in *The Oxford Chekhov* III (London: Oxford University Press, 1964) and the original Russian in A.P. Chekhov, *Vishnevii Sad*, ed. Donald R. Hitchcock (London: Bristol Classical Press, 1992).
2 The approximate dating is that of Ronald Hingley in *The Oxford Chekhov* (London: Oxford University Press, 1967), II, pp. 282–83, who explains that the text of the play, without a title, came to light only after Chekhov's death and there is no hard evidence for exactly when it was written.
3 Gordon McVay (ed. and trans.), *Chekhov: A Life in Letters* (London: Folio Society, 1994), p. 344.
4 J.L. Wisenthal (ed.), *Shaw and Ibsen: Bernard Shaw's* The Quintessence of Ibsenism *and Related Writings* (Toronto: University of Toronto Press, 1979), p. 244.
5 McVay, *Chekhov*, p. 338.
6 Quoted in David Allen, *Performing Chekhov* (London: Routledge, 2000), p. 173.
7 Such divisions were the norm in Russian theatre at the time, known as *yavleniya* or 'French scenes', according to Laurence Senelick, *The Chekhov Theatre* (Cambridge: Cambridge University Press, 1997), p. 44.
8 Chekhov may have revised *The Wood Demon* as early as 1890, but most scholars believe he rewrote it as *Uncle Vanya* in 1896 for publication the

following year: see *Oxford Chekhov*, III, p. 300. In the description of *The Wood Demon* that follows, I am relying on Hingley's translation of the play in this edition, pp. 203–72.

9 McVay, *Chekhov*, p. 340.

10 James N. Loehlin, *Chekhov*: The Cherry Orchard (Cambridge: Cambridge University Press, 2006), p. 53; Loehlin reproduces images of the set for Acts I and IV, pp. 12, 38.

11 Of such adaptations, the most recent version of *The Cherry Orchard* is by Tom Murphy, published by Methuen Drama in 2004. Harvey Pitcher, citing a letter from Violet Martin to her writing partner Edith Somerville, noted that 'it is late nineteenth-century Ireland which provides something comparable to the particular social relations that are to be found in Chekhov's play': *The Chekhov Play* (London: Chatto and Windus, 1973), p. 158.

12 McVay, *Chekhov*, p. 342.

13 Ibid., pp. 70–71.

14 For all Lopakhin's personal unease about his peasant origins, Chekhov intended the current class difference between him and the servants to be quite marked in performance, as he explained to Stanislavski: 'Dunyasha and Yepikhodov stand in the presence of Lopakhin. After all, Lopakhin is very much at his ease, behaves like a squire and calls the servants "thou", while they call him "you"', *Oxford Chekhov*, III, p. 329.

15 'The main difference between Russia and the West may be understood [. . .] when put into the context of inheritance rights and clan systems. Already in Muscovy a testator was free to will in favour of his wife and daughters. Peter the First, following the English example, tried to limit testation rights of the nobility and enforce inheritance of the eldest sons, but did not succeed – the Russian nobility and the Russian public in general clung to the institutions of partitioning inheritances and of bequeathing to women': Hans-Heinrich Nolte, 'Female Entrepreneurs in Nineteenth-Century Russia', *Business History*, 52.4 (2010), 678–79. I am most grateful to my colleague Sarah Smyth for this reference.

16 See Senelick, *The Chekhov Theatre*, p. 68.

17 Ibid., p. 71.

18 Dench had a similar piece of business in the 1981 BBC TV production directed by Richard Eyre, where on the whole she played a more sympathetic Ranevskaya.

19 Quoted by J.L. Styan, *Chekhov in Performance* (Cambridge: Cambridge University Press, 1971), p. 255.

20 Loehlin, *Chekhov*, p. 48; the photo showing this scene is reproduced on p. 12.

21 Hingley also offers an explanatory paraphrase: 'And when the serfs were freed I was already head valet', *Oxford Chekhov*, III, p. 168.

22 McVay, *Chekhov*, p. 341.

23 The translation of these two passages is that of Hingley, *Oxford Chekhov*, III, pp. 321–22, who supplies the lines that Chekhov substituted for those censored.

24 Tom Murphy in his version cleverly replaces these lines with snatches of equivalently rhetorical Irish nationalist verse: *The Cherry Orchard* (London: Methuen Drama, 2004), p. 41.
25 Senelick, *The Chekhov Theatre*, p. 78.
26 *Oxford Chekhov*, III, p. 327.
27 Ibid., p. 318.
28 Jean Benedetti (ed. and trans.), *The Moscow Art Theatre Letters* (London: Methuen Drama, 1991), pp. 174–75.
29 See Loehlin, *Chekhov*, p. 185.
30 Andrew Todd and Jean-Guy Lecat, *The Open Circle: Peter Brook's Theatre Environments* (London: Faber, 2003), p. 80.
31 Donald Rayfield, *Anton Chekhov: A Life* (London: HarperCollins, 1997), p. 260.
32 Benedetti, *Moscow Art Theatre Letters*, p. 185.
33 Ibid., p. 186.
34 Loehlin, *Chekhov*, p. 138, shows Strehler's Act II set.
35 Benedetti, *Moscow Art Theatre Letters*, p. 186.
36 Allen, *Performing Chekhov*, p. 129.
37 Loehlin, *Chekhov*, p. 151.
38 Quoted by Loehlin, *Chekhov*, p. 150.
39 Allen, *Performing Chekhov*, p. 132.
40 *Oxford Chekhov*, III, p. 329.
41 Loehlin, *Chekhov*, p. 189.
42 Rayfield, *Anton Chekhov*, p. 155.
43 *Oxford Chekhov*, III, p. 330.
44 Arnold Aronson, 'The Scenography of Chekhov', in Vera Gottlieb and Paul Allain (eds.), *The Cambridge Companion to Chekhov* (Cambridge: Cambridge University Press, 2000), p. 134.
45 Quoted in Loehlin, *Chekhov*, p. 62. Loehlin uses the productions of Brook and Stein as latter-day representatives of the Meyerhold and Stanislavski approaches: pp. 171–89.
46 Quoted in Senelick, *The Chekhov Theatre*, p. 67.

3 *HEARTBREAK HOUSE*: WAITING FOR THE ZEPPELIN

1 Letter of Bernard Shaw to Nugent Monck, 4 September 1927, quoted in Michael Holroyd, *Bernard Shaw, III, 1918–1950: The Lure of Fantasy* (London: Chatto and Windus, 1991), p. 14.
2 Bernard Shaw, *Complete Plays with Their Prefaces* (London: Max Reinhardt, the Bodley Head, 1970), I, p. 11. All quotations from Shaw, except where indicated otherwise, are taken from this seven-volume edition, (1970–74), cited parenthetically in the text.
3 See Bernard Shaw, *Arms and the Man: A Facsimile of the Holograph Manuscript*, int. Norma Jenckes (New York: Garland, 1981), p. xiv.

4 Bernard Shaw, *Heartbreak House: A Facsimile of the Revised Typescript*, int. Stanley Weintraub and Anne Wright (New York: Garland, 1981), pp. 1–3.

5 See Dan H. Laurence and Nicholas Grene (eds.), *Shaw, Lady Gregory and the Abbey: A Correspondence and a Record* (Gerrards Cross: Colin Smythe, 1993), p. xviii.

6 See Lena Ashwell, *Myself a Player* (London: Michael Joseph, 1936), p. 15.

7 A.M. Gibbs, *Bernard Shaw: A Life* (Gainesville: University Press of Florida, 2005), p. 352.

8 See Mary Hyde (ed.), *Bernard Shaw & Alfred Douglas: A Correspondence* (London: John Murray, 1982), p. 192.

9 Holroyd, *Bernard Shaw*, III, p. 18.

10 Bernard Shaw, *Collected Letters*, ed. Dan H. Laurence (London: Max Reinhardt, 1985), III, pp. 52–53.

11 Quoted in Stanley Weintraub, *Bernard Shaw 1914–1918: Journey to Heartbreak* (London: Routledge & Kegan Paul, 1973), p. 159.

12 Margery Morgan, *The Shavian Playground* (London: Methuen, 1972), p. 67. Shaw declared in a letter to Ellen Terry that 'Candida, between you and me, is the Virgin Mother and nobody else': Bernard Shaw, *Collected Letters*, ed. Dan H. Laurence (New York: Dodd Mead, 1965), I, p. 623.

13 Bernard Shaw, *The Diaries 1885–1897*, ed. Stanley Weintraub (University Park: Pennsylvania State University Press, 1986), I, p. 55.

14 The issue of Shaw's emotional relationships is analysed throughout Michael Holroyd, *Bernard Shaw, I, 1856–1898: The Search for Love* (London: Chatto & Windus, 1988); A.M. Gibbs expresses caution about assuming that the Shaws' marriage was unconsummated, *Bernard Shaw*, p. 217.

15 I have retained Shaw's spelling throughout quotations from his work.

16 For the parallels, including this one, see Martin Meisel, *Shaw and the Nineteenth-Century Theater* (Princeton: Princeton University Press, 1963), p. 317.

17 Quotations from Shakespeare here and throughout are from William Shakespeare, *The Complete Works*, ed. Stanley Wells and Gary Taylor (Oxford: Clarendon Press, 1988).

18 Shaw, *Collected Letters*, III, p. 735.

19 Shaw, *Heartbreak House: A Facsimile*, pp. 169–70.

20 Shaw, *Collected Letters*, III, pp. 685–86.

21 Weintraub and Wright in their edition of Shaw, *Heartbreak House: A Facsimile*, pp. 208–9, reproduce these sketches and suggest that they accompanied a letter of 21 August 1920 to his Swedish translator Hugo Vallentin, just two days before Shaw's letter to Simonson.

22 Weintraub, *Bernard Shaw 1914–1918*, p. 163.

23 Shaw, *Collected Letters*, III, p. 505.

24 Shaw, *Heartbreak House: A Facsimile*, pp. 51, 55.

25 Ibid., pp. xiv–xix.

26 Alan Dent (ed.), *Bernard Shaw and Mrs Patrick Campbell: Their Correspondence* (London: Victor Gollancz, 1952), p. 186.

27 For the implications of the musical term 'fantasia', see Meisel, *Shaw and the Nineteenth-Century Theater*, p. 315.
28 Holroyd, *Bernard Shaw*, III, p. 14.
29 Gibbs, *Bernard Shaw*, pp. 357–58.
30 Shaw, *Collected Letters*, III, p. 426.
31 Ariela Freedman, 'Zeppelin Fictions and the British Home Front', *Journal of Modern Literature*, 27.3 (2004), 53, quoting from *The Letters and Journals of Katherine Mansfield*, ed. C.K. Stead (London: Allen Lane, 1977); Freedman borrows the term 'Zeppelin sublime' from Guillaume de Syon, *Zeppelin: Germany and the Airship 1900–1939* (Baltimore: Johns Hopkins University Press, 2002).
32 Laurence and Grene, *Shaw, Lady Gregory and the Abbey*, p. 136.
33 Shaw, *Heartbreak House: A Facsimile*, p. 69.
34 The most obvious example of this is the controversial Epilogue to *Saint Joan*.
35 Dent, *Bernard Shaw and Mrs Patrick Campbell*, p. 198. The letter to Lady Gregory is included in Laurence and Grene, *Shaw, Lady Gregory and the Abbey*, pp. 137–38.
36 Shaw, *Collected Letters*, III, 637.
37 See, for example, Anne Wright, *Literature of Crisis, 1910–22* (London: Macmillan, 1984).
38 Irving Wardle, 'Cutting out the Talk on the Way to Apocalypse', *The Times*, 11 March 1983.
39 L.W. Conolly, *The Shaw Festival: The First Fifty Years* (Don Mills, ON: Oxford University Press, 2011), p. 103.
40 Ibid., p. 134.
41 I have discussed this contrast in my *Bernard Shaw: A Critical View* (Basingstoke: Macmillan, 1984), p. 116.
42 Bernard Shaw, *Collected Letters*, ed. Dan H. Laurence (London: Max Reinhardt, 1988), IV, p. 557.
43 Brian Gardner (ed.), *Up the Line to Death: The War Poets 1914–1918*, rev. edn. (London: Methuen, 1976), pp. 10–11, 34–36.

4 *LONG DAY'S JOURNEY INTO NIGHT*: THE TYRONES AT HOME IN AMERICA

1 For an account of the embargo and the controversy over Carlotta's actions in overruling it, see Brenda Murphy, *O'Neill: Long Day's Journey into Night* (Cambridge: Cambridge University Press, 2001), pp. 2–11.
2 Quoted from O'Neill's work diary in Virginia Floyd, *Eugene O'Neill at Work* (New York: Frederick Ungar, 1981), p. 296.
3 Eugene O'Neill, *Complete Plays*, III, *1932–1943* (New York: Library of America, 1988), p. 4. All quotations from O'Neill are taken from this three-volume edition, with citations given parenthetically in the text.
4 Eugene O'Neill, 'Strindberg and Our Theatre', *Provincetown Playbill* 1 (1923–24), www.imagi-nation.com/moonstruck, accessed 18 June 2004.

5 Although the house at 325 Pequot Ave is generally referred to as Monte Cristo Cottage – the name it is known by now as a National Historic Landmark – Doris Alexander points out that this was actually the name given to the O'Neills' more modest first house in New London: Doris Alexander, *Eugene O'Neill's Last Plays* (Athens: University of Georgia Press, 2005), p. 102.

6 Louis Sheaffer, *O'Neill: Son and Playwright* (London: Dent, 1968), p. 14.

7 Quoted in Louis Sheaffer, *O'Neill: Son and Artist* (London: Paul Elek, 1973), p. 404.

8 Nat Miller seems to have been a composite figure based partly on John McGinley, father of O'Neill's close friend, Arthur, though largely on Frederick P. Latimer, editor of the *Telegraph*, the New London paper for which O'Neill briefly worked in 1912: see Sheaffer, *O'Neill: Son and Playwright*, p. 228. The McGinley family were Irish in origin but 'left-footed', that is, Protestant Irish: see Arthur Gelb and Barbara Gelb, *O'Neill* (New York: Harper Row, 1987 [1962]), p. 89.

9 Florence Eldredge, 'Reflections on Long Day's Journey into Night: First Curtain Call for Mary Tyrone', in Virginia Floyd (ed.), *Eugene O'Neill: A World View* (New York: Frederick Ungar, 1979), p. 287.

10 John Henry Raleigh, 'O'Neill's *Long Day's Journey into Night* and New England Irish-Catholicism', *Partisan Review*, 26.4 (1959), p. 578.

11 Quoted in Gelb and Gelb, *O'Neill*, p. 95.

12 Sheaffer, *O'Neill: Son and Playwright*, p. 48.

13 Ibid., pp. 8–9.

14 The one audiovisual record of this production is a brief excerpt from Act II, scene 2, performed on the *Ed Sullivan Show* in January 1958.

15 I rely here both on my memory of this production in the theatre and on the ABC television broadcast of 1972, both directed by Peter Wood.

16 This production, which opened at the Broadhurst Theatre on Broadway in 1986 and subsequently transferred to London, was broadcast on television in 1987.

17 A version of this production with two cast changes was broadcast on television in 1982, directed by William Woodman, and my observations are based on this and on reviews of the original staging: see Brenda Murphy, *O'Neill*, pp. 72–75, 142–47.

18 Edward L. Shaughnessy, *Down the Nights and Down the Days: Eugene O'Neill's Catholic Sensibility* (Notre Dame: University of Notre Dame Press, 1996), p. 216.

19 Reproduced in Floyd, *Eugene O'Neill at Work*, p. 295.

20 See Brenda Murphy, *O'Neill*, pp. 24–25.

21 Elinor Hughes, ' Long Day's Journey into Night', *Boston Herald*, 16 October 1956; Brooks Atkinson, 'Theatre: Tragic Journey', *New York Times*, 9 November 1956.

22 Wolcott Gibbs, ' The Theatre', *The New Yorker*, 24 November 1956.

23 Brenda Murphy, *O'Neill*, p. 130.

24 See Bill Bryson, *At Home: A Short History of Private Life* (London: Doubleday, 2010), pp. 144–45. The kitchen may have been an exception; there is an illustration of kitchen electrical appliances operating from wall sockets from around 1900: see Rybczynski, *Home*, p. 144.

25 W.B. Yeats (ed.), *The Oxford Book of Modern Verse* (Oxford: Clarendon Press, 1936), p. ix.

26 For a fine reading of the dramatic effectiveness of the poetry in this scene, see Jean Chothia, *Forging a Language* (Cambridge: Cambridge University Press, 1979), pp. 178–80.

27 This is the conjectural date of Sheaffer, *O'Neill: Son and Playwright*, pp. 280–81.

28 Michael Manheim, *Eugene O'Neill's New Language of Kinship* (Syracuse: Syracuse University Press, 1982), p. 11.

29 Laurin Porter, "'Why do I feel so lonely?'" Literary Allusions and Gendered Space in *Long Day's Journey into Night*', *Eugene O'Neill Review*, 30 (2008), pp. 37–47.

30 Johan Callens, 'Spatial Practices: The Wooster Group's Rhode Island Trilogy', in Allison Oddey and Christine White (eds.) *The Potentials of Spaces* (Bristol: Intellect, 2006), p. 153.

31 Geraldine Fitzgerald, ' Another Neurotic Electra: A New Look at Mary Tyrone', in Floyd, *Eugene O'Neill*, pp. 291–92.

32 Brendan Gill, 'Unhappy Tyrones', *The New Yorker*, 12 May 1986.

33 Frank Rich, ' The Stars Align for "Long Day's Journey" ', *New York Times*, 15 June 1988.

34 See Sheaffer, *O'Neill: Son and Playwright*, p. 89.

35 Floyd, *Eugene O'Neill at Work*, p. 288.

36 Ibid., p. 297.

37 Matthew W. Wikander, 'O'Neill and the Cult of Sincerity', in Michael Manheim (ed.), *The Cambridge Companion to Eugene O'Neill* (Cambridge: Cambridge University Press, 1998), p. 231.

38 Brenda Murphy, *O'Neill*, p. 94.

39 Quoted by Brenda Murphy, *O'Neill*, 94.

40 For details of the Bergman production, see Egil Törnqvist, 'Ingmar Bergman and Long Day's Journey into Night', in Haiping Liu and Lowell Swortzell (eds.), *Eugene O'Neill in China* (New York: Greenwood Press, 1992), pp. 241–48.

41 Michael Feingold, ' Shorter Darker Day', *Village Voice*, 13 May 1986.

5 *A STREETCAR NAMED DESIRE*: SEE-THROUGH
REPRESENTATION

1 Quoted in Vivienne Dickson, 'A Streetcar Named Desire: Its Development through the Manuscripts', in Jac Tharpe (ed.), *Tennessee Williams: A Tribute* (Jackson: University Press of Mississippi, 1977), p. 159.

2 Tennessee Williams, *A Streetcar Named Desire: A Play in Three Acts* (New York: Dramatists Play Service, 1953), p. 95. Quotations from the play throughout this chapter are taken from this acting text for reasons discussed below, with references included parenthetically in the text, abbreviated as *Streetcar*.

3 For the background, see Larry Blades, 'The Returning Vet's Experience in *A Streetcar Named Desire*: Stanley as a Decommissioned Warrior Under Stress',

The Tennessee Williams Annual Review, 10 (2009), www.tennesseewilliamsstudies.org/journal/work.php?ID=89, accessed 15 October 2012.

4 Tennessee Williams, *Plays 1957–1980* (New York: Library of America, 2000), p. 395. All quotations from the plays of Williams other than *Streetcar* are taken from this two-volume edition, with references included parenthetically in the text as Williams, *Plays* i for Tennessee Williams, *Plays: 1937–1955*, and Williams, *Plays* ii for the second volume.

5 I am borrowing the term 'simultaneous set' from Thomas Postlewait, who defines it as follows: '[S]imultaneous design in the modern theatre presents a *representational* stage setting of two or more fixed locales that are identifiable without dialogue and visible to the audience throughout the performance, though lighting and movement procedures may highlight or obscure different parts of the set at different times': 'Spatial Order and Meaning in the Theatre: the Case of Tennessee Williams', *Assaph: Studies in the Theatre*, 10 (1994), pp. 51–53.

6 I rely here on Brenda Murphy's analysis of the relation between the preproduction script and the published version: *Tennessee Williams and Elia Kazan* (Cambridge: Cambridge University Press, 1992), p. 22.

7 Ibid., p. 167. There is a TS of the final revised promptbook, dated January 1949, in the New York Library of the Performing Arts, NCOF + 93–1105.

8 Most subsequent printings of the play have been derived from the New Directions first edition. The Penguin text, however, edited by E. Martin Browne, in A Streetcar Named Desire *and Other Plays* (1962), is a curious hybrid text: it is based on the New Directions reading text, but includes bowdlerising changes forced on the British premiere by the Lord Chamberlain in 1949, even though that production was in fact using the acting text. I have used the Library of America edition (Williams, *Plays* i, 469–564) to note differences between the reading text and the acting version (*Streetcar*).

9 Brenda Murphy, *Tennessee Williams and Elia Kazan*, p. 33.

10 Jo Mielzener, *Designing for the Theatre* (New York: Bramhall House, 1965), p. 141.

11 In his memoirs, Williams gives a grotesque account of a party in his apartment in the Vieux Carré to which he invited friends from the Garden District: *Memoirs* (London: Penguin, 2006 [1975]), pp. 100–1.

12 Elia Kazan, 'Notebook for A Streetcar Named Desire', in Toby Cole and Helen Krich Chinoy (eds.), *Directors on Directing* (London: Peter Owen and Vision Press, 1964), p. 364.

13 See Donald Spoto, *The Kindness of Strangers: The Life of Tennessee Williams* (London: Methuen Drama, 1990 [1985]), pp. 68–71, 128–31.

14 Mielzener, *Designing for the Theatre*, p. 18.

15 Brenda Murphy, *Tennessee Williams and Elia Kazan*, p.25.

16 Ibid., p. 31.

17 'Backstage at "Streetcar" Provides Own Drama, Too', *Chicago Sun-Times*, 16 January 1949, quoted in Randolph Goodman, *Drama on Stage* (New York: Holt, Rinehart and Winston, 1961), p. 316.

18 Harry W. Smith, 'Tennessee Williams and Jo Mielzener: The Memory Plays', *Theatre Survey*, 23 (1982), p. 227.

19 See Brenda Murphy, *Tennessee Williams and Elia Kazan*, pp. 28–31 for a detailed analysis of the use of music in the production.

20 Felicia Hardison Londré, 'Poetry in the Plumbing: Stylistic Clash and Reconciliation in Recent American Stagings of *A Streetcar Named Desire*', *Cercles: Revue Interdisciplinaire du Monde Anglophone*, 10 (2004), p. 124, www.cercles.com/n10/londre.pdf, accessed 19 October 2012.

21 Philip C. Kolin, *Williams:* A Streetcar Named Desire (Cambridge: Cambridge University Press, 2000), p. 65.

22 Actually, the censor hesitated over the cutting of this line. In the margin of the Lord Chamberlain's copy, the comment is 'a pity to cut this but I suppose we should': British Library LCP /1949/2, 111-1-6. The reference is duly omitted from the Penguin text.

23 A number of avant-garde directors have moved the bathroom onstage in order to expose that intimacy that the text only suggests: see Frédéric Maurin, '"Oh! You do have a bathroom! First door to the right at the top of the stairs?": la salle de bains dans la mise en scène d'*Un tramway nommé désir*', *Études Anglaises*, 6.1 (2011), pp. 86–100.

24 In another instance of the word 'rutting', Pablo's 'I am cursing your rutting luck!' (*Streetcar*, 95), the censored English text has 'goddam luck': Tennessee Williams, *A Streetcar Named Desire and Other Plays*, ed. E. Martin Browne (London: Penguin, 1962), p. 216. It is interesting that the Lord Chamberlain evidently preferred profanities to obscenities.

25 The observations of this production here are based on a recording made on 13 December 2009 at the Brooklyn Academy of Music, where the show was staged as part of the New Wave Festival, accessed at the New York Public Library for the Performing Arts.

26 Susan Koprince, 'Domestic Violence in *A Streetcar Named Desire*', in Harold Bloom (ed.) *Tennessee Williams's* A Streetcar Named Desire (New York: Bloom's Literary Criticism, 2009), p. 49.

27 Cole and Chinoy, *Directors on Directing*, p. 372.

28 Ibid., p. 373.

29 A more physically suggestive detail was omitted from the acting text: 'He kneels beside her and his fingers find the opening of her blouse' (Williams, *Plays* 1, 564).

30 Quoted in Gene D. Phillips, S.J., '*A Streetcar Named Desire:* Play and Film', in Philip C. Kolin (ed.), *Confronting Tennessee Williams's* A Streetcar Named Desire (Westport, CT: Greenwood Press, 1993), p. 232.

31 Ibid., p. 231.

32 *Life*, 15 December 1947.

33 Quoted in Elia Kazan, *A Life* (London: André Deutsch, 1988), p. 330.

34 See Dickson, '*A Streetcar Named Desire*: Its Development through the Manuscripts' in Tharpe, *Tennessee Williams*, pp. 154–65.

35 C.W.E. Bigsby, *A Critical Introduction to Twentieth-Century American Drama* (Cambridge: Cambridge University Press, 1984), II, p. 58.

36 Ibid.

37 Ibid., pp. 58–59.
38 Miller, *Collected Plays*, p. 23.
39 Ibid., p. 162.
40 Brenda Murphy, *Tennessee Williams and Elia Kazan*, p. 29.
41 For an overview of such interpretations, see John S. Bak-, 'Criticism on *A Streetcar Named Desire*: A Bibliographic Survey 1947–2003', *Cercles: Revue Interdisciplinaire du Monde Anglophone*, 10 (2004), 3–32, www.cercles.com/n10/bak.pdf, accessed 24 October 2012.
42 Cole and Chinoy, *Directors on Directing*, p. 365.
43 Quoted in Kolin, *Williams*, p. 12.
44 See Spoto, *The Kindness of Strangers*, p. 39.
45 See Ronald Hayman, *Tennessee Williams: Everyone Else Is an Audience* (New Haven, CT: Yale University Press, 1993), pp. 114–15.
46 Strindberg, *Miss Julie and Other Plays*, p. 57.
47 Ibid., p. 80.
48 Michael S.D. Hooper, *Sexual Politics in the Work of Tennessee Williams* (Cambridge: Cambridge University Press, 2012).
49 John M. Clum, *Acting Gay: Male Homosexuality in Modern Drama* (New York: Columbia University Press, 1992), pp. 150–51.
50 Williams, *Memoirs*, pp. 53–54.
51 John Cheever, *The Journals* (London: Vintage, 2010 [1991]), pp. 12–13. I am very grateful to my colleague Gerald Dawe for making me aware of this passage.
52 Clum, *Acting Gay*, pp. 166, 149.
53 Hooper, *Sexual Politics*, p. 76.
54 Kolin, *Williams*, pp. 143–44. Kolin is here quoting from the text of *Belle Reprieve* published in W.B. Worthen (ed.), *The Harcourt Brace Anthology of Drama* (Fort Worth: Harcourt Brace College Publishers, 1995).
55 Ibid., 145.
56 Maurin, '"Oh! You do have a bathroom"', 86.

6 *ENDGAME*: IN THE REFUGE

1 Samuel Beckett, *Eleutheria*, trans. Barbara Wright (London: Faber, 1996), p. 5. All quotations from the play are taken from this text, cited parenthetically in the text. For the original French text of the play and the circumstances that led to its publication, see Jérôme Lindon, 'Avertissemment', in Samuel Beckett, *Eleutheria* (Paris: Éditions de Minuit, 1995).
2 Katharine Worth, *Samuel Beckett's Theatre* (Oxford: Clarendon Press, 1999), pp. 26–28, plates 3–4, between pp. 117–18.
3 Quoted from the TS held in Reading in S.E. Gontarski, *The Intent of Undoing in Samuel Beckett's Dramatic Texts* (Bloomington: Indiana University Press, 1985), p. 33.
4 Rosemary Pountney, *Theatre of Shadows: Samuel Beckett's Drama 1956–76* (Gerrards Cross: Colin Smythe; Totowa, NJ: Barnes and Noble, 1988),

p. 149. The term 'vaguen' appears as a MS injunction by Beckett to himself on a draft of *Happy Days*.

5 Two-act TS Reading version of the play, quoted in Gontarski, *Intent of Undoing*, p. 45.

6 Ibid., pp. 46–50.

7 Ibid., pp. 52–53.

8 Harry White, '"Something is taking its course": Dramatic Exactitude and the Paradigm of Serialism in Samuel Beckett', in Mary Bryden (ed.), *Beckett and Music* (Oxford: Clarendon Press, 1998), p. 160.

9 Dougald McMillan and Martha Fehsenfeld, *Beckett in the Theatre* (London: John Calder; New York: Riverrun Press, 1988), p. 209.

10 Ibid., p. 204.

11 Maurice Harmon (ed.), *No Author Better Served: The Correspondence of Samuel Beckett and Alan Schneider* (Cambridge, MA: Harvard University Press, 2000), p. 24.

12 In the American Grove Press first edition, published in 1958, Beckett translated the French 'refuge' as 'shelter', but used 'refuge' in the Faber edition: see S.E. Gontarski (ed.), *The Theatrical Notebooks of Samuel Beckett, 1, Endgame* (London: Faber, 1992), p. 50.

13 Gontarski, *Intent of Undoing*, p. 40 (my translation).

14 Jonathan Kalb, *Beckett in Performance* (Cambridge: Cambridge University Press, 1989), p. 81.

15 Ibid., p. 79.

16 Gontarski, *Intent of Undoing*, p. 47.

17 Peter Allt and Russell K. Alspach (eds.), *The Variorum Edition of the Poems of W.B. Yeats* (New York: Macmillan, 1966), p. 427.

18 Harmon, *No Author Better Served*, p. 22.

19 Samuel Beckett, *Complete Dramatic Works* (London: Faber, 1986), p. 113. All quotations from Beckett's plays are taken from this edition, cited parenthetically in the text. For the original French text, I have used Samuel Beckett, *Fin de partie* (Paris: Editions de Minuit, 1957).

20 See Gontarski, *Intent of Undoing*, pp. 31–32.

21 Vivian Mercier, *Beckett/Beckett* (New York: Oxford University Press, 1977), p. 84.

22 Jean-Paul Sartre, *In Camera and Other Plays*, trans. Kitty Black and Stuart Gilbert (Harmondsworth: Penguin, 1982), p. 223.

23 Theodor W. Adorno, 'Trying to Understand *Endgame*', trans. Michael T. Jones, http://people.missouristate.edu/WilliamBurling/612%20Drama/Adorno%20Endgame.pdf, accessed 29 November 2012.

24 Gontarski, *Intent of Undoing*, p. 48.

25 Compare the reminiscences of voice B in *That Time*: Beckett, *Complete Dramatic Works*, 388–95.

26 Gontarski, *Intent of Undoing*, p. 32.

27 For a discussion of the source and interpretation of the phrase, see Steven Connor, '"On such and such a day … in such a world": Beckett's Radical

Finitude', in *Samuel Beckett Today/Aujourd'hui: Borderless Beckett/Beckett sans frontières*, 19 (2008), p. 43.

28 *The Tempest*, 1.2.365–66 in Shakespeare, *Complete Works*.

29 Mercier, *Beckett/Beckett*, pp. xiii, 74.

30 Kenneth Tynan, 'A Philosophy of Despair', *Observer*, 7 April 1957. When the play was given its London premiere in English in 1958, staged with *Krapp's Last Tape*, Tynan's review was a witty parody in dialogue form, sending up himself as well as the plays: see 'Slamm's Last Knock', *Observer*, 2 November 1958.

31 Letter of Beckett to Alan Schneider, 21 June 1956: Harmon, *No Author Better Served*, p. 11.

32 See the extended sequence in Beckett, *Fin de partie*, 103–4, where Clov denies that the boy is looking towards the house with the eyes of the dying Moses, as Hamm suggests he might be, but rather is regarding his own navel.

33 See the parallel text edition, Robert Pinget, *La manivelle/The Old Tune* (Paris: Editions de Minuit, 1960), pp. 24–25.

34 Ibid., pp. 20–21.

35 For a fuller discussion, see my 'The Hibernicisation of *En Attendant Godot*', *Etudes irlandaises*, 33.2 (2008), 135–44.

36 Eric Shorter, 'Insignificance of Mankind by Beckett', *Daily Telegraph*, 10 July 1964.

37 Untitled TS transcript of review signed H.G.M., dated 10.7.64 in archives of Theatre Museum, Victoria and Albert Museum, London.

38 Michael Billington, 'Endgame', *Guardian*, 7 May 1976.

39 John Barber, 'Beckett at His Best in "Endgame" Revived', *Daily Telegraph*, 7 May 1976.

40 Peter Lewis, 'Play It Again Sam', *Daily Mail*, 7 May 1976.

41 This is based on the archival recording of the production in the Theatre Museum, London.

42 *Beckett on Film*, Tyrone Productions, DVD set, 2005.

43 McMillan and Fehsenfeld, *Beckett in the Theatre*, p. 171.

44 Beckett's *Film*, of course, ends with a sequence in E/O's room.

7 *THE HOMECOMING*: MEN'S ROOM

1 Michael Billington, *The Life and Work of Harold Pinter* (London: Faber, 1966), p. 43. Billington does not give a source for this quotation, but it can be assumed to be taken from extensive conversations he had with Pinter when researching his book.

2 Ibid., p. 51.

3 Harold Pinter, *Plays: One* (London: Faber, 1991), p. 86. All further quotations from Pinter's plays are taken from this four-volume edition (1991–93), cited parenthetically in the text.

4 Martin Esslin, *The Theatre of the Absurd*, rev. edn. (Harmondsworth: Penguin, 1968), pp. 265–92.

5 Harold Pinter, 'Early Draft, *The Homecoming*: Amended Version', *Pinter Review*, 1995–96, pp. 200–7. The drafts of *The Homecoming* are facsimile reproductions of the originals in the Pinter Archive in the British Library.

6 Harold Pinter, 'Early Typed Draft, *The Homecoming*', *Pinter Review*, 1995–96, pp. 16–27.

7 Ibid., pp. 23, 24.

8 Ibid., pp. 23.

9 Ibid., pp. 25.

10 Billington, *Life and Work*, p. 163.

11 Ibid., p. 164.

12 Harold Pinter, 'First Draft, *The Homecoming*', *Pinter Review*, 1997–98, p. 9.

13 Billington, *Life and Work*, p. 163.

14 Pinter, 'First Draft', p. 12.

15 Pinter in fact cut a detailed description of Sam's route out to the airport, having driven the journey himself while the play was in rehearsal and discovered that new road structures made it obsolete. See John Lahr, 'An Actor's Approach: Interview with Paul Rogers' in John Lahr and Anthea Lahr (eds.), *A Casebook on Harold Pinter's* The Homecoming (London: Davis-Poynter, 1973), pp. 152–53.

16 John Lahr, 'A Designer's Approach: An Interview with John Bury' in Lahr and Lahr, *Casebook*, pp. 27–28.

17 Harold Bloom (ed.), *Harold Pinter* (New York: Chelsea House, 1987), p. 1.

18 Martin Esslin, *Pinter the Playwright* (London: Methuen, 1982), pp. 154–56.

19 Philip Hope-Wallace, 'The Homecoming at the Aldwych Theatre', *Guardian*, 4 June 1965.

20 'A World out of Orbit', *Times*, 4 June 1965. This review is unsigned.

21 Harold Hobson, 'Pinter Minus the Moral', *Sunday Times*, 6 June 1965.

22 Pinter, 'First Draft', p. 21.

23 Ibid., p. 27.

24 John Lahr, 'An Actor's Approach: Paul Rogers', in Lahr and Lahr, *Casebook*, p. 165.

25 Jeremy Kingston, *Punch*, 16 June 1965.

26 J.C. Trewin, 'Mr Pinter Says that There's No Place like Home', *Illustrated London News*, 19 June 1965.

27 Lahr, 'Interview with Paul Rogers', in Lahr and Lahr, *Casebook*, p. 170.

28 Pinter, *The Homecoming*, dir. Peter Hall, American Film Theatre, 1973.

29 *Evening Standard*, 4 June 1965, quoted by Yael Zarhy-Levo, 'Pinter and the Critics' in David Raby, *Cambridge Companion to Harold Pinter* (Cambridge: Cambridge University Press, 2001), p. 217.

30 Bert. O. States, 'Pinter's *The Homecoming*: The Shock of Nonrecognition', in Bloom, *Harold Pinter*, pp. 9–10.

31 Simon Trussler, *The Plays of Harold Pinter* (London: Victor Gollancz, 1973), p. 134.

32 See Lahr and Lahr, *Casebook*, pp. 142, 170, for suggestions that Teddy, Lenny or Joey may have been sons of MacGregor.

33 Esslin, *Harold Pinter the Playwright*, pp. 157, 159.

34 Vera M. Jiji, 'Pinter's Four Dimensional House: *The Homecoming*', *Modern Drama* 17.4 (1974), p. 433.

35 Irving Wardle, 'The Territorial Struggle', in Lahr and Lahr, *Casebook*, pp. 43–44.

36 Irving Wardle, interviewing Peter Hall, refers to the 'cigarette-lighting [sic] group opening up like a flower', Lahr and Lahr, *Casebook*, p. 20; the effect is well shown in a still from Hall's 1991 revival of the play, reproduced in Raby, *Cambridge Companion*, p. 150.

37 Kathleen Tynan, 'In Search of Harold Pinter', *Evening Standard*, 25 April 1968, quoted in Elizabeth Sakellaridou, *Pinter's Female Portraits* (Basingstoke: Macmillan, 1988), p. 118.

38 Quoted in Henry Hews, 'Probing Pinter's Play', *Saturday Review*, 8 April 1967.

39 Sakellaridou, *Pinter's Female Portraits*, p. 116.

40 Lahr and Lahr, *Casebook*, pp. 20–21.

41 Billington, *Life and Work*, p. 175.

42 Sakellaridou, *Pinter's Female Portraits*, p. 111. Penelope Prentice goes still further, describing Ruth as 'a model of virtue, one whose strength is threatened and tested from without but who understands her circumstances, herself, and the people around her and then acts wisely to gain the best available end': *The Pinter Ethic* (New York: Garland, 2000), p. 148.

43 Drew Milne, 'Pinter's Sexual Politics', in Raby, *Cambridge Companion*, p. 206.

44 Walter Kerr, 'The Theater: Pinter's "Homecoming"', *New York Times*, 6 January 1967.

45 William Goldman, *The Season: A Candid Look at Broadway* (New York: Limelight Editions, 1984 [1969]), p. 112. The judgment that Pinter became commercial with the success of *The Homecoming* is that of Alan Schneider, director of *The Birthday Party*, quoted by Goldman, p. 45.

8 *ARCADIA*: SEEING DOUBLE

1 Kenneth Tynan, 'Withdrawing with Style from Chaos', in *Show People* (London: Weidenfeld and Nicholson, 1979), p. 47.

2 Harold Pinter, 'Art, Truth & Politics', *PMLA*, 121.3 (2006), pp. 811–18.

3 Mel Gussow, *Conversations with Stoppard* (London: Nick Hern, 1995), p. 37.

4 For the Magritte source, see Ira Nadel, *Double Act: A Life of Tom Stoppard* (London: Methuen, 2004), p. 219. The title, however, involves a literal pun; the action takes place after a visit to look at a Magritte painting at 'an exhibition of surrealistic art at the Tate Gallery': Tom Stoppard, *After Magritte* (London: Faber, 1971), p. 35.

5 Tom Stoppard, *The Real Thing* (London: Faber, 1982), p. 18.

6 Ibid., p. 40. The writer Derek Marlowe, a friend of Stoppard's, declared: '[H]e can't create convincing women. His female characters are somewhere between playmates and amanuenses.' Quoted by Tynan, *Show People*, p. 63.

7 Ibid., p. 36.

8 Frank Rich, 'Stoppard's Real Thing in London', *New York Times*, 23 June 1983.

9 Stoppard, *The Real Thing*, p. 69.

10 Tom Stoppard, *Arcadia* (London: Faber, 1993), p. 1. All further quotations are taken from this edition and cited parenthetically in the text.

11 Tom Stoppard, *Travesties* (London: Faber, 1975), p. 26.

12 See James Gleick, *Chaos: Making a New Science* (London: Heinemann, 1988), pp. 57–118.

13 Nadel, *Double Act*, p. 430.

14 Nadel, *Double Act*, pp. 428–29, cites Louise Page's play *Adam Was a Gardener* and Lindsay Clarke's *The Chymical Wedding*.

15 'Unstoppered Stoppard', *Village Voice*, 9 April 1995, quoted in Martin Meisel, 'The Last Waltz: Tom Stoppard's Poetics of Science', *The Wordsworth Circle*, 38.1/2 (2007), p. 18.

16 Though Stoppard is on record as personally disagreeing with Septimus's point of view – 'over the years I've wasted grief on what's lost' – he added that 'it's a valid correction Septimus makes in the sense that one has to accept the world as it is and not the world as it could have been'. Quoted in John Fleming, *Tom Stoppard's* Arcadia (London: Continuum, 2008), p. 59, from Fleming's own interview with Stoppard in *Theatre Insight*, 10 (1993), pp. 19–27.

17 For the best full-scale comparison of the two, see Martin Meisel, 'Shaw, Stoppard, and "Audible Intelligibility"', *SHAW: The Annual of Bernard Shaw Studies*, 27 (2007), pp. 42–58. In one interview, Stoppard said that he found 'the comparison embarrassing, by which I mean flattering. Shaw raises conversation to the power of drama, and he does it for three acts. I sometimes do it for three pages, though the tone is very different; but my theatrical instincts are flashier': Paul Delaney (ed.), *Tom Stoppard in Conversation* (Ann Arbor: University of Michigan Press, 1994), p. 188.

18 Tom Stoppard, *The Invention of Love* (London: Faber, 1997), p. 95.

19 '*Arcadia* se lit comme une oeuvre inspirée de Shaw (et notamment de *Heartbreak House*)': Élisabeth Angel-Perez, 'Newton/notneW: comédie et chaomédie dans *Arcadia* de Tom Stoppard', *Modern Drama*, 61.3 (2011), p. 327.

20 Meisel, 'The Last Waltz', 19.

21 Fleming, *Tom Stoppard's* Arcadia, p. 65.

22 Nadel, *Double Act*, pp. 430–31.

23 For the iconography of the image, see Erwin Panovsky, 'Et in Arcadia Ego: Poussin and the Elegiac Tradition', in *Meaning in the Visual Arts* (Harmondsworth: Penguin, 1993 [1955]), pp. 340–67, and for an interpretation of its relevance to Stoppard's play, see Hanna Scolnicov, '"Before" and "After" in Stoppard's Arcadia', *Modern Drama*, 47.3 (2004), pp. 480–94.

24 See Jim Hunter, *Tom Stoppard* (London: Faber, 2000), p. 223, for the tentative identification of the French writer of the essay as Jean-Baptiste Fourier.

25 See the plates in Gleick, *Chaos*, between pp. 172 and 173.

26 See particularly Angel-Perez, who shows how 'comédie' becomes 'chaomédie', and Meisel on 'Stoppard's poetics of science' in 'The Last Waltz'.

27 Suzan-Lori Parks, *Topdog Underdog* (New York: Theatre Communications Group, 2002), p. 7. I will be quoting from this text throughout the next chapter.

9 *TOPDOG/UNDERDOG*: WELCOME TO THE FAMILY

1 Una Chaudhuri, 'Topdog/Underdog', *Theatre Journal*, 54.2 (2002), p. 289.
2 Robert Brustein, 'A Homeboy Godot', *New Republic*, 13 May 2002.
3 Ben Brantley, 'Brothers in a Game Where the Hand Is Faster Than the Eye', *New York Times*, 27 July 2001.
4 Artemis Furie, '*Topdog/Underdog*', *Show Business*, 12 April 2002.
5 Suzan-Lori Parks, *The America Play and Other Works* (New York: Theatre Communications Group, 1995), p. 8. Quotations from this edition are cited parenthetically in the text.
6 Alisa Solomon, quoted in Deborah R. Geis, *Suzan-Lori Parks* (Ann Arbor: University of Michigan Press, 2008), p. 45.
7 Quoted in Susan Letzler Cole, *Playwrights in Rehearsal* (New York: Routledge, 2001), p. 99.
8 Ben Brantley, reviewing the Broadway transfer, 'Not to Worry, Mr Lincoln, It's Just a Con Trick', *New York Times*, 8 April 2002.
9 Ian Johns, '*Topdog/Underdog*', *The Times*, 13 August 2003.
10 'James Fouchard's scenic design is alive with atmosphere. When arcade-style lighting materializes around the edges of the set, the effect is striking, suggesting how both brothers have become trapped inside an amusement park with a single, fatal attraction': Tim Smith, 'Everyman Theatre Offers Local Premiere of Gritty 'Topdog/Underdog', *Baltimore Sun*, 2 May 2013.
11 Rick DesRochers, 'The Mythology of History, Family and Performance', interview with George C. Wolfe and Suzan-Lori Parks, Public Access, August 2001, Program of the Joseph Papp Public Theatre/New York Shakespeare Festival, collected in Philip C. Kolin and Harvey Young (eds.) *Suzan-Lori Parks in Person* (New York: Routledge, 2014).
12 Here and throughout I follow Parks's spelling, which generally omits apostrophes as well as reproducing the sounds of Black English.
13 An extremely hostile review of the play's first production quoted this passage and commented: 'This is dialogue whoring after a favorable *New York Times* review', Mimi Kramer, 'The New Sardoodledom', *New York Press*, 1–7 August 2001.
14 Comments on the original production in the Joseph Papp Public Theatre are based on the recording, made on 30 August 2001, and on the Broadway transfer to the Ambassador Theatre on the recording made on 8 August 2002, both of them held in the New York Library for the Performing Arts.
15 See Jason Bush, 'Who's Thuh Man? Historical Melodrama and the Performance of Masculinity in *Topdog/Underdog*', in Kevin J. Wetmore and Alycia Smith-Howard (eds.), *Suzan-Lori Parks: A Casebook* (London: Routledge, 2007), pp. 73–88.
16 Richard Majors and Janet Mancini Bilson, *Cool Pose: The Dilemma of Black Manhood in America* (New York: Lexington Books, 1992), pp. 4, 88.
17 Quoted in Cole, *Playwrights in Rehearsal*, p. 99.
18 Brustein, 'A Homeboy Godot'.

19 See Patrick Maley, 'What Is and What Aint: *Topdog/Underdog* and the American Hustle', *Modern Drama*, 56.2 (2013), pp. 186–205.

20 Brantley, 'Brothers in a Game Where the Hand Is Faster Than the Eye'.

21 Sean O'Casey, *Seven Plays* (Basingstoke: Macmillan, 1985), p. 68.

CONCLUSION: HOME BASE

1 Caryl Churchill, *Love and Information* (London: Nick Hern Books, 2012).

2 See 'Caryl Churchill's Love and Information Begins Performances Tomorrow at NYTW', 3 February 2014, www.broadwayworld.com/off-broadway.

3 Henrik Ibsen, *A Doll's House*, adapted by Simon Stephens (London: Bloomsbury Methuen Drama, 2012).

4 The night I saw the production in the Duke of York's Theatre in August 2013, there was a technical hitch that meant the revolve had to be restarted a number of times, very frustrating for the actors and audience but a gift for an academic scribbling notes on the composition of the set.

5 Una Chaudhuri, *Staging Place* (Ann Arbor: University of Michigan Press, 1995), p. 29.

6 Tracy Letts, *August: Osage County* (London: Nick Hern Books, 2008).

7 Susanna Rustin, 'Why A Doll's House by Henrik Ibsen Is More Relevant Than Ever', *The Guardian*, 10 August 2013.

Bibliography

Adorno, Theodor W., 'Trying to Understand *Endgame*', trans. Michael T. Jones, http://people.missouristate.edu/WilliamBurling/612%20Drama/Adorno%20Endgame.pdf.

Alexander, Doris, *Eugene O'Neill's Last Plays* (Athens: University of Georgia Press, 2005).

Allen, David, *Performing Chekhov* (London: Routledge, 2000).

Allt, Peter, and Russell K. Alspach (eds.), *The Variorum Edition of the Poems of W.B. Yeats* (New York: Macmillan, 1966).

Angel-Perez, Élisabeth, 'Newton/notneW: comédie et chaomédie dans *Arcadia* de Tom Stoppard', *Modern Drama*, 61.3 (2011), 326–39.

Ashwell, Lena, *Myself a Player* (London: Michael Joseph, 1936).

Atkinson, Brooks, 'Theatre: Tragic Journey', *New York Times*, 9 November 1956.

Bak, John S., 'Criticism on *A Streetcar Named Desire*: A Bibliographic Survey 1947–2003', *Cercles: Revue Interdisciplinaire du Monde Anglophone*, 10 (2004), 3–32, www.cercles.com/n10/bak.pdf.

Barber, John, 'Beckett at His Best in "Endgame" Revived', *Daily Telegraph*, 7 May 1976.

Beckett, Samuel, *Complete Dramatic Works* (London: Faber, 1986).

    Eleutheria (Paris: Éditions de Minuit, 1995).

    Eleutheria, trans. Barbara Wright (London: Faber, 1996).

    Fin de partie (Paris: Editions de Minuit, 1957).

Beckett on Film, Tyrone Productions, DVD set, 2005.

Benedetti, Jean (ed. and trans.), *The Moscow Art Theatre Letters* (London: Methuen Drama, 1991).

Benjamin, Walter, *Selected Writings,* vol. 3: *1935–1938*, ed. Howard Eiland and Michael W. Jennings, trans. Edmund Jephcott, Howard Eiland et al. (Cambridge, MA: Belknap Press of Harvard University Press, 2002).

Bentley, Eric (ed.), *The Theory of the Modern Stage* (Harmondsworth: Penguin, 1968).

Bergman, Ingmar, *A Project for the Theatre*, ed. Frederick J. Marker and Lise-Lone Marker (New York: Frederick Ungar, 1983).

Bigsby, C.W.E., *A Critical Introduction to Twentieth-Century American Drama, II* (Cambridge: Cambridge University Press, 1984).

Billington, Michael, 'Endgame', *Guardian*, 7 May 1976.

The Life and Work of Harold Pinter (London: Faber, 1996).

State of the Nation (London: Faber, 2007).

Blades, Larry, 'The Returning Vet's Experience in *A Streetcar Named Desire*: Stanley as a Decommissioned Warrior Under Stress', *The Tennessee Williams Annual Review*, 10 (2009), www.tennesseewilliamsstudies.org/journal/work.php?ID=89.

Bloom, Harold (ed.), *Harold Pinter* (New York: Chelsea House, 1987).

Tennessee Williams's A Streetcar Named Desire (New York: Bloom's Literary Criticism, 2009).

Brantley, Ben, 'Brothers in a Game Where the Hand Is Faster Than the Eye', *New York Times*, 27 July 2001.

'Not to Worry, Mr Lincoln, It's Just a Con Trick', *New York Times*, 8 April 2002.

Breuer, Lee, 'Looking for a Miracle: Reflecting on Ibsen's *A Doll's House*', Mabou Mines *DollHouse*, DVD, 2008.

Brustein, Robert, 'A Homeboy Godot', *New Republic*, 13 May 2002.

The Theatre of Revolt (London: Methuen, 1965).

Bryden, Mary (ed.), *Beckett and Music* (Oxford: Clarendon Press, 1998).

Bryson, Bill, *At Home: A Short History of Private Life* (London: Doubleday, 2010).

Chaudhuri, Una, *Staging Place* (Ann Arbor: University of Michigan Press, 1997).

'Topdog/Underdog', *Theatre Journal*, 54.2 (2002), 289–92.

Cheever, John, *The Journals* (London: Vintage, 2010 [1991]).

Chekhov, Anton, *Plays*, trans. Michael Frayn (London: Methuen, 1988).

Vishnevii Sad, ed. Donald R. Hitchcock (London: Bristol Classical Press, 1992).

Chothia, Jean, *Forging a Language* (Cambridge: Cambridge University Press, 1979).

Churchill, Caryl, *Love and Information* (London: Nick Hern Books, 2012).

Clum, John M., *Acting Gay: Male Homosexuality in Modern Drama* (New York: Columbia University Press, 1992).

Cole, Susan Letzler, *Playwrights in Rehearsal* (New York: Routledge, 2001).

Cole, Toby, and Helen Krich Chinoy (eds.), *Directors on Directing* (London: Peter Owen and Vision Press, 1964).

Connor, Steven, '"On such and such a day . . . in such a world": Beckett's Radical Finitude', *Samuel Beckett Today/Aujourd'hui: Borderless Beckett/Beckett sans frontières*, 19 (2008), 35–50.

Conolly, L.W., *The Shaw Festival: The First Fifty Years* (Don Mills, ON: Oxford University Press, 2011).

Delaney, Paul (ed.), *Tom Stoppard in Conversation* (Ann Arbor: University of Michigan Press, 1994).

Delaney, Shelagh, *A Taste of Honey* (London: Methuen, 1982 [1959]).

Dent, Alan (ed.), *Bernard Shaw and Mrs Patrick Campbell: Their Correspondence* (London: Victor Gollancz, 1952).

Diderot, Denis, *Writings on the Theatre*, ed. F.C. Green (Cambridge: Cambridge University Press, 1936).

Dugdale, John (comp.), *File on Shepard* (London: Methuen Drama, 1989).

Durbach, Errol, A Doll's House: *Ibsen's Myth of Transformation* (Boston: Twayne, 1991).

Egan, Michael (ed.), *Henrik Ibsen: The Critical Heritage* (London: Routledge, 1972).

Esslin, Martin, *Pinter the Playwright* (London: Methuen, 1982).

The Theatre of the Absurd, rev. edn. (Harmondsworth: Penguin, 1968).

Feingold, Michael, 'Shorter Darker Day', *Village Voice*, 13 May 1986.

Ferguson, Robert, *Henrik Ibsen* (London: Richard Cohen, 1996).

Fleming, John, *Tom Stoppard's* Arcadia (London: Continuum, 2008).

Floyd, Virginia, *Eugene O'Neill at Work* (New York: Frederick Ungar, 1981).

Floyd, Virginia (ed.), *Eugene O'Neill: A World View* (New York: Frederick Ungar, 1979).

Freedman, Ariela, 'Zeppelin Fictions and the British Home Front', *Journal of Modern Literature*, 27.3 (2004), 47–63.

Furie, Artemis, '*Topdog/Underdog*', *Show Business*, 12 April 2002.

Gardner, Brian (ed.), *Up the Line to Death: The War Poets 1914–1918*, rev. edn. (London: Methuen, 1976).

Gardner, Lynn, 'Mabou Mines *DollHouse*', *Guardian*, 27 August 2007.

Geis, Deborah R., *Suzan-Lori Parks* (Ann Arbor: University of Michigan Press, 2008).

Gelb, Arthur, and Barbara Gelb, *O'Neill* (New York: Harper Row, 1987 [1962]).

Gibbs, A.M., *Bernard Shaw: A Life* (Gainesville: University Press of Florida, 2005).

Gibbs, Wolcott, 'The Theatre', *The New Yorker*, 24 November 1956.

Gill, Brendan, 'Unhappy Tyrones', *The New Yorker*, 12 May 1986.

Glaspell, Susan, *The Complete Plays*, ed. Linda Ben-Zvi and J. Ellen Gainor (Jefferson, NC: McFarland, 2010).

Gleick, James, *Chaos: Making a New Science* (London: Heinemann, 1988).

Goldman, William, *The Season: A Candid Look at Broadway* (New York: Limelight Editions, 1984 [1969]).

Gontarski, S.E., *The Intent of Undoing in Samuel Beckett's Dramatic Texts* (Bloomington: Indiana University Press, 1985).

Gontarski, S.E. (ed.), *The Theatrical Notebooks of Samuel Beckett*, I: Endgame (London: Faber, 1992).

Goodman, Randolph, *Drama on Stage* (New York: Holt, Rinehart and Winston, 1961).

Gottlieb, Vera, and Paul Allain (eds.), *The Cambridge Companion to Chekhov* (Cambridge: Cambridge University Press, 2000).

Grene, Nicholas, *Bernard Shaw: A Critical View* (Basingstoke: Macmillan, 1984).

'The Hibernicisation of *En Attendant Godot*', *Etudes irlandaises*, 33.2 (2008), 135–44.

The Politics of Irish Drama (Cambridge: Cambridge University Press, 1999).

Gussow, Mel, *Conversations with Stoppard* (London: Nick Hern, 1995).

Harmon, Maurice (ed.), *No Author Better Served: The Correspondence of Samuel Beckett and Alan Schneider* (Cambridge, MA: Harvard University Press, 2000).

Haugen, Einar, *Ibsen's Drama: Author to Audience* (Minneapolis: University of Minnesota Press, 1979).

Hayman, Ronald, *Tennessee Williams: Everyone Else Is an Audience* (New Haven, CT: Yale University Press, 1993).

Hews, Henry, 'Probing Pinter's Play', *Saturday Review*, 8 April 1967.

Hingley, Ronald (ed. and trans.), *The Oxford Chekhov*, 9 vols. (London: Oxford University Press, 1964–75).

Hobson, Harold, 'Pinter Minus the Moral', *Sunday Times*, 6 June 1965.

Holroyd, Michael, *Bernard Shaw*, 5 vols. (London: Chatto and Windus, 1988–92).

Hooper, Michael S.D., *Sexual Politics in the Work of Tennessee Williams* (Cambridge: Cambridge University Press, 2012).

Hope-Wallace, Philip, 'The Homecoming at the Aldwych Theatre', *Guardian*, 4 June 1965.

Hornby, Richard, *Patterns in Ibsen's Middle Plays* (Lewisburg: Bucknell University Press, 1981).

Hughes, Elinor, 'Long Day's Journey into Night', *Boston Herald*, 16 October 1956.

Hunter, Jim, *Tom Stoppard* (London: Faber, 2000).

Hyde, Mary (ed.), *Bernard Shaw & Alfred Douglas: A Correspondence* (London: John Murray, 1982).

Ibsen, Henrik, *A Doll's House*, adapted by Simon Stephens (London: Bloomsbury Methuen Drama, 2012).

Jiji, Vera M., 'Pinter's Four Dimensional House: *The Homecoming*', *Modern Drama* (1974), 17.4, 433–42.

Johns, Ian, '*Topdog/Underdog*', *The Times*, 13 August 2003.

Kalb, Jonathan, *Beckett in Performance* (Cambridge: Cambridge University Press, 1989).

'Nora the Killer Doll', *New York Times*, 7 November 2004.

Kazan, Elia, *A Life* (London: André Deutsch, 1988).

Kennedy, Dennis (ed.), *Oxford Encyclopedia of Theatre and Performance*, 2 vols. (Oxford: Oxford University Press, 2003).

Kerr, Walter, 'The Theater: Pinter's "Homecoming"', *New York Times*, 6 January 1967.

Kingston, Jeremy, *Punch*, 16 June 1965.

Kolin, Philip C., *Williams:* A Streetcar Named Desire (Cambridge: Cambridge University Press, 2000).

Kolin, Philip C. (ed.), *Confronting Tennessee Williams's* A Streetcar Named Desire (Westport, CT: Greenwood Press, 1993).

Kolin, Philip C., and Harvey Young (eds.), *Suzan-Lori Parks in Person* (New York: Routledge, 2014).

Kramer, Mimi, 'The New Sardoodledom', *New York Press*, 1–7 August 2001.

Lahr, John, and Anthea Lahr (eds.), *A Casebook on Harold Pinter's* The Homecoming (London: Davis-Poynter, 1973).

Laurence, Dan H., and Nicholas Grene (eds.), *Shaw, Lady Gregory and the Abbey: A Correspondence and a Record* (Gerrards Cross: Colin Smythe, 1993).

Lefèbvre, Henri, *The Production of Space*, trans. Donald Nicholson-Smith (Oxford: Blackwell, 1991).

Letts, Tracy, *August: Osage County* (London: Nick Hern Books, 2008).

Lewis, Peter, 'Play It Again Sam', *Daily Mail,* 7 May 1976.

Liu, Haiping, and Lowell Swortzell (eds.), *Eugene O'Neill in China* (New York: Greenwood Press, 1992).

Loehlin, James N., *Chekhov:* The Cherry Orchard (Cambridge: Cambridge University Press, 2006).

Londré, Felicia Hardison, 'Poetry in the Plumbing: Stylistic Clash and Reconciliation in Recent American Stagings of *A Streetcar Named Desire*', *Cercles: Revue Interdisciplinaire du Monde Anglophone*, 10 (2004), 124–35, www.cercles.com/n10/londre.pdf.

Majors, Richard, and Janet Mancini Bilson, *Cool Pose: The Dilemma of Black Manhood in America* (New York: Lexington Books, 1992).

Maley, Patrick, 'What Is and What Aint: *Topdog/Underdog* and the American Hustle', *Modern Drama*, 56.2 (2013), 186–205.

Manheim, Michael, *Eugene O'Neill's New Language of Kinship* (Syracuse: Syracuse University Press, 1982).

Manheim, Michael (ed.), *The Cambridge Companion to Eugene O'Neill* (Cambridge: Cambridge University Press, 1998).

Marker, Frederick J., and Lise-Lone Marker, *Ibsen's Lively Art: A Performance Study of the Major Plays* (Cambridge: Cambridge University Press, 1989).

Maurin, Frédéric, '"Oh! You do have a bathroom! First door to the right at the top of the stairs?": la salle de bains dans la mise en scène d'*Un tramway nommé désir*', *Études Anglaises*, 6.1 (2011), 86–100.

McAuley, Gay, *Space in Performance* (Ann Arbor: University of Michigan Press, 1999).

McFarlane, James Walter (ed.), *The Oxford Ibsen*, 8 vols. (London: Oxford University Press, 1960–77).

McMillan, Dougald, and Martha Fehsenfeld, *Beckett in the Theatre* (London: John Calder; New York: Riverrun Press, 1988).

McVay, Gordon (ed. and trans.), *Chekhov: A Life in Letters* (London: Folio Society, 1994).

Meisel, Martin, 'The Last Waltz: Tom Stoppard's Poetics of Science', *The Wordsworth Circle*, 38.1/2 (2007), 13–20.

  Shaw and the Nineteenth-Century Theater (Princeton: Princeton University Press, 1963).

  'Shaw, Stoppard, and "Audible Intelligibility"', *SHAW: The Annual of Bernard Shaw Studies*, 27 (2007), 42–58.

Mercier, Vivian, *Beckett/Beckett* (New York: Oxford University Press, 1977).

Meyer, Michael, *Ibsen* (Stroud: Sutton Publishing, 2004).

Mielzener, Jo, *Designing for the Theatre* (New York: Bramhall House, 1965).

Miller, Arthur, *Collected Plays* (London: Cresset, 1958).

Moi, Toril, *Henrik Ibsen and the Birth of Modernism* (Oxford: Oxford University Press, 2006).

Morgan, Margery, *The Shavian Playground* (London: Methuen, 1972).

Murphy, Brenda, *O'Neill: Long Day's Journey into Night* (Cambridge: Cambridge University Press, 2001).

Tennessee Williams and Elia Kazan (Cambridge: Cambridge University Press, 1992).

Murphy, Tom, *Plays: Two* (London: Methuen Drama, 1993).

The Cherry Orchard (London: Methuen Drama, 2004).

Nadel, Ira, *Double Act: A Life of Tom Stoppard* (London: Methuen, 2004).

Nolte, Hans-Heinrich, 'Female Entrepreneurs in Nineteenth-Century Russia, *Business History*, 52.4 (2010), 6/8–79.

Norris, Margot, *Suspicious Readings of Joyce's* Dubliners (Philadelphia: University of Pennsylvania Press, 2003).

Northam, John, *Ibsen's Dramatic Method* (London: Faber, 1953).

O'Casey, Sean, *Seven Plays* (Basingstoke: Macmillan, 1985).

Oddey, Allison, and Christine White (eds.), *The Potentials of Spaces* (Bristol: Intellect, 2006).

O'Neill, Eugene, *Complete Plays*, 3 vols. (New York: Library of America, 1988).

'Strindberg and Our Theatre', *Provincetown Playbill* 1 (1923–24), www.imagination.com/moonstruck/clsc34w1.html.

O'Toole, Fintan, *The Politics of Magic* (Dublin: Raven Arts, 1987).

Panovsky, Erwin, *Meaning in the Visual Arts* (Harmondsworth: Penguin, 1993 [1955]).

Parks, Suzan-Lori, *The America Play and Other Works* (New York: Theatre Communications Group, 1995).

Topdog Underdog (New York: Theatre Communications Group, 2002).

Perrot, Michelle (ed.), *A History of Private Life*, 4: *From the Fires of the Revolution to the Great War*, trans. Arthur Goldhammer (Cambridge MA: Belknap Press, Harvard University Press, 1990).

Pinget, Robert, *La manivelle/ The Old Tune* (Paris: Editions de Minuit, 1960).

Pinter, Harold, 'Art, Truth & Politics', *PMLA*, 121.3 (2006), 811–18.

'Early Draft, *The Homecoming*: Amended Version', *Pinter Review*, 1995–96, 200–7.

'Early Typed Draft, *The Homecoming*', *Pinter Review*, 1995–96, 16–27.

'First Draft, *The Homecoming*', *Pinter Review*, 1997–98, 1–30.

The Homecoming, dir. Peter Hall, American Film Theatre, 1973.

Plays, 4 vols. (London: Faber, 1991–93).

Pitcher, Harvey, *The Chekhov Play* (London: Chatto and Windus, 1973).

Porter, Laurin, '"Why do I feel so lonely?" Literary Allusions and Gendered Space in *Long Day's Journey into Night*', *Eugene O'Neill Review*, 30 (2008), 37–47.

Postlewait, Thomas, 'Spatial Order and Meaning in the Theatre: The Case of Tennessee Williams', *Assaph: Studies in the Theatre*, 10 (1994), 45–73.

Pountney, Rosemary, *Theatre of Shadows: Samuel Beckett's Drama 1956–76* (Gerrards Cross: Colin Smythe; Totowa, NJ: Barnes and Noble, 1988).

Prentice, Penelope, *The Pinter Ethic* (New York: Garland, 2000).

Puchner, Martin, 'Toying with Ibsen', www.hotreview.org/articles/toyingwithibsen.htm.

Quigley, Austin, *The Modern Stage and Other Worlds* (New York: Methuen, 1985).

Raby, David, *Cambridge Companion to Harold Pinter* (Cambridge: Cambridge University Press, 2001).

Raleigh, John Henry, 'O'Neill's *Long Day's Journey into Night* and New England Irish-Catholicism', *Partisan Review*, 26.4 (1959), 573–92.

Rayfield, Donald, *Anton Chekhov: A Life* (London: HarperCollins, 1997).

Rebellato, Dan, *1956 and All That: The Making of Modern British Theatre* (London: Routledge, 1999).

Rice, Charles, *The Emergence of the Interior* (London: Routledge, 2007).

Rich, Frank, 'The Stars Align for "Long Day's Journey"', *New York Times*, 15 June 1988.

'Stoppard's Real Thing in London', *New York Times*, 23 June 1983.

Robinson, Marc, *The American Play 1787–2000* (New Haven, CT: Yale University Press, 2009).

Robinson, Marc (ed.), *The Theater of Maria Irene Fornes* (Baltimore: Johns Hopkins University Press, 1999).

Rustin, Susanna, 'Why A Doll's House by Henrik Ibsen Is More Relevant Than Ever', *The Guardian*, 10 August 2013.

Rybczynski, Wytold. *Home: A Short History of an Idea* (London: Heinemann, 1988).

Sakellaridou, Elizabeth, *Pinter's Female Portraits* (Basingstoke: Macmillan, 1988).

Sartre, Jean-Paul, *In Camera and Other Plays*, trans. Kitty Black and Stuart Gilbert (Harmondsworth: Penguin, 1982).

Scolnicov, Hanna, '"Before" and "After" in Stoppard's *Arcadia*, *Modern Drama*, 47.3 (2004), 480–94.

Senelick, Laurence, *The Chekhov Theatre* (Cambridge: Cambridge University Press, 1997).

Shakespeare, William, *The Complete Works*, ed. Stanley Wells and Gary Taylor (Oxford: Clarendon Press, 1988).

Shaughnessy, Edward L., *Down the Nights and Down the Days: Eugene O'Neill's Catholic Sensibility* (Notre Dame: University of Notre Dame Press, 1996).

Shaw, Bernard, *Arms and the Man: A Facsimile of the Holograph Manuscript*, int. Norma Jenckes (New York: Garland, 1981).

Collected Letters, 4 vols., ed. Dan H. Laurence (London: Max Reinhardt, 1965–88).

Complete Plays with Their Prefaces, 7 vols. (London: Max Reinhardt, the Bodley Head, 1970–74).

The Diaries 1885–1897, 2 vols., ed. Stanley Weintraub (University Park: Pennsylvania State University Press, 1986).

Heartbreak House: A Facsimile of the Revised Typescript, int. Stanley Weintraub and Anne Wright (New York: Garland, 1981).

Sheaffer, Louis, *O'Neill: Son and Artist* (London: Paul Elek, 1973).

O'Neill: Son and Playwright (London: Dent, 1968).

Shepherd-Barr, Kirsten, *Ibsen and Early Modernist Theatre 1890–1900* (Westport, CT: Greenwood Press, 1997).

Shorter, Eric, 'Insignificance of Mankind by Beckett', *Daily Telegraph*, 10 July 1964.

Shuttleworth, Ian, 'Bleeding Nora', *FT Magazine*, 31 January 2004.

Smith, Harry W., 'Tennessee Williams and Jo Mielziner: The Memory Plays', *Theatre Survey*, 23 (1982), 223–35.

Smith, Tim, 'Everyman Theatre Offers Local Premiere of Gritty 'Topdog/ Underdog', *Baltimore Sun*, 2 May 2013.

Solomon, Alisa, *Re-Dressing the Canon: Essays on Theater and Gender* (London: Routledge, 1997).

Spoto, Donald, *The Kindness of Strangers: The Life of Tennessee Williams* (London: Methuen Drama, 1990 [1985]).

States, Bert O., *Great Reckonings in Little Rooms* (Berkeley: University of California Press, 1985).

Stierstorfer, Klaus, *Constructions of Home: Interdisciplinary Studies in Architecture, Law and Literature* (New York: AMS Press, 2010).

Stoppard, Tom, *After Magritte* (London: Faber, 1971).

Arcadia (London: Faber, 1993).

The Invention of Love (London: Faber, 1997).

The Real Thing (London: Faber, 1982).

Travesties (London: Faber, 1975).

Strindberg, August, *Miss Julie and Other Plays*, trans. Michael Robinson (Oxford: Oxford University Press, 1998).

Styan, J.L., *Chekhov in Performance* (Cambridge: Cambridge University Press, 1971).

Tharpe, Jac (ed.), *Tennessee Williams: A Tribute* (Jackson: University Press of Mississippi, 1977).

Todd, Andrew, and Jean-Guy Lecat, *The Open Circle: Peter Brook's Theatre Environments* (London: Faber, 2003).

Tőrnqvist, Egil, *Ibsen:* A Doll's House (Cambridge: Cambridge University Press, 1995).

Trewin, J.C., 'Mr Pinter Says That There's No Place Like Home', *Illustrated London News*, 19 June 1965.

Trussler, Simon, *The Plays of Harold Pinter* (London: Victor Gollancz, 1973).

Tynan, Kenneth, 'A Philosophy of Despair', *Observer*, 7 April 1957.

Show People (London: Weidenfeld and Nicholson, 1979).

'Slamm's Last Knock', *Observer*, 2 November 1958.

Ubersfeld, Anne, *L'ecole du spectateur* (Paris: Editions sociales, 1982).

Lire le théâtre (Paris: Editions sociales, 1977).

Reading Theatre, trans. Frank Collins (Toronto: University of Toronto Press, 1999).

Wardle, Irving, 'Cutting out the Talk on the Way to Apocalypse', *The Times*, 11 March 1983.

Weintraub, Stanley, *Bernard Shaw 1914–1918: Journey to Heartbreak* (London: Routledge & Kegan Paul, 1973).

Wetmore, Kevin J., and Alycia Smith-Howard (eds.), *Suzan-Lori Parks: A Casebook* (London: Routledge, 2007).

Wilder, Thornton, *Our Town and Other Plays* (London: Penguin, 2000 [1938]).

Wiles, David, *A Short History of Western Performance Space* (Cambridge: Cambridge University Press, 2003).

Williams, Raymond, and Marie Axton (eds.), *English Drama: Forms and Development* (Cambridge: Cambridge University Press, 1977).

Williams, Tennessee, *Memoirs* (London: Penguin, 2006 [1975]).

Plays 1937–1955 (New York: Library of America, 2000.

Plays 1957–1980 (New York: Library of America, 2000).

A Streetcar Named Desire: A Play in Three Acts (New York: Dramatists Play Service, 1953).

A Streetcar Named Desire: A Play in Three Acts, Lord Chamberlain's copy, British Library LCP /1949/2, III-1-6.

A Streetcar Named Desire: A Play in Three Acts, unpublished TS promptbook, New York Library of the Performing Arts, NCOF + 93–1105.

A Streetcar Named Desire and Other Plays, ed. E. Martin Browne (London: Penguin, 1962).

Wisenthal, J.L. (ed.), *Shaw and Ibsen: Bernard Shaw's* The Quintessence of Ibsenism *and Related Writings* (Toronto: University of Toronto Press, 1979).

'A World Out of Orbit', *Times*, 4 June 1965.

Worth, Katharine, *Samuel Beckett's Theatre* (Oxford: Clarendon Press, 1999).

Wright, Anne, *Literature of Crisis, 1910–22* (London: Macmillan, 1984).

Yeats, W.B. (ed.), *The Oxford Book of Modern Verse* (Oxford: Clarendon Press, 1936).

Zola, Émile, *Le naturalisme au théâtre: les théories et les exemples* (Paris: Charpentier, 1881).

Index

Figures in bold indicate the sections where individual plays are discussed in detail.